FAITH IN CATHOLIC CLASSROOMS

Patrick S. Fahy FMS

FAITH IN CATHOLIC CLASSROOMS

Theory and practice

St Paul Publications

FAITH IN CATHOLIC CLASSROOMS: Theory and practice

First published, May 1992

National Library of Australia
Cataloguing-in-Publication data:
Fahy, P.S. (Patrick Stephen).
Faith in Catholic Classrooms: theory and practice.
Bibliography
Includes index
ISBN 0 949080 63 2
1. Catholic Church — Education. 2. Catholic schools. 3. Christian education of children.
I. Title.
377.82

Cover design: Bruno Colombari SSP

Nihil Obstat: Rev. John Thornhill SM
Censor Deputatus

Imprimatur: ✠ Bede Heather DD, LSS
Bishop of Parramatta, 19th November 1991

The Nihil Obstat and Imprimatur are official declarations that the work contains nothing contrary to Faith or Morals. It is not implied thereby that those granting the Nihil Obstat and Imprimatur agree with the contents, statements, or opinions expressed.

Published by
ST PAUL PUBLICATIONS — Society of St Paul,
60-70 Broughton Road — PO Box 230 — Homebush, NSW 2140

Typeset and printed by Society of St Paul, Wantirna South, Victoria

---

St Paul Publications is an activity of the Priests and Brothers of the Society of St Paul who proclaim the Gospel through the media of social communication

To: Betty Fahy
Wife and Mother
Encourager of learning.

From: A grateful son,
"Thanks Mum".

To: Mary, mother of Jesus,
aware of the needs of all,
attentive to her Son.

From: A grateful son and Church
"Thanks Mum".

Feast of Mary's Assumption, 1991

ACKNOWLEDGEMENT

Brother Patrick S. Fahy, FMS PhD, wishes to acknowledge as contribution to this work the advice and encouragement of colleagues at the

AUSTRALIAN CATHOLIC UNIVERSITY

an eight campus university spread over 3000 kilometres of eastern Australia.

It provides tertiary education for teaching, nursing, business, theology, religious education, arts and sciences within a Christian-Catholic values ethos.

Thanks are due also to: Professor George F. Madaus, Boston College; Professor Thomas H. Groome, Boston College; Professor Richard P. McBrien, Notre Dame University; and Mrs Pip Kalajzich, typist of the manuscript.

CONTENTS

CHAPTER 1

FAITH IN CATHOLIC CLASSROOMS

The title of this book can obviously be understood at two levels. Firstly the level of faith as *confidence*, confidence that Catholic classrooms are in fact achieving what they set out to achieve academically and religiously, the issue of *effectiveness*. Secondly the word faith can be understood in the context of a religious faith, the growing realisation of a *personal relationship with a living God*. In the Catholic context this is obviously faith in the risen Jesus, his Father and The Holy Spirit they send (Acts 2:17) as interpreted by Catholic tradition. Faith in Catholic classrooms therefore raises questions of the place of *religious faith* and *faith development* in the *classrooms* and *curriculum* of Catholic schools.

Confidence in Catholic classrooms entails a *dual confidence* in both their academic standards and faith development. For this reason this book will have a dual focus. Firstly, the academic effectiveness of Catholic classrooms, how well do they reflect the values of sound curriculum. Secondly, the proper place of *faith-theology-education* within a model of religious education, for a full and effective faith development among pupils.

The inclusion of a specific 103 classrooms may seem unusual but it serves to highlight the methodology (conceptual analysis and empirical cross checking against a sizeable sample of actual classrooms). Only on this dual basis can any valid hope for a theory of Catholic schools or religious education be built.

Effectiveness is a key concept in both secular and religious learnings. The book will explore the Secular School Effectiveness debate on home and school effects and show that the pitfalls and inadequacies that limited those studies were also those that hampered the Catholic School Effectiveness debate in its early stages. Fortunately more adequate approaches from secular school studies have now been applied to Catholic schools and homes and have provided more optimistic results. The book will review and evaluate these studies to allow greater confidence in the findings for the Catholic School Effectiveness debate.

Religious faith and its relationship to the Catholic school curriculum has been a focus of recent debate. Documents from the Congregation for Catholic Education (*The Catholic School* (1977) and *The Religious Dimensions of a Catholic School* (1988) have been widely published and have added to the informed debate.

The latter document asserts:

'Intellectual development and growth as a Christian go forward hand in hand ... a relationship exists between faith and human culture. Human culture remains human and must be taught with scientific objectivity. But lessons ... to those students who are believers will not divorce faith from this culture.' *(Congregation, 1988: 41-42.)*

These are prophetic words for this study, theoretical and empirical of faith in Catholic schools.

Various models of the religious education curriculum have been proposed and the place of education-in-faith vs education-in-religion suggested. These studies are reviewed and evaluated in the light of recent theological discussions on faith. Some of the implications of these studies are the subject of *empirical study* in this book, especially those related to the place of religious faith in Catholic classrooms. *This study is unique in having total participation of students in 103 Catholic religious education classrooms* with a wide range of religious and academic variables, and uses these to test faith and learning models.

The *empirical study* at the base of this book involves total staff population (N = 448), total Year 10 (Sophomore) and Year 12 (Senior) students (N = 3431) in 23 Australian Catholic schools. While limited in sample the sophisticated analysis goes beyond most of the secular school studies and all of the Catholic school studies. The ability to analyse total schools, 103 individual religious education classrooms and 3431 students is a key feature enabling a proper test of theoretical speculations.

The review of empirical studies of Catholic schools will focus on USA, England, Ireland and Australia where the majority of the work has been done. The limitations of some earlier studies and the undue influence of their findings on religious educators unskilled in the interpretation of statistical approaches led to a pessimistic view of Catholic schools. This view is now being corrected by more reliable and valid studies that are showing Catholic schools to have a unique, positive 'effect' (not necessarily causal but certainly concomitant), on key *faith variables*.

The *faith variables* defined and discussed in the book are based on approximate measures of reliable and valid scales. It is impossible to 'capture' someone's faith level by an empirical measure. Faith is a complex and beautiful relationship between the person and God. No paper and pencil test can capture that. But it is claimed that carefully prepared, trialed and tested items can get a *rough approximation* to the underlying faith reality. For example one personal free choice item such as:

'Christ is a real person in my daily life',

answered in an anonymous free environment has been found with 14 other items to give a reliable and valid measure of something I have decided to call *Christian Faith of Students*. Related items in a personal tone included:

'I see God as a loving Father'

'The Holy Spirit influences my present life'.

They were not creedal, notional statements, but phrased in a way to make a personal free faith response possible. The theory of knowledge (epistemology) behind this evaluation and these scales is outlined in more detail below in this chapter.

Just to give a sense of the major variables covered by the study I will list them without comment. Chapter 5 will provide the research evidence for each.

1. Christian Faith of students
2. Catholic practice of students
3. Social Justice Awareness of students
4. Christian community of staff
5. Vocational awareness of students
6. Vocational interest of students
7. Student self-esteem
8. Academic Achievement of students

With these and 20 other scales as predictors the dynamics and model of a more adequate view of religious education fitting these students in 103 classrooms will be explored.

Catholic schools do not exist solely for the goals of religious education. To be good Catholic schools they have to be good schools: the academic achievement of students is a vital outcome for future success in employment and/or tertiary study. Accordingly this study of faith (confidence) in Catholic classrooms must include some evaluation of major USA and Australian studies of Catholic school academic achievement. The studies of Coleman, Hoffer and Kilgare (1982) in the USA and Flynn (1985) in Australia will be compared and evaluated to yield the best available conclusions on academic achievement in Catholic classrooms.

For those of us who can recall, the launching by the USSR of Sputnik, the first artificial earth satellite in October, 1956 was a marvellous event. We would watch it passing steadily through the array of fixed stars and rush inside to a radio to catch the 'beep, beep' of its signal. As marvellous as it was then we had no inkling of the transformation that that considerable scientific and technical achievement by the Soviets was to have upon the educational and technical systems of the Western world. For the obvious inference from the Soviet's success was that we were falling behind and lacked the depth of technical and scientific knowledge needed for 'a great leap forward'. Criticism was levelled at the schools and the quality of curriculum in all subjects. It was commonly thought the schools were ineffective and we had to find out why and how to correct this tendency. Thus was launched the Secular School Effectiveness debate with a key study by James Coleman and associates (1966) in the USA being one among many. In England Michael Rutter and co-workers (1979), also studied school effectiveness with a novel approach. This study will critically review these studies and lay a foundation for the Catholic School Effectiveness debate.

1. OUTLINE OF STUDIES AND LIMITATIONS

The Secular School Effectiveness Debate has developed a body of theory and method that has informed the investigations of the Catholic School Effectiveness tradition. Such a tradition adds to the achievement and learning outcomes of the secular debate the meaningful dimension of the Christian faith vision in the Catholic tradition. Key figures within this Catholic School Effectiveness debate are researchers such as Greeley and Rossi (1966); Greeley, McCready and McCourt (1976) in the USA; Hornsby-Smith (1978) in England and Leavey (1972a, 1972b), Flynn (1975, 1977, 1985), and Fahy (1980a,1980b) in Australia. All this research and others beside witness to a growing interest in the effectiveness of Catholic schools both on faith and academic criteria. Coleman (1982) and Flynn (1985) discuss the academic criteria and will be examined in this study. This book will critically investigate the body of research to discern the worth or value of competing claims and provide some new criteria by which Catholic School Effectiveness may be estimated.

First some of the limitations of the study should be noted.

Under this heading it may be important to note some things you will *not* learn about Catholic School effectiveness.

Firstly, because the samples for these studies have all been drawn from Catholic secondary schools in USA, UK and Australia you will learn nothing about needs and processes of Catholic primary or tertiary institutions.

Secondly, because of the difficulty of getting matched parental responses, you will learn of parents and home background only through the eyes of their children.

Thirdly, because of the complexities of getting estimates of the mass media effects it will not be possible to assess that pervasive influence.

It is appropriate now to turn to basic definitions of the key concepts of the study, effectiveness, efficiency, and religious effectiveness to be used in the book. Also a number of key assumptions will be outlined.

2. BASIC DEFINITIONS

Effectiveness vs efficiency

Efficiency comes out of an industrial model applied to schools whereby a minimisation of cost for a given output is sought. Thus should a given program of remedial education for a disadvantaged group fail to show significant learning improvement it should be axed irrespective of other positive benefits. Effectiveness however is a broader concept.

Madaus (1980, p.22) defines it as ...

> A school may be said to be effective to the same extent that there is a congruence between its objectives and its achievements. In other words, it is effective to the extent that it accomplishes what it sets out to do.

The work of Flynn (1985) has shown the importance of process measures such as climate and ethos which vary with the religious outcomes of Catholic schools.

Flynn (1985) shows that these climate and internal school processes play an important role in the overall effectiveness. They account for a quite sizeable proportion of the *variance* (a statistical variation term to be explained in Chapter 2) in criterion measures. Climate or press variables include such things as achievement, friendly relations between staff and students, fair and reasonable discipline policy, school morale and staff morale, religious and social educational goals.

Catholic school

The Catholic school is founded on a dual vision, it seeks to become a community of parents, teachers and learners that attempts a genuine integration of both human learning and religious faith, around the person of Jesus Christ.

Growth in understanding of the meanings of human learning truly integrated with a religious meaning system, freely chosen, leads to maximum personal development for all peoples no matter which tradition. For Catholics this is found in their own faith educational systems. One special format for this process is the Catholic school, not denying that there are other suitable formats.

This definition of Catholic school as seeking to construct a meaning system by integrating human learning and religious faith will be important when we come to recent theoretical perspectives in religious education.

The meaningfulness and effectiveness of the Catholic school has a number of dimensions. There is a dual supportive role of family and school, the influence of the religious climate and ethos, religious practice in school and home, student personality and happiness variables, peer group influences to name a few. There has been a long and spirited debate seeking to separate the effectiveness of home and school on religious variables. This study claims to be the *first* to do this on an univocal basis at the actual level of religious education classrooms.

There is a further assumption here that has not been sufficiently examined, namely:

> that the Christian school has a unique, positive effect upon students' Christian faith and practice in addition to that which it has in common with family background, parents' Mass attendance, student personality and peer group influences. (Fahy, 1980a, p. 3)

The purpose of this study is to critically examine this assumption. All these environments – home, school, peer group and personality factors, impinge on the evolving life of the adolescent. By knowing their relative impact we will be in a better position to understand the dynamics of the Catholic school and classroom.

What is being examined here is central to the goals of Catholic schools. If the assumption that schools have a unique effect is not supported by this study then, the extensive human and financial resources being expended on Catholic schools may not be justified. Presumably family or parish based catechesis should receive greater attention. Then catechesis as such should be removed from the school classroom and confined to voluntary out-of-class activities. This would entail a major shift in the direction of religious education/ catechesis at least for the countries studied here.

If on the other hand the assumption that schools and classrooms do have a unique effect is supported then real encouragement would be given to the work of Catholic teachers, those directly involved in the religious education department as well as those contributing to the overall school climate. There would be the ability to focus on the specific factors which seem to make classrooms effective in promoting Christian faith and practice.

If a specific classroom effect can be demonstrated for Christian faith and values then this will justify efforts to keep faith-related activities within the classroom context. This is a major point of present debate in theories of religious education. Whether or not a dichotomy such as 'education-in-faith and education-in-religion' or 'catechesis' and 'religious education' should be accepted needs to be examined for the implications for the classroom.

Religious education

Religious education is a broad term encompassing education within any faith tradition. A more appropriate term for Christians would be Christian Religious Education (Groome, 1980) yet this still lacks specificity for a particular tradition. 'Lutheran Religious Education' or 'Catholic Religious Education' would be valid. Within the Catholic tradition the term catechesis is more common. With all these cautions, this present study focuses solely on the Catholic tradition of the

Christian Church. It will be appropriate to use the shorthand term 'Religious Education' to mean those deliberate activities which initiate young believers into the Catholic tradition of the Christian Church, and which involve an integration of cognitive understandings and growth in a living faith relationship with Jesus. In this sense catechesis will be used in this book as a faith sharing between believers founded on a common understanding of religious symbols and categories. The theological set of understandings that we bring to any faith sharing (however simple) will extend as well as limit our ability to communicate our personal faith visions. Catechesis involves both theological knowledge (however simple) as well as communication of faith vision (however simple).

In this sense *religious education*, strictly speaking, is a generic term applicable to all religious traditions, but will be used in this book to examine the Catholic tradition. Within that tradition religious education seeks for a link between religious knowledge and a living faith relationship.

Faith

Faith is a universal phenomenon in the sense that all women and men have the potentiality to be believers. Rahner insists:

> Every human being, even previous to the explicit preaching of the Christian message, is always potentially a believer and already in possession, in the grace that is prior to freedom, of what he is to believe (i.e. freely accept): God's direct self-communication in Christ' (Rahner, 1975, p.496).

Rahner further insists that in speaking of faith we need to think of two kinds of knowledge, one communicated purely from outside and one touching the depth of human reality. Faith is intimately connected with this deeper kind of knowledge, experienced in the depths of human reality as grace (Rahner, 1975, p.497). What is fundamental is the hidden direct revelation of God in our lives. To lead to faith is to assist understanding of this deep experience, to put names, categories or symbols on what has already been experienced. Rahner calls the fundamental direct relationship with God, 'grace'. The faith process is the ongoing explication in human language of this core 'grace experience'. Thus faith is *personal knowledge of God.* (McBrien, 1980, p. 25). Christian faith, therefore, is personal knowledge of God *in Christ*. Because *knowledge is an integral aspect of faith it must always be made available in the context of a particular theological framework. This has implications for classroom religious education. Religious knowledge is only truly communicated in a set of specific theological categories or symbols.*

3. THEOLOGICAL METHOD

How we interpret what are essentially theological insights into Catholic schools depends in part on the theological method we adopt. The procedure used here is Revisionist Method developed by David Tracy (1975) from the earlier correlation method of Tillich (1957). It is best defined as:

> reflection upon the meanings present in common human experience and the meanings present in the Christian tradition. (Tracy, 1975, p. 35)

Tracy (1975) argues that only by examining the depth of our common human experience will the fundamental questions and the answers that human delving can glean come to the surface. They are then ready to be put in confrontation/mutual correction with the questions and answers reflected upon in the common search of the Christian life, texts and tradition. All of these question/answers need to be held in critical correlation until a new synthesis emerges under the action of God's Spirit inspiring human effort.

In this study the human experience of senior students and staff in 23 Catholic high schools is researched in detail using empirical social science scales linked to a number of key elements of the Catholic tradition, namely faith, religious practice, social justice awareness, religious goals and climate of classrooms. By empirical means these estimates of faith criteria are then held in critical correlation with other home, school, peer-group factors to seek a new insight into the effectiveness of the same classrooms. The Revisionist method provides a theological method which underlies this approach.

4. THE CHURCH AND SOCIAL SCIENCE KNOWLEDGE

This section will examine the theory of knowledge (epistemology) of this study and explain a number of assumptions.

Social science and religious issues

Many Church people are suspicious, often rightly so, of a too ready use of empirical social science procedures applied to religious questions. Such suspicion may well stem from a reaction against the Enlightenment's philosophical movement of the last century which unduly stressed the autonomy of reason over faith. The English Logical Positivists, Locke (d. 1704) and Hume (d. 1776) were key figures in the movement. They stressed logical and empirical analysis and so denied any place for a God as a part of this movement. Their view of empirical social science was that it yields pure, objective, certain knowledge free of any bias. Thinking people are rightly suspicious of such a rigid view of knowledge. Religious people reject the atheistic value base that underlies this approach.

The adoption of an empirical social science epistemology in this present study *in no way* commits one to the Logical Positivist position. Rather than a pure objectivity, this study claims a relative balance of objectivity and subjectivity whereby the data is viewed through the inherent biases of the group of people designing the survey and those responding.

This more cautious view of empirical social science takes account of the tentative, biased, historically and culturally conditioned view of our knowledge and is more in line with the philosophy of Hegel (d. 1831). A projection of his views sees computer processed data as still conditional on the biases of the people and processes of collection. House (1977) has argued for this persuasive (not absolutely certain) view of empirical evaluation knowledge.

Hegel's view looks for a thesis, antithesis, mutual confrontation and correction until a new synthesis emerges. Thus with regard to the framing of the survey questions the use of a team of people helps to minimise bias that could be more significant with a single researcher. Thus the data gathered by empirical social science, although different from normal historical data, still partakes of the conditional and probable nature of social science knowledge. Careful checks by a group, pretesting of surveys help to minimise bias from a single observer. This is founded in Hegel's philosophy.

Some claim that empirical social science can never fully capture the complex reality of religious faith and relationships. *This is true* for any attitude measure can not *capture* but only *approximate* the underlying complex tendency towards a person or object. However, it is possible to obtain an estimate of the strength of affect towards any person or thing if a reliable and valid scale of items is formed. In faith areas suitable empirical scales can be formed which, while not capturing underlying faith realities, can give reliable and valid estimates of the complex faith dimensions. A lot depends on the range of items initially selected if a reasonably full mapping of the area is to be achieved. It is the claim of this book that the set of scales formed do in fact map the major components of the faith, home, school, peer group environments of Catholic adolescents.

Social science method and bias

The social science method employed here is that of empirical evaluation. Many Catholics reject such social science because of the claim made to be 'objective data', 'value free data'. What those social scientists failed to realise was that every human activity is touched with bias. We bring our unconscious assumptions and biases to all that we do. When the social scientists design their surveys they include their biases by the items they include and the ones they omit. When they choose their methods of analysis there are inbuilt assumptions as we shall see for some of Andrew Greeley's research in Chapter 3. So there is no such thing as a purely objective social science survey. All data and interpretations are touched by the bias of the social scientist, process of collection, analysis and interpretation.

However, it is possible to reduce the bias by a number of procedures. Firstly, having chosen the area of interest, one should seek assistance from sample subjects to generate items. Sort and sift these but leave nothing out. Add your own items of interest if issues of importance do not surface.

Secondly, distribute the survey to a wide representative group so that major opinions will be detected and minor idiosyncrasies will even out.

Thirdly, be sure that the survey is anonymous and take careful steps in the procedure so that subjects see that the survey has been distributed in a random manner.

Fourthly, generate scales (groups of items) with a higher reliability and validity than individual items and use them in higher analyses. In this way the bias inherent in a piece of empirical social science is minimised, but not eliminated completely.

Such empirical data can complement historical, anecdotal data from other sources and give a picture of a social organisation by taking into account simultaneously the opinions of a large number of organisation members. This is more valid than views from only a few people.

Let us move now to the scope of this present study to see how it minimises bias and what key questions it attempts to answer.

5. SCOPE OF SURVEY

This book operates at three levels: Firstly, a theological and theoretical study of faith and religious education models, secondly, a meta-evaluation of secular and Catholic school effectiveness studies, that is asking how valid are the studies carried out to date, and thirdly, what new light is shed on Catholic school classroom studies by the sample examined here.

The sample chosen for the study is a non-random one but does preserve a representative character for the system of schools being used as a target. It is the system of schools in Australia administered by the Marist Brothers with headquarters in Sydney. A total of 23 secondary schools were involved, 17 single-sex boys schools and six co-educational schools. In order to select a sample representative to this school system, it was decided to survey all secondary staff in these schools plus all students in Year 10 (Sophomore) and Year 12 (Senior), these being the two exit points for the Australian schools when students may well have formed some evaluative judgments about their school experience.

The sample of staff whose opinions were sought for the study are shown in *Table 1.1.*

Table 1.1

Number of secondary school staff involved in study by sex and status

	Male	Female	Total
RELIGIOUS	212	10	222
LAITY	195	85	280
TOTALS	407	95	502

It is clear that the sample is biased towards male staff. There is a balance of lay and religious opinions.

This sample outline will be useful in interpreting the Christian Community Scale and other staff concerns.

The sample of students is shown in *Table 1.2*.

Table 1.2

Number of students in the 23 schools of the study by sex and school type

	Male	Female	Total
SINGLE SEX	2821	–	2821
CO-EDUCATIONAL	287	323	610
TOTALS	3108	323	3431

It is obvious that the sample is biased towards boys in single sex schools due to the historical evolution of the Marist Brothers' educational efforts in Australia. There are however sufficient girls in co-educational schools jointly administered by Marists and female religious groups to make some comparisons possible. This choice excluding girls-only schools was a deliberate one in the light of the very thorough and multivariate study of Leavey (1972b) of 560 Sixth form girls. Leavy developed very reliable factor analytic scales. It was felt best not to cover this ground again. See Section 2.4.

The sample of 23 secondary schools is a non-random one from the total population of 94 Catholic secondary schools in three states of Australia. This lack of randomness precludes any precise generalisation to all Catholic schools even in these three states. However, the *specificity of the sample* to one Religious Order system and the depth of the analysis may yield findings for this school system which would have persuasive implications for wider policy issues in other systems of Christian education, here and overseas.

Indeed this notion of evaluation as persuasion (House, 1977, p. 5-7), not as convincing argument, is at the heart of the evaluation method being applied in this study.

6. GOD AND REALMS OF MEANING

But there are other hypotheses about the nature of schools and indeed the nature of knowledge. Peter Berger and Thomas Luckmann (1966) discuss a view of knowledge as a system of symbols (language, science etc.) that constitute a symbolic universe, a network that legitimates and justifies the existing social order. In this view a school is effective if it is an organisation that hands on the tradition, the knowledge and the language needed to maintain the social order. Groome (1980) would call for a critique of the social order by critical reflection and praxis judged under the ultimate norm of the Reign of God. Berger and Luckmann would argue this is just one more symbolic universe. One can only break out of that mould of a humanly created symbolic universe if *God does indeed break through to give meaning to human existence*. If He does not break through then human existence is essentially meaningless, confined to ultimate destruction in death. (McBrien, 1980, pp. 101-139). The basic Christian hope is that *God does break through in Jesus* to provide ultimate meaning to our limited efforts in living, education or death. Therefore it is essential for the Christian to examine schools against this theological background and ask questions of ultimate meaning. Are the

Christian schools being effective in assisting both staff and students achieve a sense of meaning in their own life? Meaning is defined as a genuine integration of human and religious values drawn from the gospel. Meaning includes exposure to all the disciplines of human study themselves rich in ultimate meaning. As we saw, Philip Phenix (1964) has made a penetrating study of the major disciplines of learning and has shown from human reflection the essential meaning base behind them. Phenix (1964, p.38) saw that the challenge for schools lies …

> in recognising the centrality of meaning in human life and in creating a curricula deliberately designed to overcome the prevalent forces of meaninglessness.

He begins with an analysis of human nature and insists that a key category for the human person is a search for *meaning*. Meaning is defined (1964, p. 21) as 'rationality, reason and mind often tending to be too narrowly construed as referring to the processes of logical thinking.'

Phenix (1964, p. 21) points to the wide range of meanings of human life,

> in activities of organic adjustment,
> in perception, in logical thinking,
> in social organisation, in speech,
> in artistic creation, in self awareness,
> in purposive decision, in moral judgement,
> in the consciousness of time,
> and in the activity of worship
> all these comprise the life of man and woman.

He goes on to assert that if the essence of human nature is in the life of meaning then the proper aim of education is to promote the growth of meaning.

He divides the curriculum into six realms of meaning with similar scholarly disciplines grouped together.

1. *Symbolics* – the symbols of ordinary discourse (*language*), symbols of numeric analysis (*mathematics*), non discursive symbolic forms (*ritual, dreams, myth, legend, graphic symbols*).
2. *Empirics* – physical sciences (*physics, chemistry, geology, biology*) (has added dimension of destiny with life), *psychology,* (the science of mind), *social science* (the world of culture and society).
3. *Esthetics* – *music* (individual musical compositions), the *visual arts* (painting, drawing, graphic arts, sculpture and architecture), *human movement* (creative sense of movement, dance), *literature* (literature communicates values).
4. *Synnoetics* – (where one has a direct insight into the beings or oneself as concrete wholes existing in relation) *personal knowledge* (insights about myself and others), personal knowledge about my own history or growth, knowledge of another on an intimate one-to-one basis, a comprehending of the other.
5. *Ethics* – *ethical meanings* or *moral knowledge* (right deliberate action, what a person ought voluntarily to do), moral action based on freedom - how to promote.
6. *Synoptics* – attempts to integrate all knowledge, based on a view of time, human events of the past studied by *history, religion* seeks to integrate all meanings, 'go to the limits' and seek the *ultimate*, religious faith, rituals, silence, God as personal, the problem of evil, redemption, *philosophy* is the interpretation of meaning, (a dialectic method, evaluation and synthesis).

These then are the elements around which Phenix builds his model of meaning as the base of the curriculum. He argues for each of these as significant in its own right yet even more so in relation to each other in an integrated whole. There is a constant stress on the scholarly disciplines of the 'school' being integrated into a coherent synthesis by the link with meaning and purpose. We will see in this book if a close empirical social science study of the religious and academic areas of Catholic schools will support or weaken his model.

Another philosopher intent on the meaning of human life and indeed of all Creation in an evolutionary process is of course *Teilhard de Chardin* (1959, 1964, 1965, 1966). From his research on Peking man and the evolution of the human form, Teilhard has developed a simple view of all matter and life evolving (well in accord with science and Christian faith). He proposes a model of matter, energy and life moving towards a final Omega point. The stages are: (1959, pp. 200-204)

Alpha Point	– The beginning, the Big Bang, 15,000 million years ago.
Cosmogenesis	– evolution of stars and galaxies into observed structures.
Geogenesis	– the evolution of rock structures from star remnants, into rocks and continents.
Biogenesis	– the evolution of plant and animal life forms. The power of radial energy, the Spirit of love, guiding the evolution.
Noogenesis	– the evolution of human persons. A realm of thought and love begins to grow around the earth.
Christogenesis	– this realm of thought and love finds its highest expression in evolution most fully into the mind and Spirit of Jesus.
The Omega point	– when all will, through Jesus and in the Spirit, be drawn back to God the Father who is 'all in all'.

The progressive evolutionary model fits well with modern scientific models and links them with a solid Christian theological framework. Evolution is God's method of Creation drawing us back to God. God brought the Big Bang into existence out of nothing and has guided all evolution with his Love (radial energy).

All schools are an essential component of the evolution and spread of knowledge and love (Noosphere) and in addition Catholic schools have a dual role of integrating that evolution of knowledge and love into the mind and Spirit of Christ (Christogenesis). Thus the valid insight of Phenix into the meaning system of the curriculum is closely linked to the evolutionary Christian view of Teilhard and together they provide a firm foundation for conceptualising the purpose of Catholic (Christian) schools.

With this base then the present study proposes to make use of the social science system model, as an assumption of the statistical procedures but to move beyond it in interpretation. Interpretation will be based upon a theistic meaning system for *effectiveness*, essentially tied to the theological categories of a present reality and critical in-breaking of the Reign of God. In this theistic view effectiveness is defined as:

> Effectiveness of an organisation is the degree to which it assists its members and those it serves achieve a sense of personal and corporate meaning growing in knowledge and love into the image of Christ and his Spirit.

For Christian schools committed to a dual integration of human learning with religious faith that meaning will need to be seen as full human development linking human learning with a personal faith in Jesus expressed in a shared community of believers (the Church). This view of Christian school effectiveness enables it to use appropriate social science procedures but not be bound by them in its interpretation of what are essentially faith relationships.

Only the ultimate mystery of God can give meaning to the faith journey of the parents, staff and students of Catholic schools but the empirical procedures can at least track some of the footprint edges of that journey.

In the next chapter we will look at the secular school effectiveness debate to compare some of the studies and their procedures. This will give the current state of methodologies that may usefully be applied to the Catholic school effectiveness debate. It will also prevent falling into some of the same pitfalls.

CHAPTER 2

THE SECULAR SCHOOL EFFECTIVENESS DEBATE

If school effectiveness is about helping students develop meaning in significant objectives, then knowledge and skills in areas of human learning should be important. Phenix (1964) and Chardin (1959) show the connection between human disciplines, realms of meaning and religious values.

This chapter examines this question from the viewpoint of the secular school effectiveness debate, seeks to identify the key studies and their findings and then reviews various critiques of the initially very pessimistic findings. A final section will suggest some new elements of method which may help the Catholic school effectiveness debate avoid pitfalls such as:

1. lack of clear definition of effectiveness,
2. inappropriate measures, norm-referenced aptitude tests vs curriculum-sensitive measures,
3. inappropriate methods of analysis with unjustified assumptions.

As noted above it was the Soviet challenge to Western technology in the shape of the small, antenna crowned satellite, Sputnik, that led in 1957 to a massive effort to upgrade educational systems in the Western countries. Nowhere was this more marked than in the USA where major curriculum development projects such as Physical Sciences Study Curriculum (PSSC) Chemical Education Material Study (CHEM Study), Biological Sciences Curriculum Study (BSCS) were carefully developed and trialed. Involving both upgraded content linked to the discipline and clear connection with student learning theory they were soon trialed, modified and adapted by other countries. In an attempt to assess general impact of these and other school/home effects many studies were done.

The most influential study was one directed by James Coleman called the Equality of Educational Opportunity (1966) sponsored by the US Government. Extensive reanalyses took place in subsequent years (Jencks, 1972). Also some international studies of school effectiveness and compensatory education have added to the debate. There has been a focus on poor and minority groups of students.

The findings of these studies, taken together, paint a fairly gloomy picture and seem to lead to a denial in the traditional belief of the efficacy of schools. A critique of the assumptions and methods of these studies will however reveal that that judgment should be suspended until more reliable evidence is gathered.

1. COLEMAN (1966) STUDY

There was in the USA in the mid 1960s a growing concern for the poor and the disadvantaged. One expression of this concern was a massive survey, Coleman, Campbell, Hobson, McPartland, Mood, Weinfield and York (1966) entitled *The Equality of Educational Opportunity* which sought to show how the inequalities of school resources, in predominantly black or white areas, were having an adverse impact upon pupils' achievement, at least as measured by norm-referenced tests of achievement. The general presumption was that variation in school resource factors would help to explain variance in students' achievement scores and point to areas where more finance could restore equality. (Variance is a statistical measure of the spread of scores in a measure. (See Research Note at the end of this chapter.)

The study was the largest survey of American public education in history. It involved 4000 schools, 60 000 teachers, 645 000 pupils, categorised into six racial and cultural groups. Norm-referenced standardised tests of ability were administered to pupils from grades one, three, six, nine and 12. The teachers completed questionnaires about their academic background, teaching experience and attitudes. School principals and local administrators reported on facilities ranging from average teacher salary to numbers and age of textbooks, library and school resources from over 4000 schools.

One example, illustrating the lengths to which Coleman and his co-workers went to estimate actual usage of school resources was with library books. They took samples of school library books and actually counted, from the circulation card, how many times the book had been borrowed in the last year. This data was entered together with all the other information into the regression equation for this school's resources.

Yet the results of this massive effort were quite unexpected. Instead of demonstrating a marked inequality between schools related to differences in resources, the study found that

> ... schools bring little influence to bear on a child's achievement that is independent of his (home) background and general social context; ... this very lack of an independent effect means that the inequalities imposed on children by their home, neighbourhood and peer environment are carried along to become the inequalities with which they confront adult life at the end of school (Coleman *et al.*, 1966, p. 325).

This was a startling finding from the largest and seemingly best run educational evaluation in history. The trust that had been placed on the institutions of schooling to be a social leveller, to raise the children of the lower classes so they could compete more equally with those from more fortunate home backgrounds, seemed ill founded.

The whole reason for the existence of schools seemed to be in question. If they could not redress inequalities imposed by home and social background why should society continue to support them? Schools were seemingly having little unique effect upon pupil achievement, at least as measured by standardised norm-referenced tests of ability. Were the tests at fault or the schools or both?

Coleman's conclusion seemed intolerable and led many other researchers to reanalyse his data. Smith (1972) with extensive reanalysis came to the same general conclusion. Perhaps the criteria was in error. Jencks and his co-workers (Jencks, Smith, Acland, Bone, Cohen, Gintis, Heyns, Michelson, 1972) in a related study chose the criteria of post-school job income but reached similar findings that the home background and social background were all important.

Thus in the late 1960s and early 1970s a pessimistic picture regarding the effectiveness of schools developed and seemed to provide a basis for a denial of traditional beliefs about the impact of schooling. Ivan Illich published an influential book called *Deschooling Society* (1970) with a philosophical justification for this general pessimistic view of schooling. This pessimism seemed to influence religious educators, such as Westerhoff (1972, 1976) who rejected a 'schooling-instructional paradigm' for religious education. It must be remembered however that Westerhoff was writing about the one day Protestant Sunday school model and it should not be extended too readily to the five day school model with integrated secular/religious curriculum.

2. RUTTER'S 15000 HOURS

Another major school effectiveness study, this time from England, was conducted by a team led by Michael Rutter (Rutter, Maghan, Mortimore, Ouston and Smith, 1979) called *Fifteen thousand hours: Secondary schools and their effects on children*. The 15000 hours was an estimate of time in school from age of five until leaving school. Over a three year period the team conducted an intensive survey of 12 secondary schools in the inner-London area. A very wide range of data was collected with a shift away from physical resources towards more social variables (degree of academic emphasis or press for achievement by both staff and pupils, range of incentives and rewards), behaviour of students (in terms of delinquency rates, regularity of attendance and the proportion staying on at school beyond the legally enforced period), were also considered. The team also actually went into classrooms to gather data on teacher-pupil process interaction.

Rutter adopted a systems model for classification of his variables into intake, process and outcome which led him finally to propose tentatively some causal processes at work in the schools. Dunkin and Biddle *A Study of Teaching* (1976) provide a similar systems approach.

Rutter based his analysis of variables on a series of procedures culminating in multiple linear regression. He is thus unable to extract the unique contribution of his predictor measures to the criteria. Regression is an approach where a set of predictor variables seek to 'explain' the variance in key criteria. When there are several criteria regression cannot separate the unique contribution of blocks of predictors to overlapping criteria. Only the symmetric decomposition of variance (Beaton, 1974) can do this uniquely.

In spite of these limitations, what were Rutter's principal findings? Firstly, there was wide variation in the 12 schools in the students' behaviour, regularity of attendance, proportion staying on beyond the legal period, their success in public exams and delinquency rates suggesting specific school effects.

Secondly, these differences in outcome were systematically related to the social variables of the school as an institution. Factors such as the degree of academic emphasis, teacher behaviour in lessons, a range of incentives and rewards, good conditions for pupils, pupils able to accept responsibility were all significantly associated with good outcomes (academic and behavioural).

Thirdly, a combined measure of overall school process, which Rutter termed ethos, or a set of values, attitudes and behaviour was found to be a powerful predictor of pupil achievement and behaviour. The next chapter will show how the research from Australia some seven years previously had clearly identified this key role of ethos or climate in school effectiveness variables.

3. MORE RECENT STUDIES

A review by Purkey and Smith (1982) has commented favourably on the Rutter study (without mention of regression order of entry problem) and highlighted the importance of the school climate factor in predicting achievement.

Brookover *et al* (1979) identified three interrelated variables: i. social inputs (student body composition and other personal inputs) ii. social structure (such as school size, classroom structure) iii. social climate (school culture as the norms, expectations and feelings about the school held by staff and students). All these were found to be significantly related to achievement.

Armor *et al* (1976), Doss and Holley (1982) studied program evaluations. The findings generally indicate that most schools with effectiveness programs are characterised by i. high staff expectation and morale, ii. a considerable degree of control by the staff over instructional decisions, iii. clear leadership from the principal, iv. clear goals for the school, and v. a sense of order in the school. The present study includes specific variables on staff morale and leadership by principal as well as clear goals and order inherent in a sense of meaning.

Rutter (1979) and Brookover (1979) are all pointing to the powerful influence of *climate variables* upon school outcomes. Climate is a process variable that links expectations, attitudes, sets of values, beliefs into a dynamic mix that influences the interactions between teachers and students in a school, and has a key influence on outcome achievement and attitudes. A school viewed from a climate model seeks change not by a massive influx of resources but by helping people to change themselves. The general strategy is best characterised as one that promotes collaborative planning, collegial work, and a school atmosphere conducive to experimentation and evaluation (Hargrove *et al*, 1981; Little, 1981).

Purkey and Smith (1982, p. 68) conclude that the climate model is the most effective one for long-term, incremental cultural change in schools. They endorse the notion of schools as functioning social systems.

This place of the informal school climate and other informal curriculum variables will be examined in the final chapter of this book. There climate will be seen as operative in both the formal and informal curriculum, through morale of teachers and students, a sense of co-operative teamwork, a clear sense of a value framework for learning and relationships, a sense of just and fair discipline and a sense of order or meaning.

4. SOME CRITIQUE OF COLEMAN (1966)

Studies of the English and Irish educational systems by Madaus and his colleagues (Madaus, Kellaghan and Rakow, 1975; Brimer, Madaus, Chapman, Kellaghan and Wood, 1977; Madaus, Airasian and Kellaghan, 1980) have questioned the assumptions and methods of the Coleman (1966) study and re-analyses. The major critiques may be grouped under the following headings.

Inadequacy of outcome measures

The Coleman (1966) study uses standardised norm-referenced tests of ability as its outcome measures. A verbal ability measure is interpreted as a good measure of achievement. Madaus *et al* (1979, pp. 5-10) show how such a measure (essentially an IQ measure), which is designed to maximise differences between individual students, is not an appropriate measure for a school objective or overall curriculum influence on groups of students. It tries to spread pupils out not to see if they have acquired the curriculum content.

Implicit in this debate on adequate measures is the question of a definition of school effectiveness. Madaus *et al* (1980, p. 24) argue that 'if a school is to be regarded as effective, it must achieve the objectives it sets out to achieve.' Hence, adequate outcome measures must, firstly, be congruent with the aims and objectives of the school or specific curricula; secondly, measure specific rather than general achievement, and, thirdly, be of a format geared to the way the subject is taught.

The measures employed in the present study are congruent with the specific academic and theological objectives of Catholic schooling, are designed to measure specific religious attitudes and behaviour and are administered in a format and setting (religious education class groupings) related to the way the subject is taught. This 'Religious Education class grouping' will be an important claim by this study to break new ground.

Madaus *et al* (1980, pp. 159-169) ask the question what kind of tests might be sensitive to schooling and comes up with the notion that they should attempt to measure specific skills and content rather than general achievement. They must be geared to the specific instructional experience of the course. The authors point to 'curriculum sensitive measures' where 'curricula are defined by external examiners, which are regarded as extremely important by both students and teachers, and for which over a long period of time a tradition of what and how to teach has been built up' (p. 165). The authors point to the public examination systems of Great Britain and Ireland, and one could add Australia standing in a similar tradition. It will be interesting to compare the research on achievement between the USA (Coleman, 1981) and Australia (Flynn, 1985) in Chapter 6. Suffice it to say Madaus' critique of the earlier Coleman (1966) study on the need for more sensitive 'curriculum sensitive measures' is a major one.

Unit of analysis

Coleman used as his unit of analysis the individual school leading to a severe reduction in sample size upon division of schools into regional and ethnic groups. He 'failed to distinguish between different kinds of high schools (trade, vocational, academic, and comprehensive) or between tracks (streams) or classes within schools' (Madaus *et al*, 1980, p. 33). Subsequent studies (Brimer *et al.*, 1977) have found substantial amounts of variance in school achievement between classes suggesting that there are specific effects of being within certain class groupings. The present study recognises this critique and uses the school as the unit of analysis initially, then proceeds to analysis between religious education classes nested within schools, and finally, analysing individual students within classes. In this way variance (variation) in religious outcomes attributable to each unit, school, religious education class, and individual, may be interpreted.

School environment measures

In line with a government policy oriented study, Coleman chose static measures of school environment, such as school size, per pupil expenditure, physical resources more amenable to policy and financial intervention. These showed little relation to achievement, at least as estimated by the construct verbal ability. Brimer *et al* (1977, pp. 287-300) show, in a sample of English schools, that it is the more indirect environment measures such as school climate, academic press (parents, friends setting standards for academic work) and examination orientation which have most impact upon achievement. This present study adopts a similar position by using student climate and press measures as predictors. In addition staff climate measures such as morale, job satisfaction, goal orientation and satisfaction with school administration are included. (Fahy, 1977a, pp. 36-91). Thus the present study avoids a too physical interpretation of the school environment that limited the Coleman (1966) study.

Heterogeneity of sample

Coleman's (1966) study carried out separate analyses for regional and ethnic groups thus reducing the heterogeneity of schooling and achievement. This reduced the likelihood of finding significant relations (Madaus *et al.*, 1980, p. 33). This present study, while identifying city (urban) and country (rural) regions, analyses all schools together for maximum heterogeneity. (This implies greater variation or variance and more chance of finding a significant effect.)

Regression analysis: order of entry

Coleman's (1966) study used a regression analysis to separate components of variance in school achievement. The point here is that Coleman entered family background variables into the first stage of the regression analysis arguing that what was learnt due to home factors is logically prior to the effects of schools. School variables were entered last in the analysis. This has the effect of attributing to family factors all of their unique explanatory power upon achievement plus all that family background shares in common with other variables entered subsequently. This unduly inflates the influence of family factors over and above school factors (Madaus *et al.*, 1979, pp. 21-22). To overcome this problem a method of symmetric variance decomposition has been suggested by Beaton (1973, 1974). Mayeske's (1972, 1973) reanalyses employed this technique and while the unique effect of school variables was still low, the influence of home and school factors acting in consort was found to be important. Coleman's (1966) study therefore did not use an appropriate method for separating the effects of home and school upon achievement.

Thus these more recent studies taken together suggest that Coleman's (1966) conclusions are not fully justified. Schools are not impotent, yet neither are they the sole determinant of learning that we often assume. This present study makes use of these new methods of analysis to ask similar questions about the effectiveness of Catholic schools on specifically religious criteria, avoiding Coleman's methodological pitfalls.

5. CONCLUSION

This review of the secular school effectiveness debate has highlighted:

1. The initial impact of the Coleman (1966) study.

2. The initial finding that home background seems to be the determinant of achievement with the schools being deemed impotent.
3. The reanalyses of this data by Smith (1972) and others that confirmed the initially pessimistic finding.
4. The study by Jencks *et al.* (1972) using post-school job income that seemed to confirm Coleman.
5. The research of Mayeske *et al.* (1972, 1973) that detected some school effects when better climate measures were employed.
6. The research of Madaus *et al.* (1975, 1979) on the Irish and English systems showed significant school effects upon achievement as measured by more 'curriculum sensitive' measures.
7. A major summary and critique of school effectiveness studies by Madaus, Airasian and Kellaghan (1980).
8. A major flaw of previous studies (Coleman, 1966; Rutter, 1979) was in the method of analysis based on multiple regression. Beaton (1973, 1974) designed a symmetric decomposition of variance to avoid the unjustified bias in the regression approach.
9. Coleman (1982) revised methods and measures and compares high school achievement of public, private and Catholic schools. Symmetric decomposition of variance was employed to systematically search for differences.

The view begins to emerge that with closer attention to climate measures, to curriculum sensitive measures and a better analytic technique that a more optimistic view of school effectiveness is evident. Schools are not all powerful, yet neither are they impotent. Schools can have an impact on student attitudes and achievement, even when the home background factors are statistically controlled. This more careful, reliable research begins to suggest that schools are fulfilling their traditional role of being a social leveller, raising the educational potential of young people from lower class home backgrounds.

6. RESEARCH NOTE: VARIANCE

When we collect information on a set of schools, or the classrooms within them (or even on the pupils within the classrooms) we frequently want to know how those schools, classrooms or pupils DIFFER.

To discover this we often take MEASURES on important VARIABLES. We may be able to get PUPIL'S AGE from the school files or SENSE OF MORALE (liking for the school, teachers, would like to learn here) from a simple survey.

In any given class we would expect a NARROW RANGE FOR AGE and a WIDE RANGE FOR MORALE.

Graphically if we plotted the AGE and MORALE values for this class against a number of students having that AGE or MORALE values for this class against the number of students having that AGE or MORALE we might expect graphs something like this:

Figure 2.1: Small and large variances

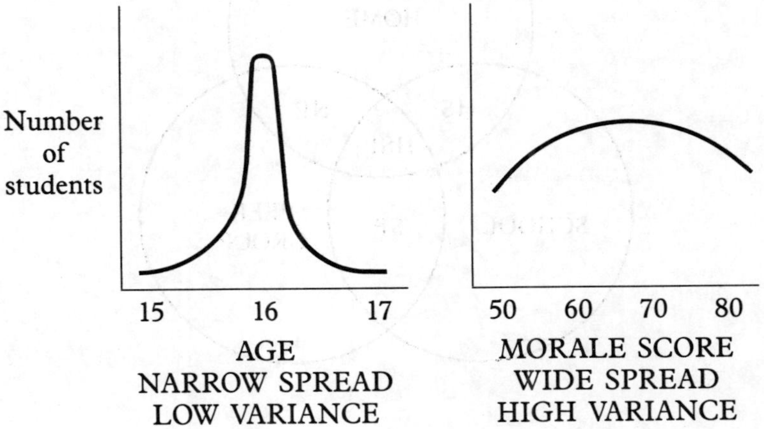

Variance is thus a mathematical way of estimating the area of a SPREAD of scores.

It is related to the other familiar concept of statistical analysis, the STANDARD DEVIATION by the relationship:

$$\text{VARIANCE} = (\text{STANDARD DEVIATION})^2$$

Computational procedures are available in any elementary statistics book and do not concern us here.

Variance is a very useful concept for it may be broken up into parts by analysis and various amounts attributed to various environments such as home, school, peer group, personality and staff factors. This enables one to get a carefully controlled estimate of the strength of these environments in the life of Catholic adolescents. This will be explained more fully in the discussion of Commonality analysis in Chapter 5.

Figure 2.2: Overlapping variance diagram (morale)

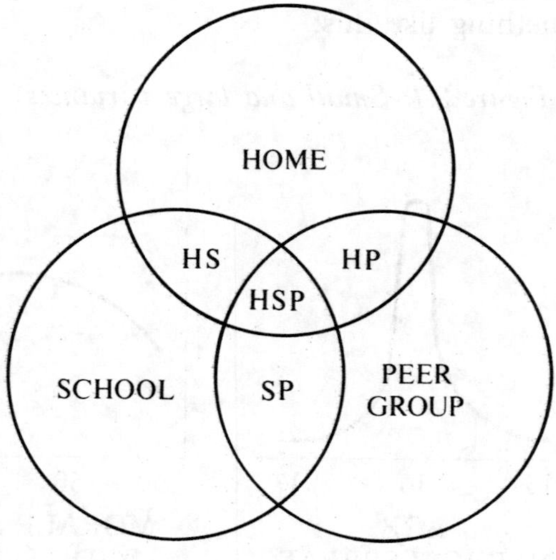

Variance in morale may be depicted as an area of measure and the overlaps between environments determined.

The approach taken here is to use reliable and valid measures of religious variables, such as social justice awareness and then use the analysis to tell how much of the variance may be attributed uniquely to home, school, peer group or personality aspects of the environment. This is symmetric decomposition of variance, a more valid approach than the former multiple regression.

CHAPTER 3

THE CATHOLIC SCHOOL EFFECTIVENESS DEBATE

We turn now to a critical review of studies relating to Catholic school effectiveness. We will see evidence of a gradual evolution of the concept of effectiveness and a development of sophistication in measures and statistical methods. I will be critical of earlier studies that drew unwarranted conclusions through inadequate methodology.

Because the central issues for a Catholic school involve integration of human learning with religious faith, the criteria to be considered here will be ones associated with religious beliefs and attitudes. The relative contribution of the significant environments, home, school, peer group, school staff and the internal world of personality factors, is the guiding question behind the review. In addition the identification of the factors within those environments which best explain students' present faith and religious activity will be highlighted.

This review of literature is divided into critical evaluation of bivariate and multivariate studies related to these two questions. Kerlinger (1973, p. 149) defines bivariate approaches as those which consider only one dependent and one independent variable at the one time in the analysis. On the other hand I will give preference to multivariate approaches that have the ability to consider multiple independent and multiple dependent measures simultaneously in a single analysis. Multivariate procedures have greater power to approximate complex systems and hence lead to more adequate models for real situations.

This review will show the following trends:

1. An increase in adequacy of measures employed.
2. A shift to more complex statistical models and a tendency to use sophisticated statistical procedures without adequate reporting of their implicit assumptions and limitations.
3. A marked impact of this research, now seen to be open to question, upon Christian education theorists and policy makers, who in general do not grasp fully the assumptions and limitations.
4. Increasing relevance of the secular school effectiveness critique upon the Catholic debate.

The review will thus lay the foundation for the claim that the present study avoids the major limitations associated with previous research in this area. The review will be divided into:

1. Bivariate American studies
2. Bivariate Australian studies
3. Bivariate Irish study
4. Multivariate Australian studies
5. Multivariate English studies
6. Multivariate American studies
7. Impact upon Christian educators
8. Conclusions

1. BIVARIATE AMERICAN STUDIES

Neuwien (1966) published a study of 218 Catholic elementary and 104 secondary schools in the United States from 13 representative dioceses. A total of 14 519 grade eight and grade twelve students were involved together with 24 502 Catholic parents who had their children in Catholic schools. Students were asked to respond to three instruments, one based upon religious understanding of truths of the Catholic faith, the second based upon attitudes to religious-moral values, social-civic values and family-marriage values, the third based upon the relative importance of stated Catholic school goals and the success of the school in achieving them. Analysis was on an item by item basis rather than construction of more reliable scales.

Differences between per cent response by different groups were discussed although no statistical tests of significance were reported. On the specific question of home and school influence upon religious outcomes the study assumed:

> that very probably family and school have the most important influence on the attitudes of students and that other influences, such as those of peer-group and community, are normally mediated by these institutions (Neuwien, 1966, p. 174).

No attempt was made to test this hypothesis or differentiate family from school effects. Students' families were categorised into three social classes (based upon father's occupational status) and six religious background groups (based upon parents' declared Catholic affiliation, parents' Catholic education and child's degree of Catholic education). Students from high social class homes with a stronger religious background were more likely to be frequent Mass attenders and less racially biased, although some differences in per cent response were only small. Increased years of Catholic schooling also seemed to be associated with more positive perceptions by students of the schools' success in achieving religious-moral objectives (Neuwien, 1966, p. 240). In summary this study generated a lot of item data on a large sample of American Catholic school students but failed to develop more reliable scales to separate the effects of home background from school influence.

A major study entitled *The Education of Catholic Americans* was published by Greeley and Rossi in 1966. It was based primarily upon a national sample of 2753 Catholics from age 23 to 57 years old. For this group their number of years of Catholic schooling was used to separate respondents into three groups, all Catholic schooling, some Catholic schooling, no Catholic schooling. Various items on religious knowledge, practice and attitudes were conceptually grouped and frequency tables in per cent form constructed. The measure of association within the bivariate table was the 'gamma coefficient' (Goodman and Kuskal, 1954).

Some of the major findings of this study were:

1. There is a moderate but significant association ... between Catholic education and adult religious behavior, an association which survives (is still present) under a wide variety of socio-economic, demographic and religious controls.
2. The association is strongest among those who come from very religious family backgrounds (defined as those in which one parent went to Communion every week).
3. There are very strong relationships between Catholic education and religious behavior for teenagers currently in school (Greeley and Rossi, 1966, p. 219).

The authors argued in several places (1966, p. 223, 228, 84-87) for a 'multiplier effect', that the religiousness of the home and school reinforce each other. The authors go so far (p. 223) as to suggest that it is only the quarter of the Catholic population coming from 'highly religious homes' who are influenced by the Catholic school.

> Catholic schools had an impact only on those who came from families in which one parent received Communion every week. Their 'success' is almost limited to these families, but among such families it is quite impressive (Greeley and Rossi, 1966, p. 87).

Such conclusions based upon national samples and apparently good statistical procedures, at least in that period, had a major impact upon the parochial school debate in the USA (Ganss, 1979) and in Australia (Flynn, 1975). The impact upon religious education theorists will be detailed after consideration of Greeley, McCready and McCourt's (1976) follow-up study. However a few reservations with the 1966 study's measures and procedures should be noted here.

Firstly, their decision to base the major part of their conclusions upon an adult population (23 to 57 years old) led them to infer influence of remembered Catholic schooling upon present religious behaviour. This seeks to estimate the long-term influence of Catholic schooling but does not differentiate the effects of post-school experience from school experience upon religious orientation. Secondly, the adequacy of their measures can be questioned. Is 'years of Catholic schooling,' further grouped into 'All, Some, None' an adequate measure of the complex reality of Catholic schools with different climates? Thirdly there was no discussion of the validity and reliability of the religious behaviour indices and no reliability coefficients were reported. The question of whether the same meaning would be attached to items used both in the 1966 and 1976 studies remains an open one. Fourthly, the 'gamma coefficient' has been little used in subsequent research and is really only a bivariate index not really capable of showing the influence of several intervening variables held constant in a single analysis. Fifthly, the procedure of asking adult respondents to recall and report on the religiousness of their parents at the time they were school children (for some 40 years prior) may well yield results biased in the direction of the respondent's present religious orientation. This, together with the reservation regarding post-school history above, would seem to be an argument for using a sample of students still within or near completion of the school experience to estimate the immediate effects of Catholic schooling and home background. The present study does this.

This review concludes that the Greeley and Rossi (1966) study used both measures and procedures open to question and did not provide a clear estimate of the relationships of family background and Catholic schooling to religious outcomes. This throws its major conclusions into question.

2. BIVARIATE AUSTRALIAN STUDIES

As part of a comprehensive study of religion in Australia Hans Mol (1968) published findings on the effects of denominational (parochial schools). His sample was a random one of 4201 persons, 1594 of whom were children and adolescents up to 20 years of age and 2607 were adults. On 15 measures of religious knowledge, belief and practice Mol found that on all but three there was a significantly more positive response by Catholics who had had some Catholic schooling when compared to those who had had none. The difference was most marked on church attendance with 80 per cent of 'Catholic-school Catholics' so classifying themselves. Mol was well aware of the danger of attributing these differences solely to the effects of Catholic schooling and recognised that 'the more religiously involved Catholics are more likely to send their children to Catholic schools than the lethargic ones' (Mol, 1968, p.24).

Mol's (1968) study was severely criticised by Anderson (1971) who accused him, among other things, of making causal claims without an experimental control group design (Campbell and Stanley, 1963). Anderson concluded:

> The analysis does not support the conclusion that there is an 'independent ... contribution' of the Catholic school system to religious behavior. The possibilities remain that attendance at a Catholic school is incidental to religious

> socialization in the family or that schooling is effective only in association with parental religion (Anderson, 1971).

Mol's (1971) rejoinder to this critique shows how he avoided any causal claims being careful to footnote the meaning of 'effect' as 'y is associated with x'. Mol claims justly that exploratory survey methods, without precise experimental controls, are more appropriate to an area, such as religious outcomes, where there is a lack of solid theory and data. However Mol's (1968, p. 32) claim that:

> Both the independent and cumulative contribution of a Catholic school system as measured by increased church-attendance, more regular prayer, stronger beliefs in God, etc. is beyond any doubt ...

stands justly criticised. Neither Mol nor Anderson had adequate measures or appropriate statistical methodology to make this claim or refute it. Neither was able to separate adequately the effect of Catholic schooling, family background or other relevant effects such as the peer group.

Also in Australia, Anderson and Western (1972) attempted to estimate the effects of denominational schooling upon religious behaviour using samples of 2000 University (college) age students. A major disadvantage of this study was the fact that questions on religious denomination and behaviour were not asked until the students' third or fourth year of college. Such responses could well be influenced by their experience in a secular university. Anderson and Western again chose to present their data in frequency tables comparing per cent religious responses across type of school background (State, Catholic and Independent). As before they could not unequivocally distinguish the effects of schooling from family background. They concluded (1972, pp. 30-31) that 'the relative contributions of (family) background and church school to the religious outlook of Roman Catholic students remain an open question.'

Thus this review of the debate in Australia as to the effects of Catholic schooling in the early part of this decade highlights two theses of this chapter, namely, that to date:

1. the measures of religious attitude and behaviour have not been sufficiently reliable or adequate and, that
2. the statistical techniques required to separate home and school effects were not yet available.

3. BIVARIATE IRISH STUDY

In Ireland Greer (1971) examined religious beliefs and church attendance of sixth form pupils and their parents. His sample included 1631 pupils and 803 parents. Using chi-square analysis of frequency tables he found significant associations between parents and pupils' belief in God. Children of parents who believed in God were significantly more inclined to believe than were children of uncertain or disbelieving parents. The association was stronger for girls than for boys. The relation between parents and pupils' Church attendance showed a similar trend. When pupils' belief in God was related to their own church attendance it was found that there were relatively large numbers of pupils who are uncertain of God's existence or disbelieve who still attend church regularly. Greer argues, with Greeley and Rossi, that parental religious practice has a considerable influence on children. The import of the Greer study for this present investigation is that students' Christian faith should be distinguished conceptually from their ritual practice and the impact of parental religiousness be examined upon each in turn.

4. MULTIVARIATE AUSTRALIAN STUDIES

In Australia Leavey (1972a, 1972b) reported on the transmission of religious and moral values in nine Catholic girls' schools. While the sample was non-random and small (560 sixth form girls) Leavey developed a number of new instruments and scales by appropriate factor analytic approaches (Nie, 1975, pp. 468-477). Her criterion religious outcome scales were students' perceptions of the integration between Christian faith and secular subjects, whether students adopted a predominantly pre- or post-Vatican II viewpoint on theological issues, the internalisation of religious and moral values, religious practice and perception of the religious education dimension of the schools' activity. All had appropriate internal reliability as estimated by Cronbach's alpha coefficient of reliability (Cronbach, 1951) and the content validity was checked by a panel of theologians. On the issue of integration Leavey found that 50 per cent of girls felt that their secular subjects had strengthened or supported their Christian faith, 46 per cent felt that there was no connection and four per cent felt secular subjects had weakened or contradicted their faith. On 13 out of 16 items Leavey found a post-Vatican II preference for theological formulations among her female sample. By constructing mean scores for the groups of girls in each school Leavey found that schools which had low scores on religious practice items tended to have low scores on all five criterion religious variables. Other schools of similar socio-economic status level tended to have high scores on all religious variables. Thus she introduced in 1972 the important concept of school religious climate which could vary between schools. She proposed that this climate could be influenced by staff-student relationships, peer group influences and the religious orientation that students bring from their home background. In turn she presented some evidence to suggest, contra to Greeley and Rossi's finding, that a Catholic school with a good climate had a positive impact upon the Christian faith and practice of students even from low religious homes. Leavey (1972b, p. 180) claimed that 'schools do have an influence independent of the home' but her conclusion rests upon examination of trends across only two schools and needs to be subjected to more rigorous study.

Although Leavey's study was based upon a small sample, rather than a national one, it demonstrates the usefulness of careful analysis with better measures for our understanding of the relationships of Catholic schools and family background in faith development. She provided more reliable scale measures of religious outcomes, used in subsequent larger studies (Flynn, 1975, 1985; Fahy, 1976, 1978). She highlighted the importance of estimating overall school climate and the need to examine differences between schools. Using the best statistical tools available to her at the time she provided some evidence for an effect of Catholic schools upon children from low religious homes and placed in doubt Greeley and Rossi's earlier conclusion.

An important extension of Leavey's (1972a) study was made in Australia by Flynn (1975) who studied a random stratified sample of pupils in 21 Catholic secondary boys' schools in the states of New South Wales and the Australian Capital Territory. His sample of 1393 students represented 45 per cent of the population of sixth form (seniors) in Catholic boys' secondary schools in these states. His measures were based on those of Leavey (1972a) and had suitable reliability and validity. He employed a number of multivariate statistical procedures including stepwise multiple regression (Kerlinger, 1973, pp.214-239) to search out significant relationships between school climate, home background and criterion measures of students' religious attitudes and academic achievement.

One major finding was the central importance of psychosocial environmental measures. The students' school morale, a cluster of variables relating to students' happiness with the school, relationships with teachers, view that teachers were well qualified and enthusiastic was particularly important. Students with a high morale tended to be those who were higher on all the religious values, belief and practice scales and who performed better in external examinations. Flynn concluded (1975, p.278) that:

> So strong is the association between morale and the religious climate of the school, that it would appear that students identify one with the other, and perceive the Christian or gospel message of their schools in the context of their experience of school itself and its procedures. The climate and morale of Catholic schools may well be a necessary pre-evangelization before effective religious education, and general education for that matter, becomes possible in the school situation.

Using from his cluster of general climate measures those related to religious outcomes of students, Flynn was able to select from his sample a number of schools with an overall pattern of positive morale, Christian faith and values and designate these as High Religious Schools. Likewise schools at the lower end on all these measures were designated as Low Religious Schools. He defined the home background as High or Low Religious Home in terms of parental religious practice and degree of encouragement for the student's religious practice. He was thus able to construct a two by two (2 x 2) analysis of variance design (Table 3.1) and test for the effects of both home and school upon a set of religious outcome scales. The outcomes were Mass Attendance (one item), Religious Practice (five items), Religious Values (six items), and Religious Outcomes, a composite scale of 22 items. On all four criteria significant main effects were found for both home and school. This means that, controlling for home background, that High Religious Schools tend to have students with higher religious outcomes. Even students from Low Religious Homes in a High Religious School have higher religious outcomes than their reference group (all students from Low Religious Homes). Likewise the significant main effect for home background, controlling for school, means that High Religious Homes tend to have children with higher religious outcomes, controlling for religiousness of the school.

Table 3.1

Design of analysis of variance used by Flynn (1975) to test independent effects of home and school upon religious outcomes of students. N = of students. (Adapted, with permission, from Figure 11.6)

	HIGH RELIGIOUS SCHOOL	LOW RELIGIOUS SCHOOL
HIGH RELIGIOUS HOME	N = 191	N = 132
LOW RELIGIOUS HOME	N = 21	N = 39

Thus for the first time in this review we have a multivariate analysis, albeit based on small numbers in some cells, with adequate religious outcome and climate measures, which suggests that both home and Catholic school background have an independent influence upon the religious attitudes and practices of Catholic school youth. It is important to note, contrary to Greeley and Rossi's finding, that Flynn found that a school with a good climate can have a positive impact upon students even from homes with little or no evident support for religion.

Flynn, (1975, p. 286) concludes:

> Concerning the effectiveness of Catholic schools in achieving their religious goals, it was found that there were very strong indications that schools in which there existed a supportive religious climate were having an influence on students' religious development independently of the home influence.

Flynn called for modification of Greeley and Rossi's notion of schools as merely a 'multiplier' of religious values of the home.

> [This notion] ... would appear today to be somewhat too sweeping. The school acts as a 'multiplier' only if it has a supportive climate of Christian community. It acts as a 'modifier' (decreasing) the religious values of the home if this climate is weak or non-existent (Flynn, 1975, p. 287).

The present study depends upon Leavey (1972a) and Flynn (1975) in terms of approach and measures but goes beyond them in using statistical methods which simultaneously consider the effects, not just of home and school factors, but also peer group and student personality variables in the partitioning of the variance of religious outcome measures. It also looks at 103 individual classrooms. Such an analysis allows a more careful estimation of the proportion of the variance in the religious outcome measures that may be attributed to different social environments of the students. The expectation is that both home and school environments will still appear as important but it may be possible to suggest some discernment as to which criteria they are most closely related. Another disadvantage of Flynn's (1975) study was his procedure of dichotomising the home and school environments into high and low categories. The present study maintains the differences between all home and school environments by keeping them as scale values to exert their full explanatory power in the analysis. Flynn (1975) did not analyse between- and within-school differences as this study does. Neither did Flynn (1975) or Flynn (1985) analyse individual religious education classrooms at the heart of the argument of this book.

In an important subsequent theoretical study, with a strong empirical basis, Flynn (1979) has examined Catholic schools and the communication of faith. He provides an important extension of Fowler's (1978) work on stages of faith development throughout the life-cycle by positing between Fowler's 'Synthetic-Conventional' (faith based upon external authority figures) and 'Individuative-Reflexive' (faith based on a personal synthesis of meaning) stages, another stage Flynn calls 'Searching faith.' He defines this as follows:

> ... from passive acceptance of faith on the authority of others, faith enters a temporary purifying phase of uncertainty, confusion and, at times, rejection. This should not be confused, however, with loss of faith (Flynn, 1979, p. 193).

Flynn sees this stage, not as characteristic of every adolescent, but of many in the mid and later secondary school years. The task of integrating faith and life experience is a life-long process and Flynn summarises research on the influences of home, peer group, culture, and Catholic schools upon adolescents' growth in faith. Flynn (1979, pp. 97-122) reviews research on religious socialisation, stressing its two-way interchange and shows awareness and support for Groome's (1977a) critique of the religious socialisation theorists, that they are not sufficiently attentive to the challenging and confronting role of the Christian vision of reality.

Flynn recognises that the Catholic school is not the only agency of education in faith but one of the many that operate from baptism to the grave. He, however, makes a strong case, from theory and empirical data, for the school's continued support and development.

> [It is] the continuing conviction of this writer that, not only does there exist a strong argument for Catholic schools on theoretical and empirical grounds, but that these schools are *more necessary today than ever in the past* ... [The] really important questions ... no longer centre around 'Are Catholic schools *necessary*' but relate to 'How can we make Catholic schools *more effective*?' in their contribution to Australian society (Flynn, 1979, p. 190).

It was against this background that Flynn began the task of collecting data from the same schools reported in the 1975 study to allow a critical comparison 10 years on. The study, Flynn (1985) The *Effectiveness of Catholic Schools*, should be seen as complimentary to this book, with different samples, and a focus on school climate rather than classrooms nested within them.

Flynn (1985) developed a theoretical framework of Catholic schools as seeking the development of the persons in their care. He (1985, p. 39) then sampled 25 schools in New South Wales and Australian Capital Territory being 50 per cent of the total population of Catholic boys secondary schools. A total of 2041 Year 12 students (Sixth Form) were included. There is a strong male bias in the Flynn sample. In 1975, the study was seen as complimentary to Leavey's (1972) study of girls' schools. So too in the Flynn (1985) study, he kept to the same sample with about 85% males and 15% girls in co-educational schools. In addition, parents (1377) and staff (717) were surveyed on their perceptions of Catholic schools. Socio-economic status data and Higher School Certificate aggregate (a weighted aggregate of performance in the best five subjects set as the final external exams for Year 12 very reliable curriculum sensitive measures) were included on the file allowing for the first time systematic comparison between religious and academic outcomes central to Catholic schools. Flynn rechecked all reliable scales with extensive factor analyses and then employed the symmetric decomposition of variance (commonality analysis) to see which criteria were uniquely explained by which sets of predictors.

Personal faith (a six item factor focused on the place of Jesus in my daily life) was most uniquely explained by Religious Education Curriculum, even when entered with home, formal curriculum, informal curriculum, quality of life blocks. This means that when the variance in religiosity of the home background is accounted for it is still the schools' *Religious Education curriculum* that is having the predominant 'unique effect'. Unique effect must be defined not as a causal effect, but as a 'concomitant variation'. The way in which students' personal faith varies from person to person matches more closely the way their perception of *Religious Education curriculum* varies than how home background or any of the others vary. Flynn concludes:

> At the time when the religiousness of students' homes has declined the Catholic school appears to be having an effect on the faith development of its students which is independent of the prior religious socialisation of the home.

Flynn (1985, p. 310) accounted for 55 per cent of the variance in Personal Faith scores. This is a very high proportion indeed, by educational standards.

Using Higher School Certificate achievement as a curriculum-sensitive measure Flynn searched for school effectiveness. Putting all religious and academic data into a single commonality analysis Flynn (1985, p. 314) was able to account for 62 per cent of the variation in the Higher School Certificate scores. This is a very high level of prediction, higher than overseas studies, which shows the critical importance of the variables Flynn selected. When he examined which block of variables had the highest unique prediction it was not the formal curriculum (classes, quality of the curriculum, staff attitudes to curriculum, student enjoyment of the classes) as Flynn expected, but the informal curriculum (morale, climate, discipline, pastoral care, out-of-school curriculum). This is a major finding of the study that the strongest unique predictor of students' level of achievement in Higher School Certificate (which provides entry to tertiary study) was found to be the informal curriculum of the school expressed through its climate and ethos. Flynn concludes (1985, p. 351):

> It appears that some schools develop a climate, or ethos, of achievement in which all students, even those of relatively ordinary natural ability do better academically.
>
> The influence of the climate of the school on the religious development of youth is widely recognised. It would appear now that the climate of schools also has a strong effect on the academic achievement of the students.

Other aspects of Flynn's findings especially those relating to Religious Education will be considered in subsequent chapters. Suffice it to say that Flynn with a random stratified sample of the schools of his previous study, has developed a wide range of reliable and valid measures. In a sound analysis he has explained very large proportions of variance in key religious and academic measures and given new convincing evidence of the effectiveness of Catholic schools on both these criteria. One criticism may be his lack of classroom groupings, a point of increasing debate in religious educational circles. This book will address the theory and empirical findings on the place of faith development in Catholic classrooms.

5. MULTIVARIATE ENGLISH STUDIES

For Catholic schools in England and Wales Hornsby-Smith (1972) has developed a sociological case for their continuance but has pointed to the lack of empirical research to assist the discussion. While citing Greeley and Rossi's (1966) findings, without criticism, he calls for sponsorship of relatively small-scale investigations in crucial areas, such as 'systematic measurement of the religious climate of schools' (Hornsby-Smith, 1972, p. 304).

Hornsby-Smith and Petit (1975) report on one such small-scale study involving 578 fifth form students in three Catholic comprehensive schools recently moved into co-educational structures. Some comparisons are also made with a London Education Authority (public) school. The 27 religious and moral items estimated general Christian Religious Morality. However no differences were found between boys/girls, high/low social class or high/low home religious background on this scale. The study found differences between schools on Christian Religious Morality, two Catholic schools being more positive than the public school and one Catholic school being less positive than the public school. This study supports the need to examine differences between schools in a systematic way. However the study, while calling for a closer look at school religious climate, is limited in its small sample, measures and inability to hold home and school factors in a single analysis.

6. MULTIVARIATE AMERICAN STUDIES

There have been three major American studies of the religious outcomes of youth. They include studies by Strommen (1974), Greeley, McCready and McCourt (1976) and the series of studies from the team of researchers at the Boys Town Center (Potvin, Hoge and Nelsen, 1976; Nelsen, Potvin and Shields, 1976; Hoge and Petrillo, 1978, 1979). A review article by Madaus and Linnan (1973) will be used to set the stage for the discussion of these studies. Most attention will be focused upon the Greeley *et al.* (1976) study for this has had the major influence upon Christian education theorists as Section 7 will suggest.

A review article by Madaus and Linnan (1973) analysed some of the problems associated with research into the effectiveness of Catholic schooling. While agreeing that Catholic schools in the USA have higher than average results on IQ and standardised achievement tests, they pointed to the inherent problem of institutional and individual selectivity – that Catholic schools tend to draw students from the above average social class groups – to conclude that outcome differences cannot be ascribed to the school *per se*. As well as cognitive, socio-economic and demographic differences in students entering Catholic schools compared to their public school counterparts, Madaus and Linnan reviewed research on religiousness of the home. They seem to agree with Greeley and Rossi's conclusion when they say:

> ... since a majority of students at entrance are predisposed to forming or already displaying the characteristics desired of graduates the school merely acts as a womb, neither accelerating nor retarding development but simply providing a safe haven where it can occur (Madaus and Linnan, 1973, p. 218).

Thus they seem to preclude any unique effect for the school upon religious outcomes. They call for measures of religious outcomes of greater content and construct validity reflecting not only cognitive but attitudinal and personal faith outcomes more in line with post-Vatican II theology. They raise some doubts as to whether empirical methods can estimate some of the more important outcomes such as the hidden curriculum (climate of schools). It would seem that Leavey (1972a, 1972b), Flynn (1975, 1985) and the present study fill this lacunae. The measures used in these studies go well beyond mere recall or knowledge of facts – with pre-Vatican II emphasis – found in a content analysis of instruments current in the USA by Madaus (cited in Madaus and Linnan, 1973, p.218).

Strommen (1974) made an important contribution by the study of 7052 youth associated with ten Christian churches in the USA. He developed the Youth Research Survey instrument of over 400 items and subjected the replies to second-order factor analysis (Strommen, 1974, pp. 127-128) to identify five basic 'cries of youth'. While these results are important, giving a real insight into youth of this period, they are of limited usefulness here since the youth were identified by congregation and not by school and no school-related data were collected. However this present study draws on Strommen's work by using some of his well-validated scales.

Perhaps the major American study on the question of the effectiveness of home and Catholic schooling upon religious outcomes is that of Greeley, McCready and McCourt (1976). *Catholic Schools in a Declining Church* really focused on two separate issues: the effectiveness of Catholic schools and the impact upon American Catholics of the birth control teaching enunciated in *Humanae Vitae* in 1968. This review will examine in detail only the school question and will be critical of the measures employed to gather data and the appropriateness of the statistical procedures used to analyse that data.

It must be borne in mind throughout this evaluation of Greeley *et al.* (1976) study that their major conclusions were in support of Catholic schools' impact on religious behaviour especially for a church in time of 'traumatic transition'. They conclude:

> Far from declining in effectiveness in the past decade, Catholic schools seem to have increased their impact. In a time of general decline in religious behavior, the rate of decline for those who have gone to Catholic schools is much slower. The correlation between Catholic school attendance (and religious behaviour) is especially strong for those under thirty (Greeley *et al.*, 1976, p. 310).

However, this review will focus not so much upon their conclusions as upon the methods and procedures used to arrive at them. Accordingly the review will consider:

1. Sample and data collection;
2. Measures used;
3. Statistical procedures employed;

and will comment on each in turn.

The initial sample of respondents employed by Greeley *et al.* (1976) consisted of 1128 American Catholic adults drawn as a national sample. The final number of analysed cases was 927; this was 82 per cent completion rate, a good figure in this kind of research. Eighty-one (81) per cent of respondents were aged between 20 and 59. Thus when subjects respond concerning their religious behaviour it must be realised that their human experience, post-Catholic school, has no doubt had an impact upon their religious beliefs and attitudes. For some this could be 40 years of life experience, the effects of which Greeley *et al.* (1976) ascribe to the foundation of their early school experience. That this is justified may be questioned.

Nowhere in either the Greeley and Rossi (1966) or Greeley *et al.* (1976) studies are reliability data reported. The latter study reports the result of a factor analysis of the religious behaviour scales in an attempt to generate more reliable

'Catholicity Factors'. Two factors are reported but the highest factor loadings are 0.28 and 0.37 respectively, rather low to be of much usefulness (p. 448).

In summary then the adequacy of the measures in the Greeley *et al.* (1976) study are in question on the grounds of unknown reliability. Also the question of the validity of items used in the 1966 study still being useful in the new social context of the mid 1970s (given the 'traumatic transition') must be raised.

In addition there are serious doubts about Greeley *et al.'s* (1976) measure for Catholic education. They use simply the measure 'years of parochial school attendance' (Greeley *et al.*, Table 6.1, p. 160). They divide this measure into three categories:

1. More than 10 years
2. One to 10 years
3. No parochial schooling.

They then call this measure 'Catholic education' (p. 160) and even 'religious education' (p. 161) without any consideration of the fact that there are other aspects to the quality and climate of Catholic education besides merely years spent in the system. There is no consideration by Greeley *et al.* (1976) that some schools may have a more positive religious climate than others as Leavey (1972a, 1972b) and Flynn (1975) found. In the 1974 sample reported in the Greeley *et al.* (1976) study 'years of Catholic schooling' yielded a '*beta* coefficient' greater than 0.10 on only two measures (Catholic Activism and Financial Contribution) out of ten examined (Greeley *et al.* (1976) p. 169). This highlights the limitations of a measure such as 'years of Catholic schooling' as a predictor of adult or adolescent religious behaviour.

Turning now to the statistical procedures Greeley *et al.* (1976) employed to test the impact of 'Catholic education' upon religious behaviour mention must be made of causal path analysis (Wright, 1960a, pp. 189-202).

Causal path analysis needs a strong body of theory to propose a *causal model*, a supposition about the situation. The data is then used to see if the model 'works'. The central problem is if there is not a strong body of theory, as in this situation, then the causal model is in danger of too much reflecting the presuppositions of the researchers. These then appear to be confirmed from the data. The problem is compounded by unreliable and invalid measures. First developed in the more exact biological sciences, causal path analysis with its strong inference is not readily applicable to less precise social science data. Only one-way recursive causal flow is allowed since feedback between any two variables precludes a valid solution of the matrix. Many religious educational settings, such as First Holy Communion, have inherent feedback. The parents' faith is strengthened by the school communion curriculum. The parents' faith influences the child. Causal path analysis is, by definition, unable to handle feedback situations such as these. This is why causal path analysis is fundamentally unsuited to social science and especially religious problems, where feedback features (Wright, 1960b, pp. 423-445). Up to the present time no path models with feedback loops exist in the literature. An alternative correlation approach such as commonality is much more suitable.

Thus in evaluating the results obtained by Greeley *et al.* (1976) it is the judgment of this reviewer that the inadequacy of the measures, particularly on the grounds of unknown reliability and validity, together with the inappropriate use of strong-inference, recursive models assuming causal relationships, make their causal path conclusions suspect.

A more recent study by Fee, Greeley, McCready and Sullivan, (1981) called *Young Catholics* studied 1259 American

Catholics 18-39 years of age. Reversing the 1966 finding Fee *et al.* found:

> (that) Catholic schools continue to be more important to the work of the Church than they were during the pre-conciliar years. Their major effectiveness seems to consist in the closer integration of a young person into the Catholic community (1981, p. 230).

However this conclusion rests on an inappropriate causal inference model and is thereby suspect. The predictor variable Close to Church in the school analysis was not factor analysed and would be very highly correlated with the criterion Catholicity scale, leading to an artificially inflated result.

Again the criterion of years of schooling is inadequate. Leavey (1972), Flynn (1975) have shown the necessity to use climate measures in assessment of effectiveness. For these reasons the Fee study must be held to be inadequate for assessing the unique effect of Catholic school and home as reliable religious measures.

In a related study of Greeley's (1982) called *Catholic High Schools and Minority Students* he seeks to explain why minority students do better academically in Catholic High Schools than in public schools. He groups his predictor variables, family characteristics (6), student characteristics (4), school characteristics (3) and sets up a causal path regression model. The variables chosen for school are ownership of religious order, student rating of teachers, discipline problems which lack the richness of the climate measures of Leavey (1972), Flynn (1975) and Madaus (1980). In addition the high inference causal path model is unsuited to this debate for the reasons given above. Greeley ignores the order of entry problem. For this reason the findings of this study are suspect.

Potvin, Hoge and Nelsen (1976) examined a national sample (N = 1121) of 13 to 18 year olds who classified themselves as Protestant, Catholic, Jew, Other religion or no religious affiliation. Three hundred and thirty (29 per cent) designated themselves as Catholics. Items were factor analysed to yield five factors:

Personal-experiential (including sense of closeness to God, frequency of personal prayer and importance of religions);

Religious practice (attendance at religious services and participation in church activities);

Traditional orthodoxy (agreement that God punishes people who sin, that the Bible is God's Word and must be obeyed, that the church represents God in this world, and that God controls everything that happens);

Ascetic morality (including items on whether getting drunk, smoking marijuana, having sexual intercourse before marriage are wrong);

Social morality (including items on whether lying, stealing, taking one's own life, and treating persons of other races or nationalities as inferior are wrong).

It is difficult to judge the adequacy of these measures since full listings of the actual items, reliability and validity data are not provided. It should be noted however that the items are designed for a national sample and do not focus upon specific Christian faith dimensions such as belief in Christ, the Father or Spirit. This book does focus on these.

This section has argued that the multivariate American studies are not able to separate uniquely home and school effects in Catholic school effectiveness. The studies, particularly those conducted by teams under Andrew Greeley have serious problems of sample, reliability and validity of measures, use of inappropriate criterion measures such as 'years of Catholic schooling'. In addition there are serious problems of application of strong inference, one-way causal path techniques to problems where a clear model has not been developed from theory. The danger of superimposing one's own pre-suppositions is higher than with a lower inference symmetric decomposition of variance technique applied here.

7. IMPACT OF THIS RESEARCH UPON CHRISTIAN EDUCATORS

The above review of previous research in this area has been a lengthy one and has focused upon adequacy of measures and appropriateness of statistical methods used to analyse data. In many cases the measures and/or the statistical models employed have been shown to be open to question. It is important therefore to examine briefly the impact of these research studies upon Christian education theorists and policy makers. It will be the thesis of this section that professional Christian educators and administrators, generally lacking empirical skills, have accepted uncritically the findings of previous research and have been led to form erroneous conclusions regarding the relative influence of home, school and peer group upon the religious outcomes of students. In some places this became associated with a lack of confidence in the effectiveness of Catholic schools and a tendency towards withdrawing support.

The two studies most frequently cited by Christian educational writers are Greeley and Rossi (1966) and Greeley, McCready and McCourt (1976). The prevailing attitude is one of unquestioning acceptance of their findings. One of the hierarchy, Bishop Walter Sullivan of Richmond, Virginia responds as follows:

> I find the information provided by the Greeley-McCready-McCourt study overwhelming. Like so many American Catholics I am not used to dealing with sociological research about religious beliefs and practice ... We 'lay readers' ... must leave a critical analysis of the book's research methodology and the validity of the data to people in the field. Until someone shows otherwise, I accept the research data

> because they come from reputable, competent sociologists (Sullivan, 1976, p. 24).

In the same way James Michael Lee (1973) adopts a similar approach to the Greeley and Rossi (1966) study. Lee (1973, p. 64) says:

> In their well-executed study of Catholic elementary and secondary schools, Andrew Greeley and Peter Rossi noted ... that every major or religious effect of these schools could be explained by family variables.

Some Christian education writers are also aware of the early stages of the school effectiveness debate which cast doubt on the effectiveness of schools to promote learning over and above home background factors. Marthaler (1973, p. 163) cites the Coleman *et al.* (1966) study to show that academic achievement depends more on family background than on what happens in the classroom. He draws similar inferences for catechesis. Coleman's conclusions have been challenged and now appear not fully justified. Thus there are dangers in applying his conclusions to the area of Christian education without a more systematic investigation.

Westerhoff (1976, pp. 1-25) seems to have been influenced by Fichter's (1966) study and the Greeley and Rossi (1966) study when he argues for the 'bankruptcy of the schooling-instruction paradigm' for Christian education. He argues for more consideration of a 'faith enculturation model' without formal schooling structures.

Piveteau and Dillon (1977a, 1977b) are also critical of the schooling model, citing approvingly the Greeley and Rossi (1966, p.95) conclusion:

> In the absence of reinforcement from the family, there is no reason to expect that the school will modify values and value-oriented behavior.

In their more extensive review *Resurgence of Religious Instruction*, Piveteau and Dillon (1977b, pp. 128-129) quote approvingly the two key findings of the earlier Greeley study as follows:

> We can go so far as to say that for all practical purposes, the religious impact of Catholic education is limited to those who come from highly religious families (Greeley and Rossi, 1966, p. 85).
>
> Catholic education is virtually wasted on three-fourths of those in Catholic schools because of the absence of a sufficiently religious family milieu (Greeley and Rossi, 1966, p. 112).

Although subsequent research (Leavey, 1972a, 1972b; Flynn, 1975) has disproved these conclusions, Piveteau and Dillon at a later date still seem to accept them unquestioningly, argue (1977b, pp. 129-137) for the ineffectiveness of schools in promoting religious values and call for a model of religious education beyond schooling. We will see a wide trend in this direction in the next chapter.

The 1979 *National Catechetical Directory* (for Catholics of the United States), 'Sharing the Light of Faith,' cites among its sources the Greeley *et al.* (1976) study, the Potvin *et al.* (1976) study and the Nelsen *et al.* (1976) study. There is a real danger that Christian educational policy makers at this level will depend overmuch upon such sources and be unaware of the limitations of these studies. Indeed writers in the popular Catholic press are still citing the two Greeley studies uncritically (Maafe, 1980).

Thus it would seem that the results of the two studies Greeley and Rossi (1966) and Greeley, McCready and McCourt (1976) have been accepted without question by Christian educators who lacked the skills to criticise them adequately. This present study has called into question both the methods and the findings of these studies and itself lays a more solid foundation for policy making concerning schools and Christian education.

It remains to briefly summarise the conclusions of this review.

8. CONCLUSIONS OF THIS REVIEW

This review of research studies has led to the following conclusions.

Need for more adequate measures

While there has been a general improvement in measurement sophistication, there are still too many studies using single items or scales consisting of only a few items. The reliability of such scales is open to question. As yet there is little discussion of construct validity (Cronbach, 1971) although the critique of the National Catholic Education Association's instrument Religious Education Outcome Inventory (REOI) by Pastrick (1978) and Elford's (1978) reply raise some important issues.

The research from Australia on differential school climate (Leavey, 1972a, 1972b; Flynn, 1975, 1985, 1989) clearly shows the inadequacy of a simple measure such as 'years of Catholic schooling' as Greeley employed in both his studies. It is essential to realise that Catholic school climates vary from high to low on religious and academic criteria and that any valid study must examine systematically differences between schools and even differences between religion classroom groupings within schools.

Shift to more complex statistical models

The review has shown the shift from bivariate analyses to multivariate analyses able to handle more variables simultaneously. Even when variables are combined into 'blocks' or sets of conceptually similar variables, as Hoge and Petrillo (1978) do, there are often unjustified assumptions relating to causal connections between home, school and peer group factors. Greeley's (1976) use of causal path analysis techniques has been strongly criticised on the grounds of inadequate measures and too strong assumptions about one-way causal connections. Greeley and his co-authors have not spelled out the assumptions underlying causal modeling, in particular their choice of a one-way recursive model without a documented basis in previous theory or research. Their assumed model then imposes itself upon the data and influences the resulting conclusions.

Indeed this study questions whether causal models are appropriate at all to this field. This question relates to the epistemology assumed by this study. It does not seek precise, universal, certain knowledge in the Cartesian sense, as the causal path approach does, but rather suggestive, dialectical reasoning that arrives at action-oriented knowledge relevant to a particular setting, client and researcher bias.

This present study avoids any explicit or implicit causal model by simply seeking to partition the variance in religious outcomes into components uniquely explained by home, school, peer group and personality blocks of variables. In addition the components these blocks share in common are estimated. In this way there is no imposition upon the data of any assumed causal network as do Greeley *et al.* (1976) and Hoge and Petrillo (1978).

Impact upon Christian educational theories

Lacking the technical skills to evaluate adequately the methods employed in these research studies, Christian educational theorists have tended to accept and quote the findings uncritically. Coupled with the initial negative findings on school effectiveness by Coleman (1966), this seems to have led to a devaluation of the school as an instrument of Christian growth and development. The focus and burden of Christian education has been placed more heavily upon the home and parents at a time when we are witnessing a real breakdown in family unity across all sectors of society.

Theorists have developed alternative models and sought to widen the focus of the Church's educational ministry. These efforts are to be encouraged for Catholic education. However it is important that any reevaluation of the role of the school be based upon solid empirical and theoretical study as to the relative impact of alternative agencies upon religious development. This review has shown that some of the conclusions about the ineffectiveness of schools are unfounded and that there is a need to reexamine the question with better measures and techniques. It is at this point that the advances made by the secular debate on school effectiveness related to academic achievement have most to offer Christian educators.

School effectiveness debate

Recent research on religious outcomes has fallen into some of the same methodological pitfalls as the school effectiveness studies, especially in the choice of inadequate measures, assumptions relating to causal priority and order of entry into multiple regression analysis. In the secular debate on school effectiveness the reanalyses of Mayeske *et al.* (1972), Brimer *et al.* (1977), Madaus *et al.* (1979, 1980) provide better measures and approaches. Sufficient to note here that these research studies provide the tools for a more careful examination of the measures of religious outcomes and effectiveness of home and school. Beaton's (1973, 1974) method of symmetric variance decomposition avoids the necessity of *a priori* causal assumptions which have plagued previous research. The choice of the school as the initial unit of analysis and examination of between-school, between-classroom and within-classroom differences is a significant step forward in Christian educational research.

With this review completed it is appropriate to examine the particular question of the effectiveness of Catholic schools in the area of the religious education curriculum. There are some theoretical issues to be discussed in Chapter 4 and then some empirical evidence in Chapter 5.

CHAPTER 4

RELIGIOUS EDUCATION EFFECTIVENESS

Theoretical issues and practical questions

There has been a lively debate going on in religious educational circles about the language that should be used for the enterprise of educating religiously. You might be tempted to say 'Does it matter what it is called as long as we get on with the task of helping kids grow in knowledge and love of God in Jesus?'. In a sense that is true, yet so often we find that the language framework we adopt limits our thinking and approach to the task. Sometimes these words have connotations from the previous history of religious education that make them restrictive when applied to a narrow field such as Catholic schools. Crawford and Rossiter (1985, pp. 34-41) have synthesised the arguments for keeping the term *catechesis* for the wider adult-centred ministry of the Church and preferring the simple *religious education* for what goes on in schools.

Likewise the many other terms current in the Church; witness, ministry, evangelisation, enculturation, mission etc., need careful definition and placement within the Church's sociology of knowledge (theology). Berger and Luckmann (1967) point to the role of language in creating a symbolic universe that provides justification for the existing social order and its practices. Where there is confusion of language/ symbols it spreads down to the policies and practices of the whole social (educational) order.

The purpose of this chapter then is not to evaluate studies of religious educational effectiveness but rather to review briefly some theoretical contributions to the language question, critique these against a theological model, propose a model for religious education effectiveness in Catholic schools and highlight some questions of effectiveness that may be testable in Chapter 5.

1. BASIC DEFINITIONS

One of the basic criteria by which a Catholic school must be evaluated is the faith dimension of its students and staff. Before proceeding to examine this issue empirically it is appropriate here to address a number of questions being raised by religious educators about the place of faith in the formal and informal curriculum processes of the Catholic school.

This chapter will therefore present some initial definitions of faith, theology, belief, education and religious education. Then it will present the key elements of various religious educational theorists, lastly a critique of the various models will lead into some empirically verifiable questions to be tested in subsequent chapters.

In order to have a reasonable debate on such central issues as faith, religious education and appropriate schooling models, it is essential to have clear definitions of the key terms. These definitions will be drawn from the work of Rahner (1975), McBrien (1980) and official church documents. The terms to be defined are faith, theology, belief, education, Christian religious education, Catholic religious education, and Catholic school.

Faith

Rahner (1975), like Fowler (1978), proclaims the universality of faith and the potentiality of all to be believers. This grace of being a believer is even prior to his/her freedom of what he/she is freely to accept.

> As a result of God's universal salvific will and the offer of the supernatural grace of faith as an abiding feature of man's mode of existence as a person, every human being, even previous to the explicit preaching of the Christian message, is always potentially a believer and already in possession, in the grace that is prior to freedom, of what he is to believe (i.e., freely accept): God's direct self-communication in Christ (Rahner, 1975, p. 496).

When defining faith itself Rahner resorts to a distinction between two kinds of knowledge, one communicated purely from outside and one touching the depth of human reality.

> Faith is never awakened by someone having something communicated to him purely from outside, addressed solely to his naked understanding as such (as, for example, the statement that the chemical formula of water is H_2O). To lead to faith (or rather, to its further, explicit stage) is always to *assist understanding of what has already been experienced in the depth of human reality as grace* (i.e., as in absolutely direct relation to God) (Rahner, 1975, p. 497, [emphasis added]).

Thus, for Rahner, faith is intimately connected with understanding and hence with knowledge. To lead to faith is to assist understanding, to be able to put names, categories or symbols on what has already been experienced and continues in the evolving direct relation with God. Thus faith is essentially propositional; it is not a feeling manifested on call to equally feeling mentors; it is related to significant learning integrated with life experiences.

Rahner gives the name 'grace' to this fundamental direct relationship with God. The faith process then is the ongoing explication in human language and terms of this core grace experience. McBrien (1980) adopts a very similar view to Rahner. McBrien is critical of the assumption that would see faith as available in some non-theological state. He argues that from the nature of faith that is not the case. Faith, he says, is personal knowledge of God (McBrien, 1980, p.25). The adjective 'personal' precludes the knowledge about God that an atheistic sociologist might have by observing the behaviour of some theistic group. The personal knowledge of believers implies some sense of God's own self-disclosure and is wide enough to encompass all world religions. On this definition Christian faith is personal knowledge of God in Christ. While the fundamental grace experience is available to all men and women, faith comes into operation when they freely begin to reflect and apply knowledge categories to that experience. Thus McBrien is well in accord with Rahner's definition.

Theology

Rahner (1975, p.1687), defines theology as the science of faith. He sees it as 'the conscious and methodological explanation and explication of the divine revelation received and grasped in faith'.

McBrien, (1980, pp.25-27) seems more to stress the theological process in the individual's coming to self understanding.

> Faith is personal knowledge of God. It is our perception of God in the midst of life ... Real faith, living faith ... exists always and only in a *cognitive, reflective, scientific state* (Emphasis added) (p.25).

Again we see the stress on the cognitive state of faith. How then is it related to theology?

> Faith is not theology ... but neither does faith exist apart from, or independently of theology. Theology comes into play at that very moment when the person of faith becomes

> intellectually conscious of his or her faith (McBrien, 1980, p. 26).

McBrien moves then to a definition of theology based upon the classic one of St Anselm of Canterbury (d. 1109) 'faith seeking understanding' (*fides quaerens intellectum*). McBrien's definition is:

> Theology is that process by which we bring our knowledge and understanding of God to the level of expression (p. 26).

On this definition and previous quotation it is obvious that for believers, of whatever age , who begin to be intellectually conscious of their faith the faith-theology interplay has come into operation. Thus even young children in this family or religious school who begin to learn names or use symbols for their God are beginning this dialogue and can be truly said to be expressing their faith in simple cognitive, knowledge forms. That is in a simple theology.

Indeed from the other side of the desk whenever teachers or religious educators engage in religious education they are expressing their faith in a particular theological form. There is no such thing as 'handing on the faith' without some conceptual and philosophical framework that expresses a certain theological process. McBrien says in this connection:

> When all is said and done, religious educators, bishops, preachers, and the Church at large do not transmit or hand on faith apart from theology. They hand on faith in and through the theology they are using. In other words, they transmit particular interpretations or understandings of faith in their various and multiple forms. It is entirely beside the point, therefore, to warn religious educators against teaching theology instead of handing on the faith. *Faith exists always and only in some theological form* (McBrien, 1980, p. 26).

The implications for religious education are clear. If religious education is about assisting people develop a deeper faith awareness, in whatever faith tradition, then the definition above that faith always exists in some theological form applies. If theology is the 'process by which we bring our knowledge and understanding of God to the level of expression' then religious education must be about the *faith-theology-knowledge interplay*. It is impossible to separate out one or other component and seek to consider it either conceptually or in institutional structure, such as home, school or classroom.

Belief

McBrien (1980, p. 27) distinguishes between theology as faith brought to the level of self-consciousness whereas belief is one aspect of theology like a 'snapshot'. Theology is a process, whereas a belief is one product. A belief is a formulation of the knowledge we have of God through faith.

Education

The etymological root of the word 'education' is *educare* – to lead out – and has the sense of helping persons to develop their full potential. Educational philosophers from the time of Aristotle (d. 322 BC) have reflected on the meaning of this word and in recent times some viewpoints very relevant to this study have emerged.

Dewey (1916, p. 89) spoke of 'reconstruction or reorganisation of experience which adds to the meaning of experience.' A useful corrective to this rather too all-inclusive view was added by Ellis Nelson (1972, p. 7) who wrote,

> we should make a distinction between what an individual *may use* for educational purposes out of his total experience and the *deliberate activities* of the educator who is attempting to help students.

This is similar to the distinction between the informal, contextual environment of schools and the deliberative intentions of the teachers operative in the formal curriculum.

Gradually a sense of the inherent religious dimension of even secular education has emerged from the writings of philosophers. Oakeshott (1972) has considered education as

> that transaction between generations in which newcomers to the scene are initiated into the world they are to inhabit. That is the world of understandings, meanings, moral and religious belief (p. 22).

Others such as Friere (1970) would reject this 'banking education' as too much inclined towards a socialisation into the existing status quo. Friere calls for a more critical dialogue between teachers and students to unveil oppressive structures, and transform the world.

Alfred North Whitehead, concerned with quality education and seeing the danger of a value-free education, without reference to religion, wrote (1967, p. 14):

> We can be content with no less than the age old summary of the educational ideal which has been current at any time from the dawn of our civilization. The essence of education is that it be religious.

Thus true education since it deals with ultimate life questions for the individual and society always has an implicit religious element. With the recognition of the power of this claim for true secular education there is still scope and need for believers of any faith tradition to have the freedom to establish educational structures and programs to educate their children and followers in the particular tradition of their faith. The State has the right to ensure that its citizens are educated to a level appropriate to their useful contribution to society. But this does not give the State the right actually to take over that education. This prior right to educate always rests with the *parents* and those to whom they freely choose to delegate that right. It is important therefore for religious groups in society to establish educational institutions so that parents may exercise that right. Such educational institutions must strive to integrate secular learning with the traditions of their particular faith to meet their dual obligation to parents and State. Only an approach that helps students consider *simultaneously* the challenge of secular knowledge with an explicit faith orientation can help them develop their own personal theological stance (vide McBrien), help them avoid 'cognitive conflict' on leaving the educational setting to live out their faith creatively in an adult world.

In this context we see the importance of the concept 'to believe' as used, for example, when talking of catechesis as 'dialogue between believers'. To believe in this connection means not only to form one's own theological view but to seek to share it with others. This communication is most effective when there is some kind of match of stage of faith (Fowler, 1978; Flynn, 1979) or at least awareness of the other's stage of faith. Flynn has extended Fowler's faith categories to include a stage of 'searching faith' which some adolescents may experience. To 'engage in dialogue between believers' needs special skills by well trained adults/teachers who can establish a climate where searching youth may share their uncertain journey. In this sense rebellious youth engaged in this dialogue may well be considered as believers. As they seek to make sense out of their experience, rebellious, searching youth build up their own theological images and symbols of God and ultimate meaning. Thus their faith grows and though their categories do not match conventional Church models or terms they are nonetheless personally genuine views of God. 'To believe' is always within a theological framework and may vary widely with stage of faith at different stages of life history.

Religion

The etymological root of the word 'religion' has been debated since Cicero (d. 44 BC) and is of uncertain origin. One view suggests *religio* – fear of the Gods, awe, sacredness – and implies a sense of wonder and praise. We have seen that a person's fundamental experience of God is brought to understanding in the faith process and articulation of that understanding in language or symbols is a personal theology. So too in the lives of religious communities an interrelated process of grace, faith, theology comes into being to generate a particular religious tradition. (Christian, Hindu, Moslem etc.) Religion does not exist apart from a particular religious tradition except when one attempts to abstract a faith-free view from many specific religious traditions. When such a world religion class is being taken within an educational environment of one faith tradition then students are invited to reflect on their own religious tradition in the light of what they learn from the others. Faith in their own tradition is explicit and is refined by the comparative process. When the same process is done within an educational framework of no specific support for any one religious tradition there is a very different outcome. Unless there is a specific faith tradition in the home a sense of relativism of the various religious traditions may well develop with little encouragement for the adoption of a particular faith stance. This attempt to examine knowledge about world religions without recognition of the priority of a particular faith tradition is a denial of the true nature of education, pointed to by Whitehead above, and in a school with a religious tradition is unjust to parents and students of that tradition.

Even in schools where parents come from a variety of religious backgrounds or none at all there is a responsibility on staff to educate for life, to examine the great questions of life (origins, birth, death, suffering, life beyond the grave) and without proselytising let their own values and faith inform their teaching. All teachers promote the philosophy of their own tradition. To deny teachers with a religious philosophy the ability to express in appropriate ways their view of life is unjustified.

2. OTHER THEORISTS

Gabriel Moran

Gabriel Moran, a prolific religious educational writer, in his key initial works on Revelation, opting for the titles *Theology of Revelation (1966) and Catechesis of Revelation* (1966) still saw a viable place for the terms theology (faith seeking understanding) and catechesis (dialogue between believers) in the realm of religious education. In another work, *Religious Body* (1974, p. 153) he makes the explicit claim that

> the term religious education is one worth fighting for. What I wish to describe is education that includes religion as ecumenically understood.

and in the same work (1974, p. 146)

> ... all education is religious education and .. religious is not a component or qualifier so much as a test of whether it is education at all.

Many secular educators would not subscribe to such a view. To respect their stance it is important not to propose some kind of imperialism of faith which blankets all educational activities as religion. Yet it is equally important not to go to the opposite extreme and deny the central place in all education to religious education. We recall the view of Alfred North Whitehead, concerned with quality education and seeing the danger of a value-free education without reference to religion, who wrote (1967, p. 14):

> We can be content with no less than the old age summary of the educational ideal which has been current at any time from the dawn of our civilization. The essence of education is that it be religious.

Moran supports this view in a keynote article entitled 'The Religious Element in Education' (1984) where he placed the key theological image of covenant over and against secular educational images of growth.

Moran then is very much concerned with the language question. He even has reservations about Christian education as being too narrow, and making too many assumptions about who learns what and how.

> In contrast the term religious education makes no imperialistic claim. Religion can be understood so that each learner is religious, the context is a religious one and the intended outcome can be a religiously educated person (1974, p. 154).

Thus it is evident that greater precision in religious educational language is needed.

In Moran's (1981) *Interplay* he discusses in depth models of education and religion and asserts that religious education must be a dialogue or interplay between the two.

> It is ... important to set up a dialogical relationship so that the movement is religious to education to religious , or education to religious to education (p. 38).

'Interplay' is a key concept of this present work in its model of religious education as *'faith-theology-knowledge interplay'*. 'Play' implies an enjoyable game, a stepping apart from normal life to engage in activities with a pleasurable and fundamental meaning. Normal time does not apply but only the 'third quarter' or 'fourth set' of the game. We are in touch with eternal truths of a religious tradition. 'Inter' implies between two individuals or groups. It is a communal activity taking place in homes, classrooms, discussion groups; but always linking secular knowledge and understanding to the faith message within a particular theological framework.

Richard McBrien

What is to be the relationship of theology to religious education? Richard McBrien (1977) in *Basic Questions for Christian Educators* highlights the need to be clear, systematic and precise in our language and to be able to defend it and the philosophy which that language embodies. He points to a danger of a universalist world religion vs particularist traditions (e.g. Christianity, Jewish) of religious education.

> One cannot adopt a thoroughly universalist notion of religious education and at the same time function according to a particularist notion. (p. 26).

McBrien calls for a clear definition of the words 'religious' and 'education'. In terms of religious education McBrien sees a three fold nesting as in *Figure 4.1*.

Figure 4.1

RELATIONSHIP AMONG ELEMENTS OF RELIGIOUS EDUCATION

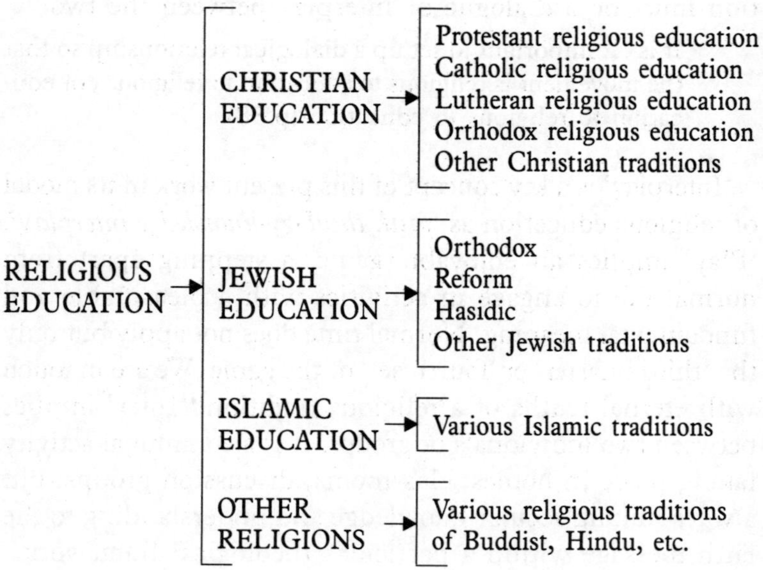

Christian education, Jewish education, Islamic and other traditions are the specific frameworks in which religious education occurs. In the same way as Christian theology is related to theology 'as such', it and religious education must always be situated within a particular tradition. Christian education – and an even more particularised form of that, Catholic education – is a subset of religious education. Some religious educators may feel that if we adopt the name Christian Educators instead of the broader religious educator we lose the ecumenical breadth implied in the adjective 'religious'. McBrien (1977, p. 28) replies:

> The specific characteristic of Christian faith is its acknowledgement of the Lordship of Jesus. But that particular perception of faith ideally expands rather than constricts the Christian's vision.

What distinguishes Christian faith from other traditions does not destroy the bond it holds in common with every other tradition. McBrien sees this as a radical hope for and commitment to, the coming of the Reign of God. Because Christ is the focus point for the ultimate drawing together of all religious traditions, Christian faith and Christian education understand themselves in universal terms. Because of this concern with

> final memory, symbolism, ritual and claims for total commitment it seems mistaken to argue, as some Christians do, that 'religious education' is a more appropriate self descriptive category than is 'Christian education' (p. 29).

McBrien has challenged us to rethink our basic categories and presumptions and made some strong points on the nature of Christian theology and Christian education.

Thomas Groome

Working independently, Thomas Groome came to establish his basic theological category on the Reign of God and a process of shared praxis (an integrated critical reflection upon the present situation in the light of the Gospel message and a shared reflection on how the vision of the Kingdom might be more fully attained). It is essentially a dialogue searching out together one's own personal and communal story, placing it in tension with the Gospel Story, and then personal and mutual reflection/ action for the sake of one's own vision and the Community Vision.

On the language question being considered here Groome opts for the title *Christian Religious Education* (1980) noting the distinctive qualities of 'Christian' for the term 'religious education'. He shows how the language debate, at least in USA, first surfaced among Protestant religious educators via a confrontation in religious education between liberal and neo-orthodox theology. The debate has been joined by Catholic theorists (McBrien, 1976; and Moran, 1977) who have brought the terms catechesis and catechetics (dialogue between believers) into prominence.

Groome makes explicit use of faith in the praxis approach with the Gospel or Church Story at the centre of the five steps. Classrooms using the praxis approach would have ample scope for simple faith discussions and sharing.

While Groome has demonstrated the practical worth of his approach in classroom, college and adult settings by conducting sessions himself at each of these levels, there has been no full scale evaluation of his approach as compared to a non-praxis approach. A very neat experimental design could be conducted with matched students and classes. Hopefully such an evaluation will be conducted in the near future.

An Australian review and critique of Groome's (1980) book by Hamilton (1981) is mainly positive. Hamilton raises a question mark however over the key symbol of the Reign of God by asking whether Jesus or The Cross might not be more central.

Graham Rossiter

The contribution of Graham Rossiter to this language debate, to the clarification of intentions and purposes of religious teachers has been quite prodigious. His major work (Rossiter, 1983), entitled *An Interpretation of Normative Theory for Religious Education in Australian Schools* sought, among other things, to suggest that bridges could well be built between government and Church-related schools, via the means of religious education curricula. A massive and very significant review of Australian research related to religious education was a welcome feature. (Also available in Rossiter, 1984) As well as the author's close knowledge of the Australian government school scene he discussed in depth other Christian groups engaged in education.

In the early part Rossiter (1983) makes a case for setting up a 'dialectic framework involving interaction between two main orientations designated as Education in Faith and Education in Religion ' (1983, p. 112). He defines these as:

> Education in Faith is defined to be the orientation of religious education which is aimed at handing on a particular religious faith tradition; that is, handing on the collective religious beliefs, traditions and practices of a group, by which the group identifies itself (or is identified) as a faith sharing community. The justification and aim of the activity came from the community of faith. Education in faith seeks to develop the personal religious faith and commitment of the pupil in the context of his or her particular religious faith. Education in faith is directed towards helping the pupil know and understand the faith tradition (1983, p. 113).

In a similar way Rossiter defines Education in Religion in this dialectical framework:

> Education in Religion is defined to be the orientation of religious education where the justification, aims, rationale and practices for the activity come from the general educational process. Education in religion seeks to deepen the individual's awareness, knowledge and understanding of religion, it focuses on how the study of religions may contribute to the general education of pupils and their personal development. Education in religion involves pupils at both cognitive and affective levels. Religious faith and commitment are neither presumed or required of pupils or teachers (1983, p. 116).

The definitions of education in faith and education in religion developed by Rossiter do not easily accord with those of catechesis and religious education developed from the literature reviewed above.

Indeed the nature of faith as personal knowledge of God as discussed above, and integral dependence on knowledge categories makes an approach that seeks to dichotomise faith away from knowledge a suspect one, at least in the Catholic tradition.

In addition, as McBrien has pointed out above, one should not distinguish Christian faith away from other traditions for Christianity holds, in common with every other tradition, the hope of a coming Reign of God. In world religions courses one needs to stand within one's own tradition and seek points of comparison and confrontation with other traditions. It is a dual knowledge and faith-depthing process. Because Christ is the focus point for the ultimate drawing together of all religious traditions, Christian faith and Christian education understand themselves in universal terms.

Rossiter (1983, p. 397) references the emphasis of the Church on the school model of instruction and seeks, with

Westerhoff to 'liberate catechesis from an unhealthy dependence on a "schooling-instructional paradigm"'. What Rossiter does not appear to realise is that Westerhoff (1976) is influenced by the erroneous school effectiveness research suggesting that schools have little impact. (Discussed in Chapters 2,3). Also Westerhoff is basing his critique of schooling on the Protestant Sunday School one-day-a-week model rather than the integrated secular and religious knowledge of week-long Catholic schools.

The place of formal religious education is clear in the Rossiter and Crawford proposals (1985, p. 40; 1987). It is to be the place for the teaching of religion, (education in religion) while catechesis is to be reserved for voluntary out-of-classroom commitment groups.

> Catechesis and the teaching of religion are complementary. The classroom religion period is the place for the teaching of religion ... Catechesis is more appropriately taken up in voluntary commitment groups and on retreats. Classroom religious education complements and prepares for catechesis (1985, p. 40).

Catechesis, defined as being a faith dialogue of believers then is seen to be best pursued in voluntary groups outside the formal religion education classroom.

We need to note the discussion above on the nature of faith if we are to see the difficulties inherent in this view of Rossiter's. We have shown that faith is a total gift of God ('to assist understanding of what has already been experienced in the depths of the human reality as grace in direct relation to God', Rahner, 1975, p. 497). Thus for Rahner faith is ultimately connected with understanding and hence with knowledge. Thus at all stages of life (infant to old age) to lead to faith is to assist *understanding*, to be able to put names, categories or symbols on what has already been experienced and continues in the evolving direct relation with God. Thus the knowledge link to faith development is deep and makes the classroom with a formal educational focus a valid and necessary place for faith expression and development.

Secondly McBrien (1980, pp. 25-27) shows that faith is not theology but that theology in a particular stance comes into play whenever a person seeks to express her/his faith in word, symbol or action.

Theology is a process by which we bring our knowledge and understanding of God to the level of expression, then religious education must be about the *'faith-theology-knowledge' interplay*. It is wrong and impossible to separate it either conceptually or in institutional structure. Yet this is precisely what Rossiter and Crawford (1985, p. 40) seek to do in this claim.

To return to the claim above, it happens that it is subject to an empirical test. In the current data set we have 3431 students grouped into 103 classrooms.And the procedure of data collection was to group these into the 103 formal religious education classrooms. Thus we have a wealth of data on both outcome and process of religious education, including a number of faith and faith-related scales to test the Crawford and Rossiter claim. The Flynn (1975, 1985) data sets could not test this claim because his data was arranged into total year groups and the distinctiveness of individual classes was lost.

This central claim of Crawford and Rossiter's is that classrooms with their compulsory nature are more suited to education in religion while voluntary groups and faith sharing catechesis belong out of the classroom. The implicit assumption is that classroom settings are less effective for faith-sharing or development. This claim will be critiqued by this study that has a unique set of 103 actual religious education classes with a wide range of students and teachers' attitude and faith views.

There is also a concern here about freedom for the student. What appears to be overlooked is that education in secular disciplines integrated with meaning insights of one's own religious tradition is in fact the highest freedom. One may then choose one's own position and life direction with the fullest freedom having heard the message.

Like all of us, Rossiter (1987) has adjusted his position from the bald categories of 1983, 1985 and has stressed the *professional* religious education with a variety of methods. Yet there is still debate over what is the *professional nature*. While looking for a 'more professional side of young people's education in the classroom', he sees the answer 'to base it within an intellectual study' respecting the basic freedoms of the individual. This does not sufficiently respect the integral role of faith in *both* formal (classroom) and informal (youth groups, camps, retreats, climate, rituals, policies of the school context) aspects. Intellectual study and opportunity for explicit faith expression need to be provided naturally by believing teachers in and out of the classrooms.

The model of faith-theology-education interplay asserts that teachers will do so out of their own theological models and will teach something (there will be carefully planned educational intellectual content). The teachers' own explicit faith and God's grace will act upon students with a free (in the mystery of God's grace) idiosyncratic response by students to build their own faith vision. This by its nature is very different from the academic subjects. As Paul says, 'I planted, Apollos watered but God gave the growth' *(1 Cor 3:6)*.

Michael Leahy

A conceptual article is provided by Leahy (1991) who makes a key distinction between the 'Church's mission of evangelisation/catechesis and the school's task of education'. The formation of the human person is incomplete without a spiritual dimension. Yet the concept of 'formation' seems ambiguous. In his terms a problem arises between 'education' which demands freedom to choose and Catholic school evangelisation which implies a closed system without freedom to choose. This is a false dichotomy since growth in faith in Christ makes one more fundamentally free in the depths of life's mystery than someone who has only secular education. To know Christ is to '... know the truth and the truth will make you free' *(Jn 8:32)*.

It is right to subject the theologically based statements of others to rational criticism but a point is reached when the faith leap must be made into the mystery of God (always fundamentally unknowable). The obligation to evangelise (help build faith) is therefore best carried out in the religious education class in the matrix of a Christian ethos of the Catholic school. Students' freedom is utterly respected and enhanced by giving them the gospel message with the best variety and forms of educational method. This includes rational criticism always ultimately based upon the faith vision of the teacher and her/his own theological framework.

If the tension between evangelisation and education is to be realised, according to Leahy (1991, p. 8) then

> 'educating students in the content of the Catholic faith in a way which respects what I have called "the norms of education" and witnessing to that faith by a range of other practices ... especially the educationally needy.'

Leahy does well to highlight the educationally needy and the need to help them religiously within the formal classroom setting.

Marcellin Flynn

Following the work of Carmel Leavey (1972a), Marcellin Flynn has made a major contribution to our understanding of the dynamics of Catholic schools in Australia. His books include *Some Catholic Schools in Action*, an empirical study of 1393 sixth form boys, 619 parents and 404 staff, in 21 Catholic schools (1975); *Catholic Schools and the Communication of Faith* (1979), a more theoretical study integrating various theorists and proposing a socialisation model for the school; and his most recent *The Effectiveness of Catholic Schools* (1985) a follow up, 10 year empirical study on 2041 senior students, 1377 parents and 717 staff. From these he has developed a model for the role and function of Catholic schools in promoting faith growth.

This section will not review Flynn's work, leaving the faith effectiveness debate to Chapter 5 and the academic Higher School Certificate results till Chapter 6. However it will discuss Flynn's contribution to the language debate of this chapter.

Flynn's key point is that religious education should not be thought of as a dichotomy involving education in faith and education in religion. Rather he says (1984, p. 20):

> Good religious education teaching today requires both the educational challenge of the education in religion perspective and the vision of the education in faith approach if it is to be good religious education.

Flynn makes a fundamental distinction between formal and informal curriculum which bears up well in his empirical studies of effectiveness, where it is clear that both the formal and informal curriculum are predictors of religious outcomes. In Figure 4.5 (p. 102), Flynn (1984, p. 20) stresses this integration.

Figure 4.5

THE RELIGIOUS EDUCATION CURRICULUM
OF CATHOLIC SCHOOLS
(Flynn, 1984). (Used with permission)

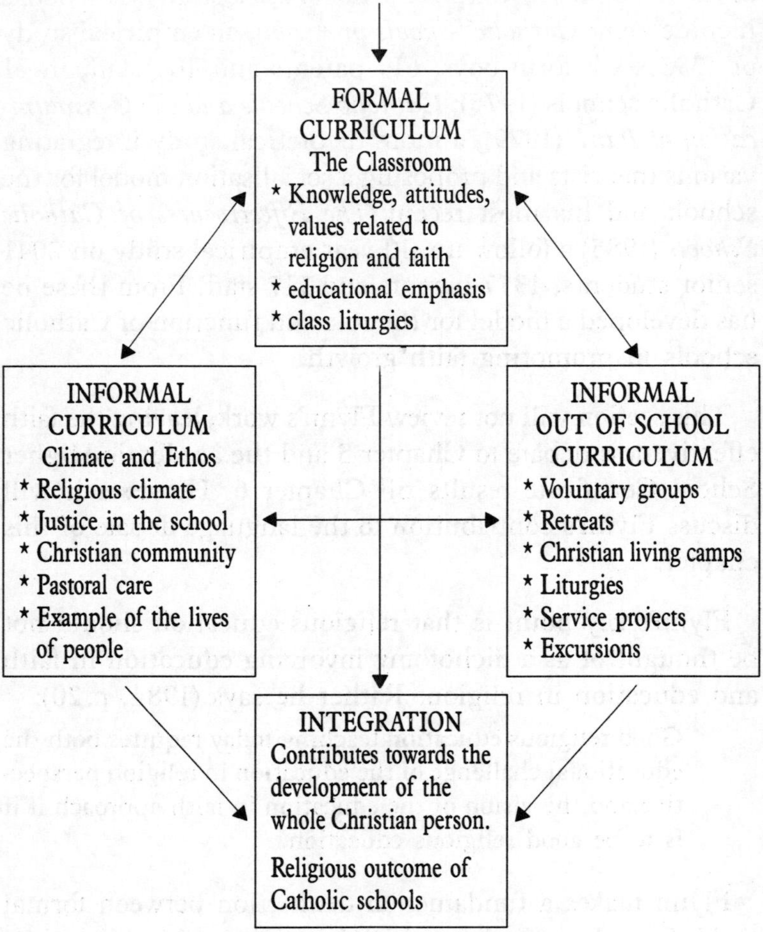

By distinguishing between the formal and informal curriculum Flynn opens up the path for research to check how effective are each of these in promoting religious outcomes. Furthermore by distinguishing climate and ethos, a key cluster of effectiveness variables, from the informal out-of-school activities such as voluntary groups he highlighted these aspects that all teachers are responsible for in Catholic schools from those that fall to only some. The key point Flynn made is the need for integration of these various aspects of the curriculum into the total development of the whole Christian person.

What is important is that each individual student takes from these various 'faith-theology-education' interplays in formal and informal curriculum to build up her/his own faith vision. This is an idiosyncratic process and combines life experience and an emerging personal theology.

Further, Flynn calls for a fidelity to Catholic tradition as the stress on Catholic theology in the 'faith-theology-education' model suggests. On the integration in classroom Flynn agrees that classroom religious education should be more educational and knowledge oriented (elements of Catholic theology) while being open to moments of faith without coercion. Thus Flynn's model integrates the sound academic learning with openness to faith development (however simple) in the classroom. He cites empirical data on student perceptions of religious education curriculum to illustrate the influence of the informal curriculum (climate and ethos) when linked with the students' perceptions of the religious education classes (formal curriculum).

3. CONCLUSION

This extensive review of religious education effectiveness and the associated theoretical issues has highlighted the following:

1. Effectiveness defined in terms of meeting objectives set involves both outcome and process measures of religious education.

2. A study of basic definitions of faith and related terms have shown the integral nature of faith to the whole Catholic school curriculum (formal and informal).

3. Other theorists show the intimate link between religion and education, the need for a theological vision and a defensible educational model.

4. Graham Rossiter's work was reviewed and critiqued with particular focus on the 'education in faith' and 'education in religion' orientations. Some reservations about the conceptual clarity of these with respect to the theological literature were noted.

5. The proposal by Rossiter that education in religion was more suited to the classroom while education in faith was more suited to out-of-class voluntary groups was seen as a key question for the future, subject to empirical and conceptual test now.

6. Marcellin Flynn's distinctions between formal (classroom) and, informal (climate) and informal (out of school activities) were seen as a way of testing the integration of faith-theology-knowledge in the lived experience of students and teachers.

Having discussed the religious educational effectiveness from a theoretical point of view we will now examine the research evidence regarding the role of both the formal and informal religious educational curriculum.

CHAPTER 5

RELIGIOUS EFFECTIVENESS OF CATHOLIC SCHOOLS

The research evidence

This chapter will examine in detail the Fahy (1980a, 1980b) study for evidence on the religious effectiveness of Catholic schools that will shed light on the Catholic school effectiveness debate of Chapter 3 and theoretical questions of Chapter 4. The study will be explained, the sample defined, the methodology outlined and then a series of tables for each faith related criterion will enable empirical conclusions to be drawn. Consideration of effectiveness on academic outcomes will be left till Chapter 6.

1. THE STUDY

The study was an in-depth one of 23 Australian Catholic high schools. The schools were predominantly single sex male, but there were also six coeducational schools. No schools were all female students. This deliberate choice of a system of schools administered by a single order of male religious was an attempt to control for any system specific effect and focus on the schools and classrooms themselves. An outline of the sample is given in Tables 5.1, 5.2.

Table 5.1

Number of students analysed by type of school, sex and year level.

Year	Single sex boys	Co-ed. school Boys	Co-ed. school Girls	Totals
YEAR 10	1789	202	228	2219
YEAR 12	1032	85	95	1212
TOTALS	2821	287	323	3431 (98% pop.)

Table 5.2

Number of teachers in sample of 23 secondary schools.

Staff	Male	Female	Total
RELIGIOUS	137	30	44%
LAY	174	107	56%
TOTALS	311	137	100%
GRAND TOTAL: 93% staff	448		

This focus on the effects of school and classroom differences marks this study off from all others, including Flynn who was unable to distinguish between religion class groupings. The study is the first one to enable determination of the unique effect of classroom religious education upon faith measures when compared to home, peer group, personality and other school factors.

2. METHODOLOGY

The methodology is based upon the symmetric decomposition of variance (or commonality analysis). This is a method which, unlike Greeley's strong inference causal path approach, makes no unjustified assumptions about causal directions or order of entry of variables into the analysis (Beaton, 1973, 1974).

A simple outline of commonality is given here. Suppose for example we had a key criterion attitude such as Social Justice Awareness, and that this attitude has been estimated on a reliable, valid scale. Suppose further, we want to know the unique effect of home factors, school factors and peer group factors upon these important justice attitudes. We do not want to know the effect of these environments each one alone, we want to enter all of them together into a single analysis to see which one is the best unique predictor when the other two are controlled for. Then we would find, for example, home background factors are the best unique predictors (unique effect) of students' Social Justice Awareness. In this example we could say the other two blocks of variables are less powerful in explaining Social Justice Awareness scores. Note the term 'unique effect'. This does not mean an effect as in causal effect, that A causes B in a one way direction. The term 'unique effect' here means that two variables share a high proportion of variation (as one variable goes up the other tends to go up concomitantly). It is saying that the two variables 'covary systematically' even when other blocks (school or peer group) are kept constant. Thus a 'unique effect' can pinpoint that group of variables which uniquely explains the major part of the variation (variance) in a criterion measure, such as Social Justice Awareness.

One other factor sometimes troubles people reading commonality graphs. The graph with the highest level of per cent variance explained is the 'best predictor'. But there is one on the end sometimes larger simply marked 'Commonality'. How is this to be read? See Figure 5.1.

When the computer looks at the three blocks of variables (home, school, peer group), it recognises that these themselves are also intercorrelated. The commonality is the sum of all the small overlaps possible but generally adds up to a substantial amount. Usually this is not easily interpretable being a mixed overlap of so many environments. In Figure 5.1 this overlap is termed Commonality.

Figure 5.0

Commonality Analysis of Three (3) Blocks of Data on Social Justice Awareness as criteria
Sample data only

The three (3) blocks of data are:
HOME BACKGROUND (H)
SCHOOL ENVIRONMENT (S)
PEER GROUP (P)

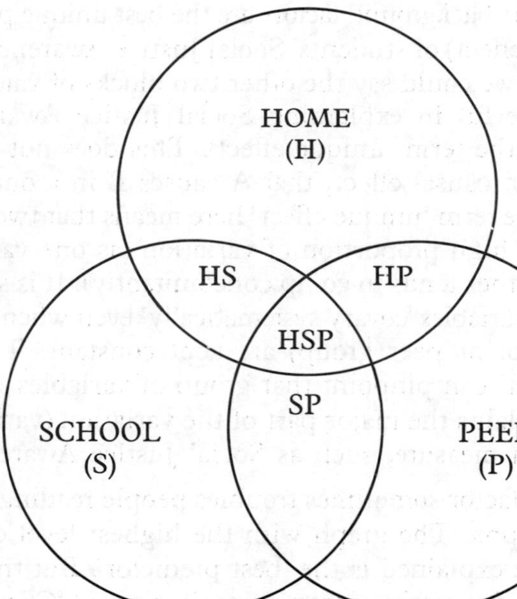

The diagram shows the amount of variation in Social Justice scores that may be attributed uniquely to (S), (H), (P) and also to the overlap or joint effects (SP), (HS), (HP), (HSP). From these uniques and overlaps may Figure 5.1 be assembled. (From Beaton, 1974).

Here is a hypothetical graph (see next page) (Figure 5.1)

Figure 5.1

Per cent of explained variance in Social Justice Awareness Attitudes Scores

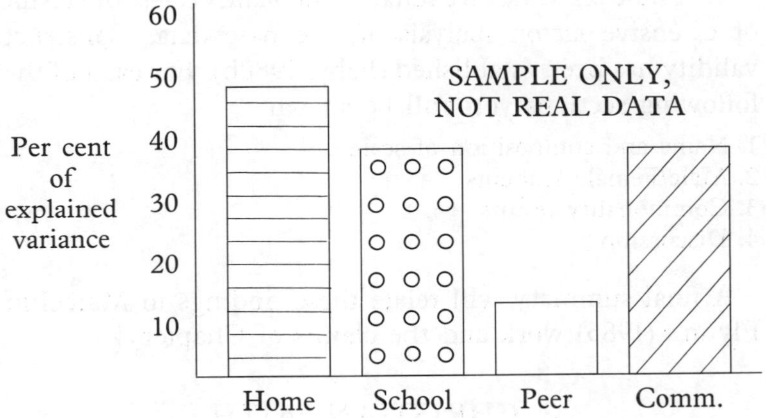

One would read this as Home Environment factors have the most positive unique effect upon Social Justice Attitudes over and above the smaller influence of school and very little peer group. The overlap commonality block is ignored.

One interpretation of this may be that students' social justice and racial attitudes ('black people are inferior by nature to white people') at least measured by this scale are most uniquely explained by experiences at home such as parents' reported discussions about racial attitudes. It in *no way* proves *causation*, it merely says students and parents' attitudes covary in a regular way even when school and peer group influence is controlled or evened out. Herein lies the power of this approach to differentiate between various environments. It suggests policy and instructional directions for maximum effectiveness in home and school using the variables in those scales.

This ends the hypothetical section.

□□□

Having completed this outline of methodology it is the task to turn now to the real data six faith-related criteria to determine which predictor/blocks best explain their variation. These six scales are reliable and valid scales, the result of extensive factor analysis on the base data. Construct validity has been established (Fahy, 1980b). For each of the following sections you will be shown:

1. Name and composition of scale
2. Male/Female students
3. Commonality results
4. Discussion

A final summary will relate these findings to Marcellin Flynn's (1985) work and the claims of Chapter 4.

3. CHRISTIAN FAITH

This key criterion scale consists of the following items in Table 5.3 for boys and Table 5.4 for girls. Figure 5.2 shows the results of the commonality analysis between five blocks, HOME, PEER GROUP, PERSONALITY, SCHOOL and STAFF. These blocks were formed by preliminary screening of 131 variables into reliable scales and then grouping into conceptual blocks.

Table 5.3

Per cent response to items defining CHRISTIAN FAITH SCALE N = 2821 students, male.

Item	Per cent Agree	Per cent Disagree	Factor Loading
Christ has become a real person to me in my daily life	33	37	0.71
I see God as a loving Father	55	21	0.62
The Holy Spirit influences my present life	29	32	0.61

I intend to base my life on the teaching and example of Christ	22	50	0.59
I would like to know more about Christ and his teachings	36	36	0.57
I believe God forgives me	74	9	0.57
I appreciate the chance to go to the New Rite of Reconciliation	32	44	0.41
I like to take an active part of singing, reading at the liturgy	26	63	0.38
Even if necessary precautions are taken, sexual relationships outside marriage are still wrong	23	63	0.36
I believe in God	62	8	0.32
I appreciate the opportunity to go on a religious camp or weekend	59	25	0.18
The religious experience of a Christian living weekend, camp or retreat has made a lasting impression on me	43	34	0.17
Christ lived 2000 years ago, in another culture and has no relevance for today (R)	13	62	−0.27
Christ has no relevance for me today (R)	12	62	−0.31
When I see all the war, poverty and cruelty that exists in the world, I have trouble believing in God (R)	34	47	−0.35

No. of items 15, Range 15-75, Scale mean 47.8, S.D. 10.8, Alpha Reliability 0.85. R = item is reversed in scale addition.

HIGH SCORE: Students with a strong commitment to aspects of their Christian faith.

LOW SCORE: Students with a weak or little commitment to a Christian faith in their lives.

Table 5.4

Per cent response to items defining CHRISTIAN FAITH SCALE
N = 323 students, female.

Item	Per cent Agree	Per cent Disagree	Factor Loading
Christ has become a real person to me in my daily life	40	31	0.71
I see God as a loving Father	62	15	0.62
The Holy Spirit influences my present life	35	30	0.61
I intend to base my life on the teaching and example of Christ	22	49	0.59
I would like to know more about Christ and his teachings	39	29	0.57
I believe God forgives me	74	7	0.57
I appreciate the chance to go to the New Rite of Reconciliation	34	45	0.41
I like to take an active part of singing, reading at the liturgy	34	53	0.38
Even if necessary precautions are taken, sexual relationships outside marriage are still wrong	34	51	0.36
I believe in God	59	7	0.32
I appreciate the opportunity to go on a religious camp or weekend	60	18	0.18
The religious experience of a Christian living weekend, camp or retreat has made a lasting impression on me	40	25	0.17
Christ lived 2000 years ago, in another culture and has no relevance for today (R)	11	58	−0.27
Christ has no relevance for me today (R)	10	62	−0.31

When I see all the war, poverty and cruelty that exists in the world, I have trouble believing in God (R)	39	42	−0.35

No. of items 15, Range 15-75, Scale mean 50.6, S.D. 9.4, Alpha Reliability 0.85. R = item is reversed in scale addition.

HIGH SCORE: Students with a strong commitment to aspects of their Christian faith.

LOW SCORE: Students with a weak or little commitment to a Christian faith in their lives.

Before commenting on the graphs and variance estimate it is instructive to consider the items defining the CHRISTIAN FAITH SCALE. The overall structure is similar for boys and girls although the girls express a significantly higher level of faith development.

The most central item which seems to define the students' basic belief is:

'Christ has become a real person to me in my daily life.'

Where students agree with this (33% boys and 40% girls), then they tend to have positive attitudes to all other religious items and a host of school and home ones also. There are a number of youth uncertain about belief in Christ as a real person (30% boys, 29% girls). If the research and conceptual analysis of Fowler (1978), Flynn (1979) is accurate then it is highly likely that many of these youth are in a stage of 'searching faith', a valid faith stage but lacking clarity of expression.

Notice the significant position of the next two items on the Father and the Spirit. These items were scattered throughout a 210 item questionnaire but the factor analyses groups items according to their correlations, so one may suggest underlying constructs in the perceptions or attitudes of these youth. It would seem then that there is a central construct in the perceptions of reality of these 3431 Catholic youth.

> That central perception perhaps not articulated in normal conversation is of the reality and influence of the Trinity in their own lives.

All other religious and secular attitudes cluster (unconsciously perhaps) around the reality of God in their lives. This is a very significant finding of this study and points to directions in our religious education.

Notice the next item about 'intending to base my life' is less well supported by youth, many of whom are unable to make that kind of commitment yet. Yet there is stronger support for wanting to know more about Christ and his teachings, a central concern for religious education. There is some appreciation for the New Rite of Reconciliation although many still stay away. Appropriate catechesis and celebration of Reconciliation is an important need of these students. Liturgical involvement is a feature only for a quarter of boys and a third of girls. The complex processes of involving youth in liturgy need further explanation.

In an era of contraception only a quarter of boys and a third of girls are supportive of one aspect of the Church's sexual morality. These free choice anonymous responses provide approximate norms for youth (Australian youth perhaps) in these areas.

Basic belief in God is high (62% boys, 59% girls), and so is a solid foundation on which to build other attitudes and understandings.

The out-of-school religious experiences are very popular and being in this factor do correlate well with the basic faith positions above. They are significant faith experiences in themselves and deserve support.

A few negative items serve as a check on the consistency of the above responses across the sample. Notice that 62% of boys and girls *disagree* that 'Christ has no relevance for me today'. This accords almost exactly with the first item if we include the *uncertain* people who may be seen now in a real sense as not rejecting the relevance of Christ but *searching* for him.

Table 5.5

Per cent of boys (N = 2821) and girls (N = 323) attitudes to Christ.

Item	BOYS			GIRLS		
	A	U	D	A	U	D
Christ has become a real person to me in my daily life	*33*	*30*	37	*40*	*29*	31
Christ has no relevance for me today	12	26	*62*	10	28	*62*
Notice:	33 + 30 = 62 (approximately)			40 + 29 = 62 (approximately)		

A = agree, U = uncertain, D = disagree

Thus it may be said from Table 5.5 that the 30% of boys and 29% of girls who were uncertain about Christ in their lives are *not rejecting him as of no relevance* but are genuinely searching for his place in their lives. This is a cogent empirical check on the reality of searching faith proposed by Flynn (1979) and further suggests that probably all who respond *uncertain* in items relating to Christ are in fact in a *searching* mode rather than a *rejecting* attitude mode. In faith research then this key finding needs to be explored:

> *Two thirds of youth are not rejecting the relevance of Christ, one third clearly recognise him as a real person while another third are in a stage of searching faith, the last third reject him at the present time.*

Now follow the results of comparing the various environments of home, peer group, personality, school, staff. In Figure 5.2 the amount of variation (variance) in the Christian faith scores that is uniquely explained by a given environment holding all the others constant is estimated. The tallest column indicates the strongest unique effect, except for Commonality (C) which is a mixture of unrelated overlaps.

The data is examined first grouped into total schools (N = 23), then into groupings of religious educational classrooms (N = 103) and finally as individual students (N = 3431). In each case the amount of Christian faith variance changes and the predictor blocks (also grouped similarly) explain different amounts.

Figure 5.2

Per cents of explained variance in Christian Faith scores uniquely accounted for by each block of predictors.

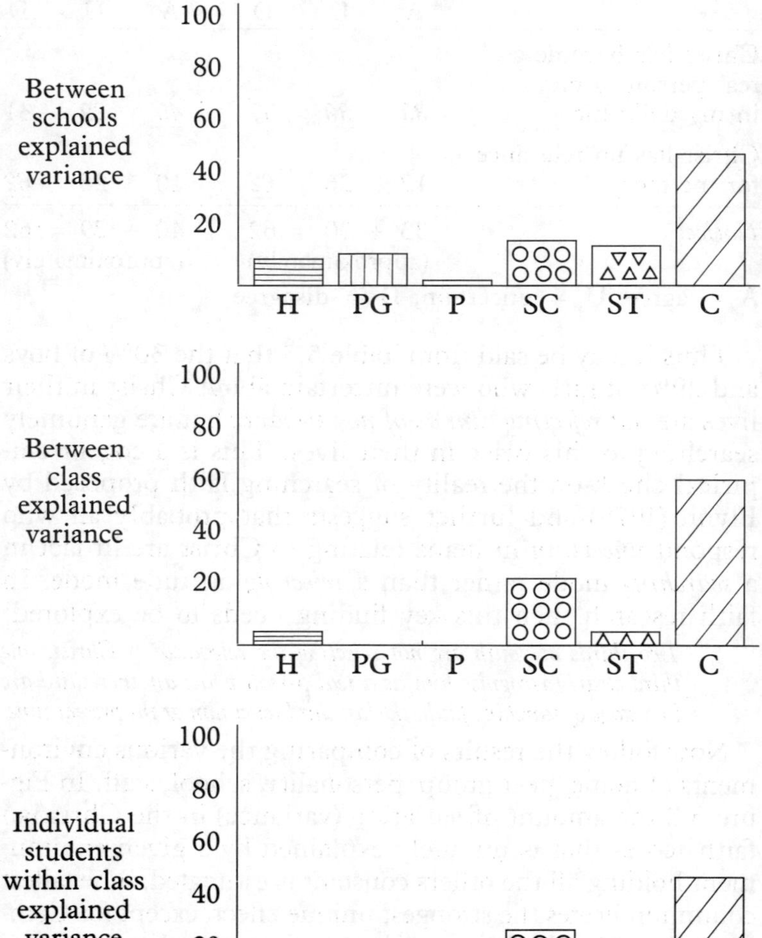

* H = HOME, PG = PEER GROUP, P = PERSONALITY, SC = SCHOOL, ST = STAFF blocks of predictors, C = COMMONALITY.

Table 5.6

Main predictors of STUDENT'S CHRISTIAN FAITH at SCHOOL, CLASSROOM and INDIVIDUAL LEVEL with per cent variances in faith scores between these groups.

SIGNIFICANT PREDICTORS OF STUDENT'S CHRISTIAN FAITH			
SCHOOL	1. Ideal importance of Religious Goals of school. 2. Level of satisfaction with religious education classes. 3. Liking for teachers. 4. View of actual importance of liberal education goals by the school.		
HOME	1. Student's view of parental warmth, trust. 2. Student's view of parental religiosity.		
LEVEL	SCHOOL $N = 23$	CLASSROOMS $N = 103$	INDIVIDUAL $N = 3431$
ABSOLUTE VARIANCE	3.1% ($p < 0.0001$)	1.3% ($p < 0.05$)	95.6%
TOTAL EXPLAINED VARIANCE*	98.3%	67.5%	47.6%

* The predictors above can explain these proportions of the variation in this key religious criteria of *student's Christian faith.*

Table 5.6 is the KEY TABLE of this study. On a reliable and well validated Christian Faith scale it shows that both school and home environments have a unique as well as overlap effect. The school factors refer to both formal (2,4) and the informal (1,3) aspects as proposed above. The home factors relate to students' perceptions of warmth, trust and parental example as believing people. Home and school have unique and complementary effects on students' Christian faith.

The lower half of Table 5.6 answers the key questions posed by this study about the effectiveness of classrooms nested within schools. When the variation in Christian Faith is analysed a total of 98.3 per cent of the absolute variance between schools may be explained by the above six (6) (4 school, 2 home) predictors. Schools and their climates differ in level of Christian faith of students (3.1 per cent absolute variance) but this is *very significant in such a controlled setting* (there being statistically only 1 chance in 10 000 of being wrong in this conclusion). The predictors identified above can account for 98 per cent of the explained faith scores at the school level. We therefore know what aspects are most strongly related to students' Christian faith and can develop specific priorities.

Turning now to the analysis of the 103 classrooms we see there is a small but still significant amount of absolute variance (Our chance of being wrong here has statistically dropped to 1 in 20). We can discern that religion classrooms nested within and therefore controlling for overall school climate, *do in fact differ*. This identifies the reality of a *unique classroom religious climate.*

This affirms that in truth there is Faith in Catholic Classrooms which differs from religion class to religion class even within the same school climate.

The six (6) predictors listed can account for 67.5 per cent of the explained variance in faith scores at the level of classrooms. This is quite high and shows the value of the six (6) predictor scales in understanding classroom faith development. Investigation of those six (6) scales shows those items most amenable to intervention.

Finally the large proportion of absolute variance attributable to individual students is a central finding. This shows the *idiosyncratic nature of faith*. Students construct their faith vision from a wide range of sources and have their own unique personal theology built up from their total life experiences.

While admitting the idiosyncratic nature of personal faith the students and their parents also stand within and are being educated into a particular faith tradition. The key stories, symbols, language and concepts of that tradition need to be taught. Individual assessment of that knowledge base by all the best educational means is valid and necessary. However attitudes being closer to the personal faith vision may only be assessed anonymously for the purpose of classroom curriculum evaluation. Skills and behaviour remain the province of the individual conscience and are not assessed individually except in so far as to maintain the order of sound classroom management. It is appropriate to assign individual grades, marks, diagnostic tables, class mark graphs *for knowledge outcomes only* since we need to reinforce knowledge of the central stories, facts, language and symbols of the tradition. From these elements and their life experiences the students will build their own specific and unique faith vision which we can never assess individually.

What aspects of school best explain the level of Christian Faith? They are all significant predictors and are:

Christian climate of the school

The students' opinion of the religious goals for the school including the building of an atmosphere of Christian community, providing meaningful liturgical celebrations, teaching religious education at a level comparable to other subjects, integrating it with other subjects and providing an example of dedicated life by lay and religious staff. For the per cent who agreed with these, see the full set of scales in Appendix A1.

Satisfaction with formal religious education

This process scale involves a sense of finding religious education classes interesting, helpful to one's religious development, a sense that the religion teacher is interested in religious education, open communication to discuss freely problems that students have and a sense of relevance of religion to life. This scale which involves more than just academic religious education learning but talks more about the atmosphere of mutual respect and genuine religious development is a reliable and valid measure of the process of religious education classroom. The full details are in Appendix A1.

Satisfaction with teacher

Only three items feature here. Most of my teachers take a genuine interest in me, generally my teachers teach well, and some of my teachers do not like me (a reverse item). Again full details in Appendix A1.

Liberal educational goals

Links to liberal ideals such as giving students experience in the main areas of human knowledge, provide scope for creative work, encouraging a love of learning for its own sake, make students aware of other religions and develop independence and critical thinking. See Appendix A1 for full details.

All four scales contribute to the high unique positive effect that the *School* block has upon *Christian Faith* scale. It is not possible to separate these four once they are entered into the commonality analysis. Therefore one would have to say that the school's influence on the faith development of its students is exerted through all of these acting together …

1. school's religious climate (informal curriculum).
2. formal religious education classes (formal curriculum).

3. atmosphere of mutual respect between teachers and pupils (informal curriculum).
4. Liberal educational climate with exposure to the wide ideas of education and a tolerance for divergent viewpoints (formal curriculum).

This is a very interesting result in the light of our discussion of Chapter 4 where it was suggested that the academic learning about religion should be confined to the formal religious education classroom whereas the out-of- classroom informal curriculum was more suited to faith sharing and faith development. The results presented here based on 103 actual religious education classrooms puts paid to the above claim. For these Year 10 (Sophomores) and Year 12 (Senior) students their faith development (as estimated by a reliable and valid scale) is uniquely related to other school variables showing that *both* the school's informal religious climate and the formal religious education classes (well taught and interesting) need to be integrated. In addition an atmosphere of mutual respect between students and teachers and an openness to a liberal educational climate are important predictors.

Likewise, the claim that a faith-sharing model is not an appropriate one for religious education classrooms neglects the fact that the whole environment in which the education is going on is steeped in faith and to make possible its legitimate expression in a simple faith-theology-education interplay is a necessary part of formal religious education. We need also to consider the informal school religious climate.

Regarding the contrast of Formal vs Informal, religious education curriculum, consider the view that the Formal religious education curriculum is more effective than the informal curriculum, the climate or ethos, in promoting religious outcomes.

The problem with this view is the non-specific 'religious outcome'. There are a number of different religious outcomes that research has identified. Flynn (1985) summarises in a single commonality table a large number of systematic comparisons.

Table 5.7 here (taken from Flynn, 1985, Table 12.14 with permission).

It is obvious that, as Flynn has defined formal and informal religious education, formal religious education relates most uniquely to the following religious criteria as a primary unique effect.

> 'Personal faith, Religious commitment, Attitudes to the Church, Religious knowledge.'

However, the home is still seen as the primary unique effect for 'religious practice' and 'moral values'. This accords well with Fahy (1980). Looking at secondary unique effects shows formal school curriculum being a primary or secondary predictor of a wide range of religious outcomes. Formal school processes are essentially linked to students' faith and values and should not be separated.

For comparison, Flynn's (1985) results are given in Table 5.7.

Table 5.7

COMMONALITY ANALYSIS: A SUMMARY
From Flynn (1985, Table 12.14)

Criterion or outcome	Primary unique effect	Secondary unique effect
1. Personal faith	Religious education Curriculum	Home
2. HSC achievement	Informal school climate	Formal school curriculum
3. Religious practice	Home	Religious education curriculum
4. Moral values	Home	Religious education curriculum
5. Religious commitment	Religious education curriculum	Home Formal school curriculum

6. Attitudes towards the Church	Religious education curriculum	Formal school curriculum
7. Justice values	Quality of school life (informal)	Religious education curriculum
8. Religious knowledge	Religious education curriculum	Home

In summary then this discussion suggests that the roles of home and school are distinct (contra Greeley and Rossi, 1966), as this analysis is able to demonstrate. There is no 'multiplier effect', that was the result of an inadequate analysis of home and school. Catholic schools can have an independent influence on faith from family religious development. They can exert their own unique positive effect over and above the home. A good Catholic School can have a positive impact on a student's faith even from a religiously poor home. A good Catholic home can have a positive impact on a student's faith even if he/she attends a religiously poor Catholic school. The ideal of course is Catholic schools and homes exerting a complementary influence in the faith development of students/children but both environments have their unique, independent yet complementary role to play.

The position arrived at here empirically and theoretically is that the 'faith-theology-education' interplay has a valid and essential place in formal religious education curriculum in classrooms and needs close integration with the informal climate and ethos. The place of dedicated religion teachers (lay and religious) working at both these levels is essential. Faith development and sharing of vision in simple ways (simple theology) must go on both in and out of the classroom in a Catholic school.

These findings should be of encouragement to both teachers and parents. We need not adopt the pessimistic view of schools provided by the secular studies or even more so those pessimistic views proposed by our Catholic researchers. With more curriculum sensitive measures, more valid and reliable scales, better methods of analysis it has been possible to show the effectiveness of Catholic schools and homes in promoting adolescent faith development. The practical content of these scales should encourage teachers and parents to make continued efforts for their adolescents' searching for God.

4. CATHOLIC PRACTICE

It is common practice to reanalyse significant data sets at some suitable later time. The second key factor to be extracted from the Fahy (1980) data set is that related to attendance at Catholic ritual activities such as Mass and Communion, frequency of Reconciliation, frequency of prayer in general and prayer to Our Lady. Table 5.8 shows the pattern of response for male students and Table 5.9 for female students. There are no differences between boys and girls on levels of Catholic practice. Even girls and boys in co-educational schools do not differ. Notice the closeness of pattern of response for male and female on Mass (56, 57%), attending weekly; Communion (37, 39%) receiving weekly etc. Some parents and educators may be troubled by these figures and blame the school for not putting more emphasis on the ritual dimension of Catholic life. But, as we shall see, the predominant unique effect upon Catholic practice is not the school, but rather what happens in the home.

Table 5.8

Per cent response to students' reported CATHOLIC PRACTICE
N = 2821 students, male

Item	Per cent (*)	Factor loading
I normally attend Mass		
on the weekend at least	56	0.67
a few times a month	11	
once a month	6	
a few times a year	11	
rarely or never	15	

I normally receive Holy Communion		
on the weekend at least	37	0.63
a few times a month	18	
once a month	9	
a few times a year	17	
rarely or never	19	
I normally go to the Sacrament of Reconciliation		
once a week	1	0.53
a few times a month	2	
once a month	14	
a few times a year	44	
rarely or never	38	
I normally pray (apart from school prayers)		
each day	21	0.51
a few times a week	24	
a few times a month	18	
a few times a year	13	
rarely or never	23	
I pray to Our Lady		
each day	11	0.55
a few times a week	18	
a few times a month	17	
a few times a year	18	
rarely or never	36	

No. of items 5, Range 5-25, Scale mean 14.6, S.D. 4.3, Alpha Reliability 0.60.

HIGH SCORE: Those students who attend Mass and sacraments regularly and who pray frequently.

LOW SCORE: Those students who do not attend Mass or sacraments frequently and who pray little.

(*) Missing data (some 4 per cent) not included in these per cents but assigned the median response (code = 3) in the scale score.

Table 5.9

Per cent response to students' reported CATHOLIC PRACTICE
N = 323 students, female

Item	Per cent (*)	Factor loading
I normally attend Mass		
on the weekend at least	57	0.67
a few times a month	14	
once a month	10	
a few times a year	11	
rarely or never	8	
I normally receive Holy Communion		
on the weekend at least	39	0.63
a few times a month	27	
once a month	10	
a few times a year	15	
rarely or never	10	
I normally go to the Sacrament of Reconciliation		
once a week	1	0.53
a few times a month	4	
once a month	42	
a few times a year	32	
rarely or never	21	
I normally pray (apart from school prayers)		
each day	23	0.51
a few times a week	15	
a few times a month	41	
a few times a year	10	
rarely or never	11	
I pray to Our Lady		
each day	9	0.55
a few times a week	18	
a few times a month	39	
a few times a year	12	
rarely or never	22	

No. of items 5, Range 5-25, Scale mean 14.9, S.D. 4.1, Alpha Reliability 0.60.

HIGH SCORE: Those students who attend Mass and sacraments regularly and who pray frequently.

LOW SCORE: Those students who do not attend Mass or sacraments frequently and who pray little.

(*) Missing data (some 4 per cent) not included in these per cents but assigned the median response (code = 3) in the scale score.

These two scales show up the very similar pattern of responses by Catholic boys and girls on these Catholic ritual items. Fifty-six per cent of boys and fifty-seven per cent of girls report attendance at weekly Mass while more (67% boys and 71% girls) go weekly or a few times a month; 37% boys and 39% girls receive Communion each week, while 55% boys and 66% girls receive weekly or a few times a month. Reconciliation is received at least a few times a year by 61% of boys and 79% girls. This may well be as part of school-initiated retreat or camp experiences. Personal prayer (apart from school prayers) at least a few times a week is meaningful to 45% of boys and about the same (38%) of girls. It is interesting that this personal prayer correlates so highly with Catholic ritual practice suggesting that, at least in the Catholic tradition, one reinforces the other.

Specific prayer to Our Lady at least a few times a month is supported by 46% of boys and significantly more (66%) girls.

A significant item in the Catholic Practice scale was that dealing with prayer to Our Lady. Mary is thus an important presence for these boys and girls. Mary is an important figure in the New Testament and the later developed Christian and Catholic tradition. Her relationship to schools stems from her role as mother and initial teacher of Jesus. In particular the story of the Wedding Feast at Cana (John 2:1-12) shows the Johannine summary of her key attributes reflected on late in the 1st Century. There are two programmatic statements:

'They have no wine'

a witness to her attentiveness to the needs of the young couple and by extrapolation the whole ongoing Christian community. She sees the needs of our schools and acts with her Son to meet these needs.

Secondly she says, (her only two sentences in the whole Gospel):

'Do whatever he tells you'

Again a programmatic statement urging us to centre our lives on Jesus, listen to Him in prayer and then be courageous to do as we hear. A fine motto for Catholic school staff and students.

There is every evidence that about half the boys and two-thirds of the girls in our Year 10 and 12 samples pray sincerely (anonymous survey) to Mary at least a few times a month. These are encouraging figures for Catholics with a special love for Mary and an understanding of her model of faith and inspirational influence upon the present church.

Thus it is important to highlight the very valid place of Mary in Catholic schools and endorse respect and devotion to her. Statues and pictures of Mary still have a place in Catholic classrooms as does suitable prayer and on feast days school-wide celebrations with genuinely involving paraliturgy or Mass. Suitable textbooks and lessons on Mary should be part of a year's curriculum. Only then will students acquire a valuable role model to whom they can turn in difficulties in adult life.

Turning now to our study of the whole Catholic practice scale:

Figure 5.3

Per cents of explained variance in Catholic practice scores uniquely accounted for by each block of predictors.

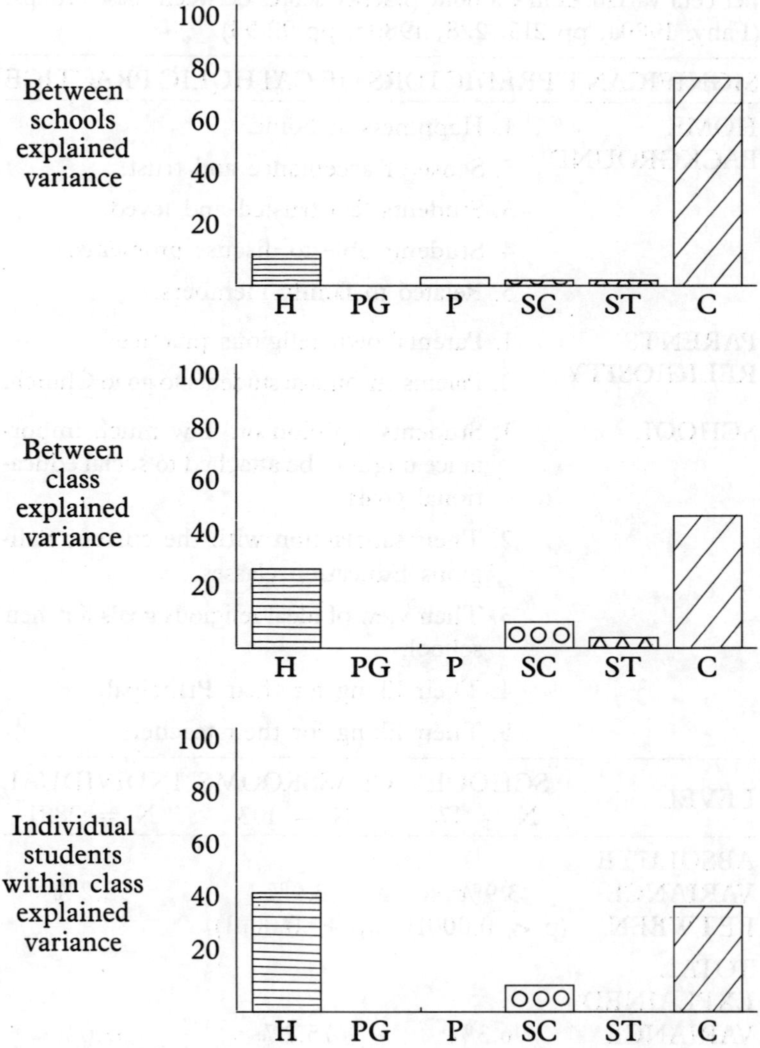

* H = HOME, PG = PEER GROUP, P = PERSONALITY, SC = SCHOOL, ST = STAFF blocks of predictors, C = COMMONALITY.

Table 5.10

Main predictors of CATHOLIC PRACTICE OF STUDENTS at SCHOOL, CLASSROOM and INDIVIDUAL LEVEL with per cent variances in Catholic practice scores between these groups. (Fahy, 1980a, pp. 213, 228; 1980b, pp. 92-93)

SIGNIFICANT PREDICTORS OF CATHOLIC PRACTICE	
HOME BACKGROUND	1. Happiness at home. 2. Sense of acceptance and trust. 3. Students feel trusted and loved. 4. Students able to discuss problems. 5. Related to family members.
PARENTS' RELIGIOSITY	1. Parents' own religious practice. 2. Parents encourage students to go to Church.
SCHOOL	1. Students' opinion on how much importance ought to be attached to social educational goals. 2. Their satisfaction with the current Religious Education classes. 3. Their view of ideal religious goals for their school. 4. Their liking for their Principal. 5. Their liking for their teachers.

LEVEL	SCHOOL N = 17	CLASSROOMS N = 103	INDIVIDUAL N = 2821
ABSOLUTE VARIANCE BETWEEN	3.9% ($p < 0.0001$)	3.9% ($p < 0.0001$)	92.2%
TOTAL EXPLAINED VARIANCE*	96.3%	75.2%	37.0%

* The predictors above can explain these proportions of the variation in this key criteria of *Students' Catholic Practice*.

It is clear that what happens in the home is the major 'unique effect' (in the sense of concomitant variation) upon children's religious practice. However at the school and classroom level there is still a very significant effect with large proportions of the variance in Catholic practice scores being explained.

Regarding Figure 5.3 and Table 5.10 the major block explaining the variance in Catholic practice is clearly the home background. However, the school at the level of religious education classroom is also significant. Perhaps the classroom teaching on the Mass and Sacraments is having some secondary role in association with home to encourage Mass and Sacramental attendance. In general however, it is the home background (parents' own Mass attendance and climate of trust and communication in the home) which are the key predictors of whether or not the students themselves will go to Mass. It would be unfair to criticise the school for the apparent lack of effectiveness in this area when it is clear that home climate is the major effect. Home seeks the support of the school in a secondary role educative of the meaning of the Mass and involvement in creative liturgies.

The other aspect of the home background which predicts students' Catholic practice is the students' perceptions of the degree of trust and communication experienced with parents and siblings. Where the home climate is a trusting, happy one with open communication children will more readily adopt the parents' faith practices.

The second block, though less powerful, shows up as the SCHOOL block at both the classroom and individual level. Searching within the block showed the following variables to comprise it.

1. Informal religious education goals
2. Social education goals – ideal
3. Satisfaction with formal religious education classes
4. Satisfaction with teachers' interest and skills
5. Liberal education goals – actual importance

While noting again the presence of both informal and formal religious education it is obvious that these two taken together have some impact on Catholic practice (although not as great as the home).

It seems as though home and school are acting together to promote Catholic practice with some degree of effectiveness (70% go at least weekly or a few times a month while about 60% of boys and girls receive Communion weekly or a few times per month).

Social educational goals is a new scale, relates to issues such as making students aware of pressing social problems, giving adequate sex instruction, creating friendly relations with other Church schools, providing a choice to discuss controversial topics, providing counselling help in personal problems. Thus a wide ranging sense of the social dimension of school seems to have some relation to Catholic practice. Perhaps where students experience trust and open communication from parents and the same kind of trust and communication by discussion and sharing on school and personal issues, they feel freer to bring their life concerns to the sacramental and liturgical ministry of the Church. If they don't experience that openness and trust at either home (especially) or school (secondary) they probably will not feel free to bring those life concerns to what may seem by association to be a cold Church.

One final remark on the reported level of Mass attendance. It may be of assistance to readers to obtain some measure of how often young Catholic people report going to Mass and Communion, central aspects of our faith. Table 5.11 shows the details.

Table 5.11

Reported per cent weekly attendance at Mass and Communion by Catholic students (1975-1985)

	Flynn (1975) N = 1393	Fahy (1980) N = 3431	Flynn (1985) N = 1834
Mass	69	56	55
Communion	30	37	44

Flynn (1985, pp. 209-210), discusses trends in Mass attendance and Communion reception over the ten years (1972-1982). The results of the present study do not fully fit his pattern and suggest that the Mass attendance of adolescents bottomed out at about 56% by the middle of the decade being considered and has not changed much. Notice that for those who do keep going to Mass there is a significant climb in Communion reception.

Thus we have seen that the primary unique predictor of Catholic religious practice in both Fahy (1980) and Flynn (1985) is in fact the degree of home (parental) religious practice and establishment of a climate of trust and communication.

The school has a secondary but important role not only in educating the students to the meaning of the liturgical ritual but more importantly establishing a similar climate of trust and communication that leads students to want to celebrate their life mystery and concerns together in the Church's liturgy.

A note is in order here about the size of the effects in this analysis. Table 5.10 above shows all five predictor blocks, but predominantly home background, explain 37.0 per cent of the individual variance in Catholic practice. This is a very strong effect by educational standards and points to the power of the home background to explain Catholic practice. There is a smaller but important 13% contribution of the school stressing the need for home and school to work together in developing a climate of trust and communication that draws students to an openness to liturgical worship.

5. SOCIAL JUSTICE AWARENESS

As well as the belief and ritual dimension of a person's faith life there is in the Christian tradition also a dimension of service to others. There is a long history in the Church of service or diakonia beginning with Acts (the choice of 'the seven' to serve in 6:1-7) to modern saints such as Mother Teresa serving the poor of Calcutta. It is of critical importance that young Christians be exposed to this tradition and encouraged to respond creatively to it. Likewise it is critical that Catholic religious educators discern those elements of faith tradition or educational strategy that most uniquely explain social justice attitudes. Only then will they be on a firm footing to develop strategies to assist students develop sound social justice awareness.

• A valid, reliable scale called Social Justice Awareness was found via factor analysis. See Tables 5.12, 5.13. As might be expected for a sample of Australian students the central item deals with righting of injustices to Aborigines, the native people of Australia, who have been here for well over 40 000 years. Boys expressed 42% agreement, girls 39% to the righting of those injustices. A more general sense of concern for other countries, brought close by TV, where there is starvation, is the second item. This receives about 50% support from the boys, and girls agree to a much higher 78%. When challenged to a more definite action such as visiting hospitals the response (25% boys; 48% girls) is weaker. A strong sense

(62% boys; 70% girls) of having tried to help the lonely or rejected is evident. About half (49% boys; 46% girls) have taken part in some school-based social justice project. Again about half (47% boys; 56% girls) think that 'other students would be prepared to help me in some charitable works' while about the same number say they have worked on such projects for needy people. Two negative items reveal two disturbing trends among boys and girls of these schools. When presented with the racist statement 'Black people are inferior by nature to white people', 14% of boys and 13% of girls agree. Thus about 1 in 7 of our Catholic youth express racist views. The schools of the study have a mixture of city and country towns. When asked further if companies should be allowed to mine on Aboriginal land 23% of boys agree and 10% of girls agree. While this is a complex issue the item does allow for a general statement in principle of viewpoint and is valid. All these items form a reliable scale of social justice awareness attitudes.

You will have noticed that the girls in general tended to have more positive attitudes on social justice issues than the boys. A statistical test confirms that they are in fact more positive on peace and justice attitudes. This could be due to their co-educational environment but when the 287 boys in the co-educational schools are examined they are found to have attitudes similar to their fellow male students in single schools. Thus we have some evidence of a genuine sex difference with girls adopting more positive peace and justice attitudes than males no matter what the school environment. It would be important to check girls in single sex schools to see if a female role is operating here independent of school environment.

The next consideration is which of the five key blocks of HOME, PEER GROUP, PERSONALITY, SCHOOL and STAFF best explains the variation in social justice scores.

Table 5.12

Per cent response to items defining SOCIAL JUSTICE AWARENESS N = 2821 students, male.

Item	Per cent Agree	Per cent Disagree	Factor Loading
White people in Australia have a Christian obligation to repair the damage done to Aborigines	42	24	0.45
I worry about people in countries where there is starvation	56	29	0.37
I would like to be part of a group that helps others e.g. by visiting hospitals, working with the poor	25	36	0.12
I have tried to be a friend to people who are lonely and rejected	62	21	0.24
I have taken part in some activities helping other people organised by the school	49	25	0.12
I think that other students would be prepared to help me in some charitable work	47	24	0.23
I have worked with other people on community projects helping needy people	49	43	0.04
Black people are inferior by nature to white people (R)	14	69	−0.36
Companies should be allowed to mine on Aboriginal land (R)	23	51	−0.50

No. of items 9, Range 9-45, Scale mean 30.4, S.D. 5.9, Alpha Reliability 0.60. R = item is reversed in scale addition.

HIGH SCORE: Students who are concerned about social justice issues and have taken some steps to help the poor.

LOW SCORE: Students who are not aware of social justice issues, have not helped the poor and may have some racial prejudice.

Table 5.13

Per cent response to items defining SOCIAL JUSTICE AWARENESS N = 323 students, female.

Item	Per cent Agree	Per cent Disagree	Factor Loading
White people in Australia have a Christian obligation to repair the damage done to Aborigines	39	20	0.45
I worry about people in countries where there is starvation	78	11	0.37
I would like to be part of a group that helps others e.g. by visiting hospitals, working with the poor	48	13	0.32
I have tried to be a friend to people who are lonely and rejected	70	12	0.24
I have taken part in some activities helping other people organised by the school	46	20	0.12
I think that other students would be prepared to help me in some charitable work	56	16	0.23
I have worked with other people on community projects helping needy people	46	45	0.04
Black people are inferior by nature to white people (R)	13	60	−0.36
Companies should be allowed to mine on Aboriginal land (R)	10	58	−0.50

No. of items 9, Range 9-45, Scale mean 36.2, S.D. 4.9, Alpha Reliability 0.60. R = item is reversed in scale addition.

HIGH SCORE: Students who are concerned about social justice issues and have taken some steps to help the poor.

LOW SCORE: Students who are not aware of social justice issues, have not helped the poor and may have some racial prejudice.

Figure 5.4

Per cents of explained variance in Social Justice Awareness scores uniquely accounted for by each block of predictors.

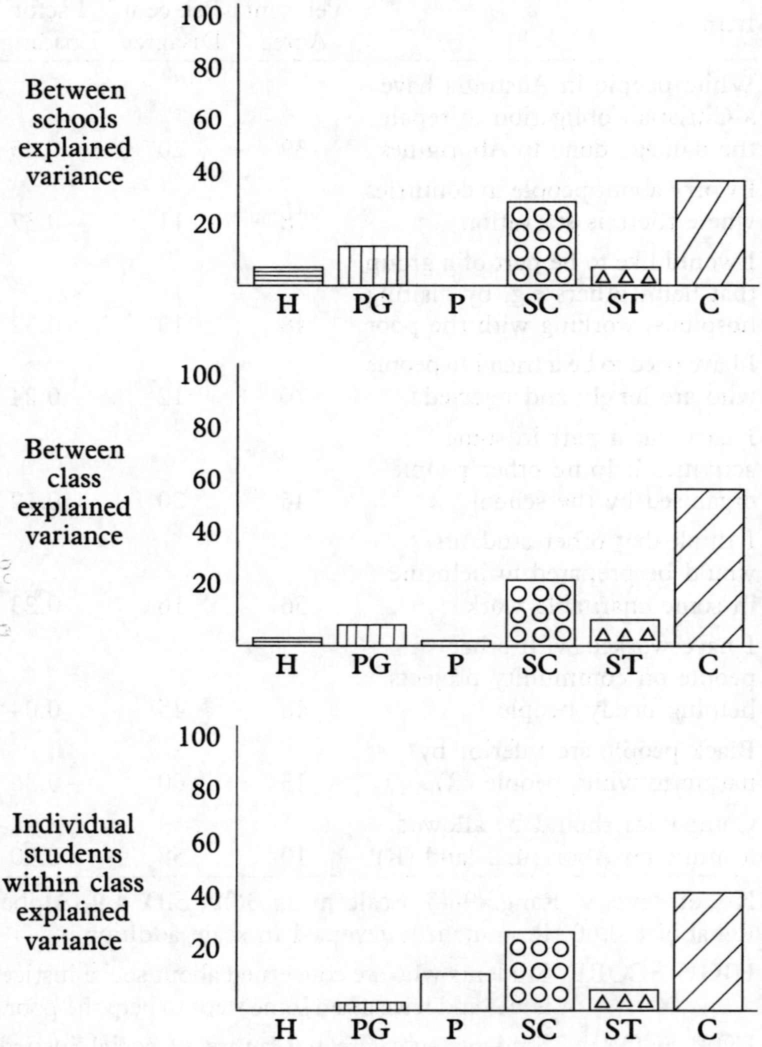

* H = HOME, PG = PEER GROUP, P = PERSONALITY, SC = SCHOOL, ST = STAFF blocks of predictors, C = COMMONALITY.

Table 5.14

Main predictors of STUDENTS' SOCIAL JUSTICE AWARENESS at SCHOOL, CLASSROOM and INDIVIDUAL LEVEL with per cent variance between these groups.

	SIGNIFICANT PREDICTORS OF SOCIAL JUSTICE AWARENESS
SCHOOL	1. Students' opinion on how much importance ought to be attached to social educational goals 2. Their satisfaction with the current Religious Education classes 3. Their view of ideal religious goals for their school 4. Their liking for their Principal 5. Their liking for their teachers
STAFF	1. Degree of acceptance of religious goals by the religious staff 2. Open and just patterns of responsibility and decision making in Catholic schools

LEVEL	SCHOOL N = 17	CLASSROOMS N = 103	INDIVIDUAL N = 2821
ABSOLUTE VARIANCE BETWEEN	3.5% ($p < 0.0001$)	5.1% ($p < 0.0001$)	91.4%
TOTAL EXPLAINED VARIANCE*	88.3%	71.4%	30.5%

* The predictors above can explain these proportions of the Absolute variance above.

Figure 5.4 and Table 5.14 show that students' social justice attitudes are best predicted mainly by school climate and curriculum factors. That the home seems to have little effect may be explained by the absence of direct parental justice measures in the study. Had these been added they would no doubt have contributed. Yet there would probably still be an effect of the school (here 88%] and classroom (here 71% of explained variance). This first approximation suggests schools with a sound, just climate do have an effect on justice attitudes. We need to explore the role of home in justice attitudes in further research.

What factors in the school predict Christian social justice attitudes in adolescents? They are:

1. students' opinion on how much importance, ought to be attached to social educational goals
2. their satisfaction with the current religious education classes
3. their view of ideal religious goals for the school
4. their liking for the Principal
5. their liking for the teachers

Among staff factors that are also significant predictors of students' social justice awareness are:

1. the degree of acceptance of religious goals by the religious staff
2. the openness by the total staff to lay people having access to positions of administrative responsibility

These latter two relationships suggest that students are more open to social justice concerns when they see religious staff giving a credible witness of the radical Gospel life-style dedicated to ideals of peace and justice. In addition they sense some aspects of the staff community as a whole, where staff are seeking just working conditions for both lay and religious. The case is being made here that students see school as society in microcosm and will adopt just attitudes in the wider society only if they perceive just attitudes and policy operative in the school setting. Even more so in the home setting. Their demand for a more socially relevant education and a relationship of mutual respect with Principal and staff is also related to their openness to wider social concerns. The key scale in this area is press for more social education and involves:

1. making students aware of pressing social problems
2. giving adequate sex education
3. creating friendly relations with other Church schools
4. providing a chance to discuss controversial topics
5. giving counselling help in personal problems

Where students perceive a more socially relevant education being provided they tend to adopt more just attitudes to the wider society.

Crawford and Rossiter (1985, p. 39) made a similar claim relating to justice and peace issues. That was:

> A priority given to justice and peace has implications for both the religious curriculum and the social reorganisation of the school... (need to make) the school itself a more just and peaceful organisation.
>
> Students' justice and peace attitudes are best predicted by both formal religious education classes and the informal climate of the school.

The analysis of the 103 religious education classrooms supports this view. There is a role for the formal instructional level as well as the informal climate of the school as the list of variables above suggests. Both social educational goals and specific religious classroom variables figure prominently. Thus, this study empirically supports Crawford and Rossiter's view.

This stresses that any education for peace and justice must operate *at two levels* seeking to change understanding and attitudes in the school and also in the wider society. Only when the school setting is reasonably just can energy be freed to reach out to wider problems. Dealing with larger problems gives a vision and direction to the more local school problems. Thus a constant dialectic operates in the process of seeking justice.

Some vision needs to energise this process. One model current in Christian circles focuses around the Reign of God.

People are called to cooperate in the building up of this Reign to stand under the judgment of God's Word and await the return of an eschatological Lord in our day (Groome, 1980; Hunermann, 1975, pp. 1349-1357). Key themes, the Reign of God is peaceful, the Reign of God is prophetic, the Reign of God brings challenge etc. may form the basis of educational programs.

There are four (4) other faith-related criteria that should also be mentioned. They are:

1. Vocational Awareness
2. Vocational Interest
3. Self-esteem
4. Staff Community

The first three of these have been discussed elsewhere (Fahy, 1982) and the last in Fahy (1977). The key points only of that discussion will be given here.

6. VOCATIONAL AWARENESS AND VOCATIONAL INTEREST

One measure of a faith-view of life is the students' appreciation of the worth of the priestly and religious lifestyle. An even more significant faith vision is expected of those showing a personal interest for themselves in such a lifestyle.

The openness to religious lifestyle was a distinct factor in the students' minds. It consisted of three items:

1. I feel brothers and sisters have a worthwhile part to play in today's world
2. I feel that a priest has a worthwhile part to play in today's world
3. I would be happy if one of my friends became a priest, brother or sister

About two thirds of boys and girls agreed with the first and second item, while a third agreed with the more personal item three. This is encouraging that in our 23 Catholic schools there is a high level of openness to the worth of the religious lifestyle. For those who expressed a more personal interest, the following three (3) items were found to be important.

1. I have thought seriously about being a priest, brother (or sister) over the last year or so (14% boys, 13% girls agree)
2. I would like to talk to someone about a religious or priestly way of life (11% boys, 9% girls agree)
3. I have spoken to an adult about being a priest, brother (or sister) over the last year or so (8% boys and 8% girls agree)

So of the 3431 youth in this study about 10% (340) show a personal interest in a religious lifestyle. This is a relatively large number, considering the small number actually seeking entry, and raises the question of how more of this 10% might be guided and encouraged to continue to an initial application for entry.

Are there differences between schools? One obvious question might be 'Is the experience of a co-educational school setting associated with lower level of interest in religious life than for youth in single-sex schools?' A series of statistical discriminant analyses between the groups of schools reveal no significant differences between single-sex boys, boys in co-educational schools and girls in co-educational schools. For the boys, where a true comparison is possible, it is clear that the co-educational environment has not diminished their openness to or personal interest in the possibility of religious or priestly life. This finding needs to be checked for girls. From this evidence, it would seem that religious orders of men and women deciding to pool resources in co-educational schools need not fear that this move will result in a decline in vocations from such schools.

Does openness to or interest in a religious lifestyle increase or diminish as youth grow older? While not a longitudinal study, there is some evidence that Year 12 youth have stronger sense of openness and more keenly felt personal interest than Year 10 students. As Catholic young people approach career life choices, they do give serious consideration to the options of religious and priestly life. This testifies to the witness value of these people in their lives.

Table 5.15

Significant predictors of Openness to and Interest in a Religious lifestyle – in order of importance. (N = 3431) (All significant 0.05 or better)

Per cent variance explained	Openness to religious lifestyle	Interest in a religious lifestyle
	Christian faith	Christian faith
	Social justice awareness	Social justice awareness
	Catholic practice	Catholic practice
	Altruism	Self-esteem (negative)
	Religious education classes	Ideal religious educational goals
	Ideal religious educational goals	Religious education classes
	Satisfaction with Principal	Ideal liberal education (negative)
	Satisfaction with teachers	
Uniquely by	Personality block 10.3%	Personality block 8.1%
Uniquely by	School block 5.2%	School block 2.0%
Common to	Personality/school 19.2%	Personality/school 7.4%
Total explained variance	49.2%	19.5%

What predicts religious vocational openness and personal religious vocational interest? Table 5.15 gives the details essentially similar for boys and girls. The high degree of similarity suggests that a natural progression from openness to interest is possible. The first three most powerful predictors are identical and show the centrality of faith, justice and Catholic religious practice in the lives of these young people. Their conscious expressed motivations accord with the ideals of Christian life. Faith and justice attitudes are predicted by school and home-based factors while practice is predominantly a home-based effect. The presence of all three here shows the complementary role that good homes and good climate Catholic schools have in the nurturing of sound religious vocation. Some personality variables such as altruism and self-esteem occur next. Self-esteem bears a complex curvilinear relationship to religious variables and will be discussed in the next section. Altruism is more straight forward. Students were asked to indicate the degree of importance they attached to a number of life priorities ranging from Forgiveness, Service, Honesty, Religion, Family Happiness (the more altruistic end) to Pleasure, Personal Power over others, Money for things I want (the more self-serving end of the scale). Table 5.15 indicates that the more altruistic students are more open to religious life, as is consistent with their vocational orientation.

A number of other school goals, satisfaction with religious education classes and atmosphere of mutual respect with principal and teachers are also important. We see again that what goes on in school, the formal religious education influence as well as in the informal climate does make a difference to religious vocational choice.

In setting up the analysis the Christian faith, Catholic practice and social justice awareness were entered into the Personality block as being aspects of personal values that impinge on religious life. This is apparent in large significant per cents of explained variance. Also apparent in the common effect between Personality and School one should also add Home for reasons discussed above. So we see the beginnings of a theory of religious life motivation with significant inputs from Home, School and Personality factors.

One final scale is instructive. Where students are more concerned about liberal education goals, such as the development of independence and critical thinking, openness to all areas of human knowledge, respect for other religions, etc. they are less inclined to consider religious life as a viable option. Perhaps current religious life, as seen by these adolescents, may seem correctly or incorrectly, to allow little room for the development of these desirable qualities of independence and critical thinking. These adolescents may be more conscious of a degree of uniformity they think is demanded of religious that allows little scope for individuality. With freedom and independence being such critical values of adolescents engaged in a process of establishing their own identity and moving away from the family setting, religious life needs to present a viable attractive model where all true human values and genuine freedom in Christ are being integrated with Gospel values.

The above set of predictors need to be fitted into a theoretical framework. One such model is of Fr. Luigi Rulla (1976) as developed by his commentator, Champoux (1977). Rulla warns us to ascertain also the unconscious motivations of aspirants and estimate any social or psychological inconsistency between the ideal self (projected onto the religious institution) and the actual self. This requires interviews which were not possible with the present study. The consistency between the conscious motivations of these young people and the ideals of religious life at least suggests the construct validity of the measures developed here and the genuineness of their interest.

Another interpretation of the negative relationship of liberal goals to interest in religious life may be that youth who are less independent minded, and more conformist (with a religious bent), may be more interested in a religious lifestyle. In Rulla's terms (Champoux, 1977, pp. 214-216) there could be unconscious motivations such as the need for a secure, non-threatening environment, the need for approval which could be dissonant with their conscious motivations. If some of our religiously-oriented youth feel uneasy with the independent decision making demanded in the complex world beyond school, they might well consider opting for the (presumed) secure and dependent lifestyle they may believe exists in religious life. Formation needs to expose and resolve these unhealthy motivations.

There are some significant omissions in Table 5.15. Firstly the peer group block failed to gain entry. One might argue that the three peer group items are inadequate but they do cover peer group pressure, group membership issues and openness to drug/alcohol usage. Boys and girls seem to be making up their minds on religious life options with little if any reference to the opinions of their peers.

Graham Rossiter (1981) has developed this theme extensively into practical strategies. For those youth considering a religious lifestyle there would seem to be a need for increased contact with religious on an informal basis. Monasteries and convents need to be seen by these youth as open, warm, friendly places where they may come to experience hospitality and sharing of spirituality. Religious communities may even be open enough to take in some young adults for short to moderately longer periods of time to share the religious living of the community, without expecting from these young adults the clarity or commitment associated with past postulancy programs.

This study of the religious life options of young Catholics suggests that the most important factor predictive of an openness to, and interest in religious life revolves about a happy home environment based upon Christian values and a school environment of mutual respect, seeking to develop a genuine Christian community. The centrality of faith, focused on Christ as a real person in their daily life, justice values, seeking to build a better world and regular Mass and Sacramental attendance are evident. This testifies to the genuineness of the 1 in 10 young, Catholic people seriously considering religious life. The elements of a model for religious life choice at a critical stage of young people's lives have been laid.

7. SELF-ESTEEM

The next most important predictor of interest in the religious lifestyle is the students' self-esteem. At first sight this appears to be related negatively but closer analysis reveals a significant curvilinear relationship between interest in a religious lifestyle and self-esteem as illustrated by Figure 5.5.

Figure 5.5

Curvilinear relationship between Interest in a Religious Vocation and students' Self-esteem (N = 3431 students)

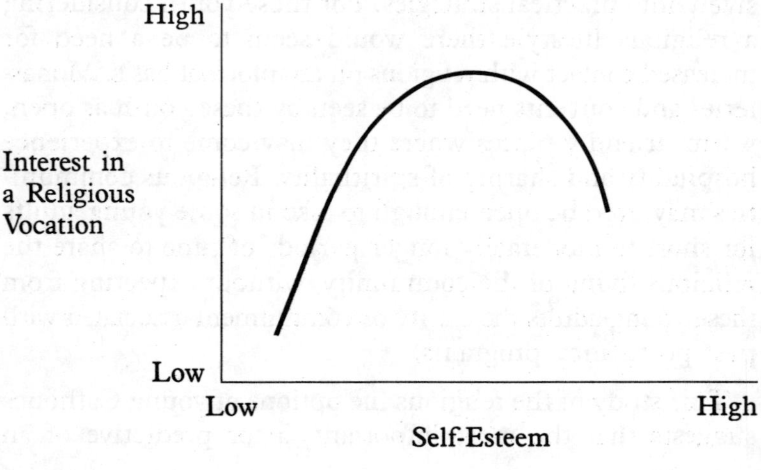

It would appear that in this sample of Australian youth, moderately positive self-esteem is associated with higher interest in a religious lifestyle while both negative and very high self-esteem tend to have significantly lower levels of interest in a religious lifestyle for themselves. This very interesting finding promoted a search for other significant curvilinear relationships with self-esteem. Two others were found of the same form, one between students' Christian Faith and Self-Esteem and the other between students' Catholic practice and their Self-Esteem, illustrated in Figure 5.6.

The very similar form of the relationship between three conceptually related yet distinct religious scales and self-esteem of students suggests that we have here real associations and not just artifacts of design or measurement. How might these very significant and interesting results be explained?

There is a tendency for low self-esteem youth to have lower levels of faith, practice and now also interest in religious life. These youth may be similar in many respects to those reported by Strommen (1974) as involved with a 'cry of self-hatred'. With little sense of self-worth, of acceptance or love by parents, peers or significant adults they cannot believe in a God who loves and cares for them. Overly conscious of their own faults and failures they have little sense of God's forgiveness. Their view of God as punishing and vengeful becomes too difficult to bear and he is blocked out of their lives. They cease going to Mass and sacraments as they feel themselves unworthy to partake in these 'holy rituals' and rationalise that they do not need such childish forms of worship. This would explain why their levels of Christian faith and practice are significantly lower than youth of more positive self-esteem.

Figure 5.6

Curvilinear relationship between Christian Faith and students' Self-Esteem (N = 2821 students)

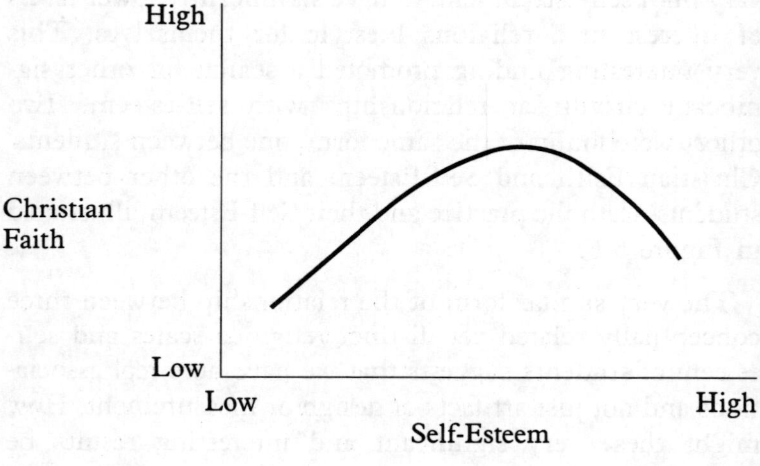

Figure 5.7

Curvilinear relationship between Catholic Practice and students' Self-Esteem (N = 2821 students)

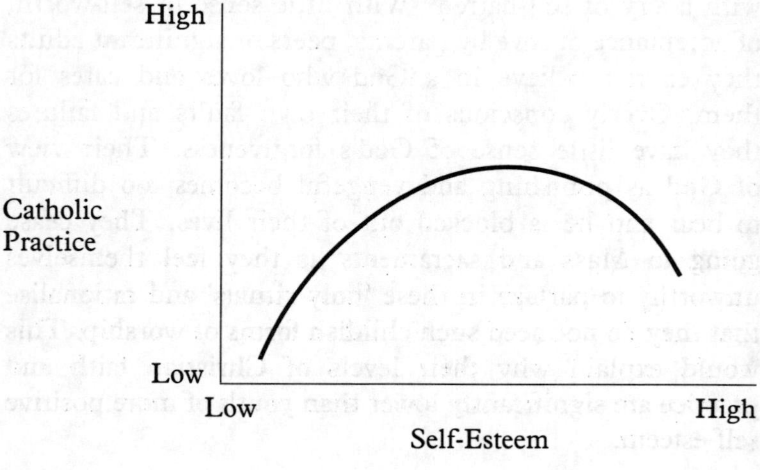

While low self-esteem youth may see some relevance in priestly and religious life, their own feelings of low self-worth tend to prevent them from considering such a lifestyle for themselves. They may have unrealistic notions of the character of religious life and lack confidence to trust in the power of God's call even if they hear it in their own lives. When asked, even by a significant adult, they tend to decline, saying 'I would not be good enough to be a religious.' These findings highlight the need to identify religiously inclined low self-esteem youth and develop their self image through such strategies as 'unconditional positive regard' (Rogers, 1961) and clearly defined and enforced limits (Coopersmith, 1967). In this present context there is also a need to present God as a loving, forgiving Father, a Son who has redeemed and reconciled us to the Father and Spirit of love that draws us out of ourselves to a new and fuller life. Low self-esteem youth need to hear and experience love and forgiveness to build gradually a more hope-filled vision of their life. There is no reason why such youth struggling to overcome their own limitations could not become mature, caring religious sensitive to the needs and hurts of others.

But what of the youth on the other end of the self-esteem scale, those with a very positive self-concept? The analysis suggests that they also have significantly lower levels of faith, practice and interest in religious life. Certainly in all cases not as low as the low self-esteem youth, but significantly lower than moderate self-esteem youth. Perhaps high self-concept youth have a sense that they can with their own resources answer all the questions that life will pose for them. They are unaware of their own faults or limitations. They see themselves as in control of their own life and destiny and see little need to make reference to, or place reliance in, a power beyond themselves. The notion of an all-powerful, Transcendent God who cares for them and is involved in human history has little appeal to them. They are not aware of their own limitations and feel little need for forgiveness or help from others or God. They come to regard Mass, the essence of which is the acknowledgement of the dependence on God in an act of worship, as irrelevant to their lives and hence they stop attending. Similarly a priestly or religious lifestyle explicitly pointing to Transcendent realities and values beyond this present life and dependent upon a religious superior would tend to have little appeal to very high self-esteem youth, caught in their own egocentricity and independence.

It is not surprising then that high Self-Esteem youth would tend to have lower levels of Christian faith, Catholic practice and Interest in a Religious Vocation. Perhaps one approach with high self-esteem youth is to confront and challenge them with basic questions such as the nature of creation and our situation as creaturely beings dependent on an all-powerful, Transcendent God. One such approach linking insights from modern scientific world-view has been developed previously (Fahy, 1980c). Whatever approach is taken there must be a fundamental respect for the freedom of the individual in the area of belief and unbelief. McBrien (1980, pp. 183-197) discusses the relative positions of the believer and unbeliever and the mutual respect necessary in their dialogue on the meaning of human experience.

Thus self-esteem is a predictor of both high and low Christian faith, Catholic practice and interest in a religious life. A plausible explanation for this has been given in terms of the needs of high and low esteem youth. The effectiveness of the Catholic school in developing improved self-esteem, once considered a key goal, needs to be tempered with a secure sense of one as creature and God as Transcendent Reality. Only then will self-esteem be situated in a secure foundation of Catholic theology and practice.

A well developed model of self-concept and schools is provided by Fahey (not this present author) (1987); from her higher studies she develops a behavioural cycle for teachers and students.

We turn now to the final predictor of religious outcomes, that is to the staff and their sense of Christian Community.

8. STAFF COMMUNITY

At the same time as the data was gathered on the 3431 students a survey was conducted of secondary staff (religious 149; lay 299) representing over 90 per cent of the population in the 23 schools. Items were included on staff morale, acceptance of religious goals for the school, openness to lay administration by religious and push for lay administration by laity. A multivariate analysis showed the centrality of the morale scale and its close positive correlation with the religious goals in an analysis accounting for 36 per cent of the variance. Because of this close relationship between explicitly Christian religious goals and staff cohesion it is reasonable to re-define this scale as Christian Community of Staff. The full details of the scale are given in Table 5.16 (as well as Appendix Al) and a brief summary is given here with per cent agree for each item.

The Christian community of staff scale includes a sense of high staff morale (78 per cent), of religious and lay working together as a staff community or 'team' (82 per cent), adequate channels of communication (74 per cent), lay staff having a genuine share in policy making (49 per cent) religious and lay enjoy being together on informal occasions (87 per cent), religious staff work with energy and enthusiasm (89 per cent), lay staff work with energy and enthusiasm (86 per cent) and general discipline is humane and reasonable (89 per cent).

Table 5.16

Per cent response to items defining CHRISTIAN COMMUNITY OF STAFF N = 448 staff.

Item	Per cent Agree	Per cent Disagree	Factor Loading
I think that staff morale in this school is high	78	9	0.79
Religious and lay work together harmoniously as a staff community or 'team' in this school	82	9	0.75
There is a high degree of integration of lay and religious to form one staff	62	12	0.68
Adequate channels of communication between the headmaster and staff exist	74	15	0.65
Lay teachers have a genuine share in the decision-making and policy-making of this school	49	31	0.60
Teachers, both lay and religious, enjoy being together at morning tea and other informal occasions	87	4	0.58
Religious staff in this school carry out their work with energy and enthusiasm	89	3	0.56
Lay staff in this school carry out their work with energy and enthusiasm	86	4	0.53
General discipline in this school is humane and reasonable	89	4	0.51

No. of items 9, Range 9-45, Scale mean 37.1, S.D. 2.8, Alpha Reliability 0.84 (religious), 0.86 (lay staff).

HIGH SCORE: Those staff with a strong sense of Christian community and cohesion.

LOW SCORE: Those staff with a weak sense of Christian community or cohesion.

When subjected to the commonality and analysis at the school level the results of figure 5.8 are obtained. It is clear that, the last criteria of Christian community of staff, is best explained by students' perceptions of school and some staff views of their environment.

Figure 5.8

Variance in Christian community scores explained by various predictor blocks.

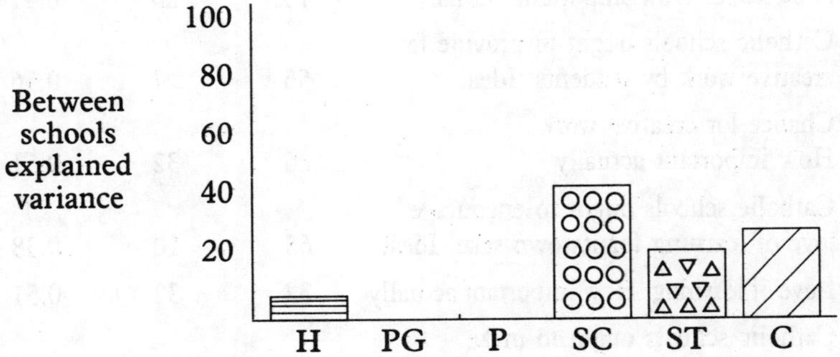

* H = HOME, PG = PEER GROUP, P = PERSONALITY, SC = SCHOOL, ST = STAFF blocks of predictors, C = COMMONALITY.

The most significant predictors of Staff Christian Community are:

1. Students' press for a more liberal education
2. Students view of the actual importance attached to religious goals of the school
3. Students' view of the importance that ought to be attached to social education goals
4. Staff degree of support for the religious goals of the school
5. Job satisfaction of lay staff
6. Press for lay administration

Each of these will be examined in turn.

Table 5.17

Per cent response to items defining LIBERAL EDUCATION GOALS IDEAL, ACTUAL N = 3431 students.

Item	Per cent Import.	Per cent Unimport.	Factor Loading
Catholic schools ought to give students experience in the main areas of human knowledge. Ideal	56	4	0.66
Experience in the main areas of human knowledge. How important actually	75	20	0.47
Catholic schools ought to provide for creative work by students. Ideal	55	7	0.56
Chance for creative work. How important actually	26	32	0.51
Catholic schools ought to encourage love of learning for its own sake. Ideal	65	10	0.38
Love of learning. How important actually	32	32	0.51
Catholic schools ought to make students aware of other religions. Ideal	54	19	0.27
Awareness of other religions. How important actually	20	53	0.41
Catholic schools ought to develop independence and critical thinking. Ideal	72	8	0.40
Independence and critical thinking. How important actually	33	30	0.53

No. of items 5 in each scale, Range 5-25.

Ideal Scale: Mean 19.0, S.D. 4.3, Alpha Reliability 0.58.
Actual Scale: Mean 14.6, S.D. 3.5, Alpha Reliability 0.52.

HIGH SCORE: Students who attach strong importance to liberal educational goals (ideal) and who see the school supporting liberal educational goals (actual).

LOW SCORE: Students who do not attach importance to liberal educational goals (ideal) and who do not see the school doing so (actual).

Table 5.18

Per cent response to items defining RELIGIOUS EDUCATION GOALS IDEAL, ACTUAL N = 3431 students.

Item	Per cent Import.	Per cent Unimport.	Factor Loading
Catholic schools ought to provide an atmosphere of Christian community. Ideal	57	14	0.62
Christian community – how important actually	56	17	0.50
Catholic schools ought to provide a chance to participate in the liturgy. Ideal	40	27	0.51
Liturgy – how important actually	38	27	0.45
Catholic schools ought to teach Religious Education classes at a level comparable to other subjects. Ideal	33	37	0.40
Religious Education comparable to other subjects – how important actually	26	38	0.59
Catholic schools ought to integrate Religious Education and other subjects. Ideal	29	43	0.43
Integrate Religious Education and other subjects – how important actually	20	51	0.59
Catholic schools ought to give an example of dedicated life through lay and religious staff. Ideal	51	24	0.90
Dedicated life of lay and religious – how important actually	38	31	0.44

No. of items 5 in each scale, Range 5-25.

Ideal Scale: Mean 15.9, S.D. 4.4, Alpha Reliability 0.75.
Actual Scale: Mean 15.1, S.D. 3.8, Alpha Reliability 0.67.

HIGH SCORE: Students who attach strong importance to religious educational goals (ideal) and who see the school supporting religious educational goals (actual).

LOW SCORE: Students who do not attach importance to religious educational goals (ideal) and who do not see the school doing so (actual).

Table 5.19

Per cent response to items defining RELIGIOUS GOALS OF STAFF N = 448 staff.

Item	Per cent Agree	Per cent Disagree	Factor Loading
I think that some Christian commitment should be expected of all teachers in Catholic schools	81	9	0.59*
The Catholic School should offer experience in Christian living through the liturgy, sacraments and prayer	92	3	0.58
Classroom prayers should be said daily in Catholic schools	85	5	0.57
The Catholic school should integrate religious and secular studies as far as possible	88	6	0.57
I think that teachers in Catholic schools should be practising Catholics	39	48	0.50
Lay teachers are able to give a witness of Christian living in the daily life of the school	90	3	0.46
Catholic schools should provide a witness of dedicated Christian life through its religious teachers	96	1	0.45

No. of items 5 in each scale, Range 5-25.

Religious: Mean 25.3, S.D. 2.2, Alpha Reliability 0.28.
Lay staff: Mean 21.9, S.D. 4.6, Alpha Reliability 0.74.

HIGH SCORE: Staff who strongly support the religious goals.

LOW SCORE: Staff who have little or no support for religious goals of the school.

* Religious agreed strongly with all items and hence had little variance in their scores. The factor loadings are for the lay staff and reflect a useful scale.

Table 5.20

Per cent response to items defining JOB SATISFACTION LAY STAFF N = 299 lay staff.

Item	Per cent Agree	Per cent Disagree	Factor Loading
Satisfied with teaching subjects	80	6	0.42
Satisfied with number of periods taught	70	16	0.52
Satisfied with size of classes	46	39	0.44
Satisfied with salary provisions	57	30	0.53
Satisfied with promotional opportunities	34	41	0.68

Item	Per cent Response	Factor Loading
Concern about superannuation:		
1. greatly concerned	57	−0.13
2.	14	
3.	12	
4.	1	
5. no concern at all	12	
Degree of involvement of lay teachers in administration:		
1. very involved	15	0.33
2.	26	
3.	24	
4.	18	
5. no involvement	11	

No. of items 7, Range 7-35, Scale mean 24.6, S.D. 1.4 Alpha Reliability 0.63.

HIGH SCORE: Lay staff well satisfied with their teaching conditions, high job satisfaction.

LOW SCORE: Lay staff dissatisfied with teaching conditions, low job satisfaction.

Table 5.21

Per cent response to items defining SOCIAL EDUCATION GOALS N = 3431 students.

Item	Per cent Agree	Per cent Disagree	Factor Loading
Catholic schools ought to make students aware of pressing social problems. Ideal	58	7	0.63
Awareness of social problems – how important actually	34	22	0.54
Catholic schools ought to give adequate sex instruction. Ideal	64	4	0.56
Adequate sex education – how important actually	26	33	0.55
Catholic schools ought to create friendly relations with other church schools. Ideal	63	12	0.36
Friendly relations with other church schools – how important actually	30	38	0.45
Catholic schools ought to provide the chance to discuss controversial topics. Ideal	69	9	0.40
Discuss controversial topics – how important actually	30	35	0.59
Catholic schools ought to give counselling help in personal problems. Ideal	68	11	0.32
Counselling for personal problems – how important actually	31	40	0.47

No. of items 5 in each scale, Range 5-25.

Ideal Scale: Mean 19.6, S.D. 3.4, Alpha Reliability 0.64.
Actual Scale: Mean 14.7, S.D. 3.7, Alpha Reliability 0.55.

HIGH SCORE: Students who want more stress on social education (ideal) and/or feel the school is giving it.

LOW SCORE: Students who do not stress social education and do not want the school to stress it (actual).

Table 5.22

Per cent response to items defining PRESS FOR LAY ADMINISTRATION N = 149 religious and N = 299 lay staff.

Religious N = 149

Item	Per cent Agree	Per cent Disagree	Factor Loading
Positions of responsibility such as Deputy Headmaster should be open to lay teachers	62	21	0.69
Suitably qualified lay teachers ought to be offered the position of Headmaster in Catholic schools	44	31	0.67

Lay Staff N = 299

Item	Per cent Agree	Per cent Disagree	Factor Loading
Positions of responsibility such as Deputy Headmaster should be open to lay teachers	74	14	0.71
Suitably qualified lay teachers ought to be offered the position of Headmaster in Catholic schools	63	20	0.73

No. of items 2 in each scale, Range 2-10.

Religious: Mean 7.8, S.D. 0.8, Alpha Reliability 0.74.
Lay staff: Mean 8.6, S.D. 0.6, Alpha Reliability 0.79.

HIGH SCORE: For religious indicates those open to lay staff as taking positions of responsibility. For lay staff it indicates a press for such positions.

LOW SCORE: For religious indicates resistance to lay staff in positions of responsibility. For lay staff indicates little desire to see lay staff in positions of responsibility.

The key factors in the staff's sense of Christian community are both school student perceptions and staff perceptions. In a single analysis it is possible to compare the relative effects of these two groups of people.

Among the student-school average scales are:

1. Students' press for a more liberal education (Table 5.17)
2. Students' view of the actual importance being attached to religious goals of the school (Table 5.18)
3. Students' view of the importance that ought to be attached to social education goals (Table 5.21) [Students with a strong desire for socially relevant education are found in schools where staff sense of community is low].

Among the staff factors are:

1. Staff degree of support for the religious goals of the school (Table 5.19)
2. Job satisfaction of lay staff (Table 5.20)
3. Press for lay administration (Table 5.18)

Why are these six (6) scales important for a sense of Christian community of staff? Let us examine each in turn.

1. Where students are pressing for more liberal education with stress on exposure to great ideas, creativity, love of learning, awareness of other religions, critical thinking and independent thought encouraged then it must be a pleasure for teachers to teach in these schools. So one would expect teacher morale and sense of community to be high in these positive learning environments.
2. Where students support the religious goals of the school again we have a situation where to a high degree student and teacher goals are congruent. Again associated with a more pleasant teaching environment and higher teacher Christian community based on these religious goals.
3. Students in the study say a lot of importance ought to be attached to sound educational goals (social problems, sex education, other Church schools, discussion of controversial topics, counselling help) but they are less happy that this is being done

in practice. Schools where students are dissatisfied with social education are schools of low staff community. Without knowing the causal direction it highlights one area to look at (students' social education) when staff are not happy with the school or each other.

4. Where there is strong staff support for the religious goals of the school then staff sense of community is high. The role of religious is very significant here with their total lifestyle witness to the values of the gospel. We have evidence here that both lay teachers and students are well aware of this fundamental dedication.

   As the number of religious active in schools continues to decline it is critical to in-service laity not just in school procedures and administration but in a spirituality of Christian education and Catholic schools. This book seeks to establish a foundation for that process. This close link of religious goals to staff morale shows we are dealing with a genuine measure of Christian Community of staff, which could be used with other scales to obtain a valid and reliable index of school staff climate.

5. Where job satisfaction is high, laity are well satisfied with the conditions and rewards of employment. This is significantly associated with sense of Christian community. A sense of justice seems to underlie this. Australia has a long history of Government assistance which supplements the sacrifices of the primary parental educators to give lay teachers a just wage. In some other countries, such as the USA, where the justified assistance is not forthcoming, it is more difficult to pay just rewards and the job satisfaction, morale, and community sense suffers. Where Catholic schools prepare youth to be good citizens of their country, a too rigid division of Church and State monies is not justified.

6. We know that religious were open to laity as deputy principals and to some extent as headmaster. The laity were split on this. One group, the high commitment group, wanted a greater share in the administration and policy making. The other group, of lower religious commitment, were little interested in responsible positions. Putting it crudely, the 'good Catholics' wanted 'more say' in how things were run. They felt frustrated that

they could not implement their ideas. The 'other teachers' were happy to 'let someone else run the shop', and to draw the rewards of their teaching. This was very consoling to the religious major superiors and Catholic educational authorities for it meant they could offer positions to the lay staff seeking them knowing they were predominantly people of fine values who would maintain the Catholic philosophy.

Just working conditions for staff, promotion of a deep spirit in faith are intimately linked with sense of Christian community for staff. It is interesting to note how these basic themes of faith and justice have emerged from both the student and staff parts of the study. It suggests this is a genuine requirement for the effectiveness of these and other Catholic schools and classrooms.

Faith and justice, two things our world stands so much in need of, and here we find them at the core of our Catholic schools, a sign that we need Catholic schools and classrooms as a leaven in our modern society; a sign that we need to make increased personal and professional efforts to help faith and justice to grow for both staff and students within the matrix of effective Catholic classrooms. Only then will the Christian meaning dimension, already a key focus, emerge more clearly as the central one.

9. CONCLUSION

The unique central nature of Religious education makes it different from all other subjects. We have seen from the complementary roles of faith, theology and education that the three must be seen as an interplay at the centre of formal curriculum. Other subjects have a value, educational and subject specific component. The values section has a close link with the Christian values central to Catholic schools. In addition there is the informal curriculum (climate, goals) which affects religious education. See Figures 5.9 and 5.10.

Figure 5.9

Model of Catholic School Curriculum Formal and Informal in relation to Home Values.

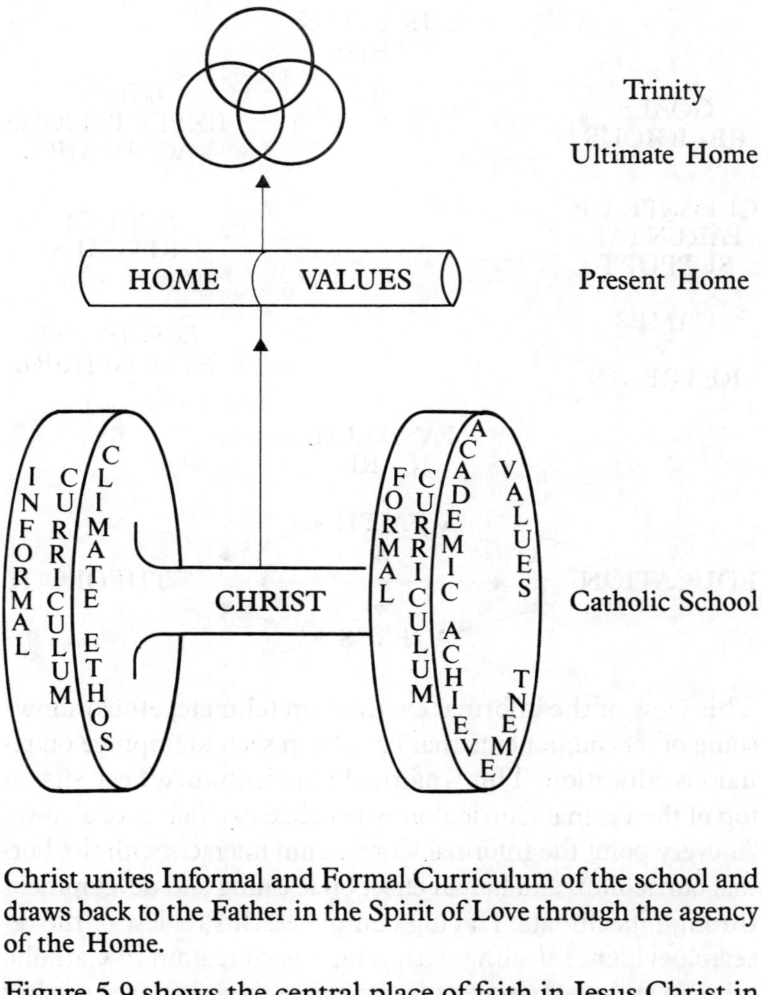

Christ unites Informal and Formal Curriculum of the school and draws back to the Father in the Spirit of Love through the agency of the Home.

Figure 5.9 shows the central place of faith in Jesus Christ in the religious education curriculum which in turn by its Christian theology and faith values has a real link with the value or meaning positions found in all other subjects (Teilhard, Phenix).

Figure 5.10

Informal Curriculum Model – Catholic Schools

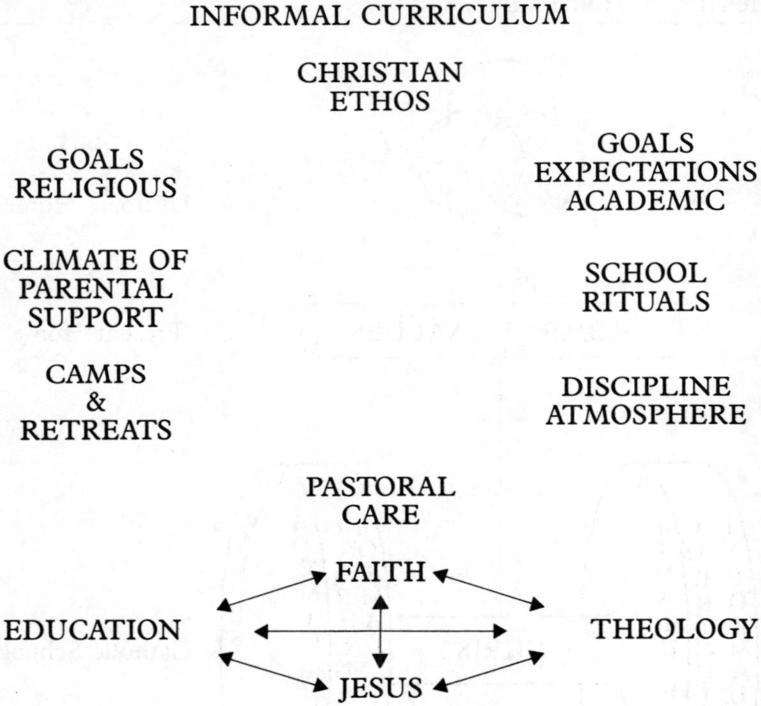

This view of the informal curriculum (climate, ethos) shows some of its components that have been seen to impinge on religious education. This 'Informal Curriculum Wheel' sits on top of the Formal Curriculum wheel like two halves of a yo-yo. At every point the Informal Curriculum interacts with the Formal curriculum and has an effect on learning and development through its climate. Having completed this review of the research evidence dealing with religious education in Catholic schools and classrooms it is time now to consider the other key criterion, that is the academic outcomes and achievement of these students. The key studies in Australia and overseas will be used to find significant predictors of academic achievement.

CHAPTER 6

ACADEMIC EFFECTIVENESS OF CATHOLIC SCHOOLS

The research evidence

Having seen the research evidence associated with religious aspects of the school it is appropriate to turn now to the question of the academic effectiveness. After all there is not much point in having a high religious climate school if it is not a good school. Schools are about learning and one essential criterion is academic learning.

It is not the intent of this study to enter into debate with public schools about relative merit (although Coleman, Hoffer and Kilgare, 1982, do make some such comparisons). We need good public schools just as we need good Catholic schools with mutual exchange of ideas. The two major studies which have looked systematically at high school achievement are Coleman *et al.* (1982) and Flynn (1985). Greeley (1982) examined a subset of the Coleman *High School and Beyond* data as it applied to minority students in Catholic schools.

Accordingly this chapter will treat in turn the main conclusions of (1) Coleman (1982) in USA with some reference to (2) Greeley (1982) in the USA and (3) Flynn (1985) on the Australian scene.

1. COLEMAN: *'High school achievement'*

Coleman's purpose was to examine various assumptions about the relative outcomes of public and private schools. The private schools were divided into national samples of Catholic (N = 84) schools and other private (N = 27). The bulk of the sample (N = 893) were public schools. As the Catholic schools turned out to be the most homogeneous in characteristics there was much less variation between Catholic schools than between Catholic and public schools. The study, in the Coleman tradition, was a massive one with N = 28 450 seniors (Year 12) and N = 30 280 sophomores (Year 10) being involved.

Coleman had an interest in the racial composition of these schools for one of the claims often heard voiced suggests that

> Catholic and private schools are accused of being racially divisive for parents can choose to send their children to these schools and effectively segregate their children from racial contact.

Coleman finds no significant evidence for this claim. On these national samples there are just as many Hispanics in Catholic as in public schools, there are slightly fewer blacks in Catholic schools, but the difference is not significant.

In terms of curriculum and courses offered there are comparable patterns with Catholic schools having more focus on languages, less focus on technical courses compared to public schools.

Staff patterns often cited as being very different in elitist schools was in fact very similar for public and Catholic. Table 6.1 shows the number of students per professional staff (Coleman, 1982, p. 79).

Table 6.1

Numbers of students per professional staff (after Coleman, 1982, p. 79) by school type.

NO. OF STUDENTS	PUBLIC	CATHOLIC	OTHER PRIVATE
Overall staff	15	16	6
Teachers	16	18	7
Counsellors	323	235	55
Librarians	597	340	212

The public and Catholic schools are very similar. True the other private schools have over twice the number of teachers proportionately. The Catholic schools have put more of their human resources into pastoral care and services such as library. But overall the staff patterns are not very different in terms of classroom teachers between public and Catholic.

In terms of curriculum Catholic schools tend to emphasise formal curriculum with a stress on such things as foreign language. Catholic schools have fewer work experience programs for the gifted seeking concrete career choice.

The attitudes to discipline are an important index of academic learning. Catholic schools are traditionally regarded as being more highly disciplined and this comes through in the results (Coleman, 1982, pp.88-89). Table 6.2 shows the pattern.

Table 6.2

Per cent of students agreeing to discipline items (after Coleman, 1982, pp. 88-89)

Item	Public	Catholic
Students should be responsible for property damage:		
Sophomores	64	77
Administrators	96	95

Effectiveness of Strictness of Discipline:		
Seniors	42	72
Sophomores	41	76
Fairness of Discipline:		
Seniors	36	47
Sophomores	38	52

Students in Catholic schools are the most likely to rate their schools as 'excellent' or 'good' in effectiveness of discipline and public school students are least likely to do so. Attitude to discipline is a marker to the whole morale of the student body. If discipline is seen as fair and reasonable a much more positive tone is present which, as Flynn shows below, influences learning outcomes.

Regarding disciplinary suspension, in the USA Coleman notes (1982, p. 100)

> A lot of legal safeguards, policies have been imposed by the Federal government and state bodies on public schools re the process before suspension.
>
> Yet it is the private schools, less bound by the strictness designed to ensure fairness, that are most likely to often be regarded as fair by the students.

Coleman comments that such legalistic approaches to ensuring fairness may be less effective than other more flexible approaches to bringing about fairness. Flynn (1975, pp. 123-124) discusses a theory of alienation by a British sociologist Barakat (1969, pp. 1-10) which contrasts the states of overcontrol and undercontrol in a social system. Overcontrol leads to powerlessness and alienation, while undercontrol leads to normlessness and permissiveness. Effective discipline finds a middle path between overcontrol and undercontrol.

The major test of school academic effectiveness is ultimately 'do they learn more' yet such a question is often confounded by the home background. If home backgrounds vary in wealth, educational background of parents, range of educational stimulus in the home (as they certainly do) then how can we be sure that a school with higher academic outcomes is not reflecting the background of its clientele rather than anything intrinsic to its own efforts. For sufficiently large samples there is a way of controlling for a whole host of family variables and then looking for significant differences between schools across achievement scores. This is like equalising across the pupils the effect of a whole collection of family variables and then seeing if academic outcomes vary from school to school.

Coleman's 17 family background variables were divided into clearly prior and not clearly prior to academic outcome (of the final achievement tests):

Clearly Prior:

- Family income
- Mother's education
- Father's education
- Race
- Hispanic – non-Hispanic
- Number of siblings
- Number of rooms in home
- Both parents present in home
- Mother working before child was in elementary school
- Mother working when child was in elementary school

Not Clearly Prior:

- Encyclopedia or other reference books in home
- More than 50 books in home
- Typewriter in home
- Owns pocket calculator
- Frequency of talking with mother or father about personal experiences.
- Mother thinks student should go to College after high school
- Father thinks student should go to College after high school

(Coleman, 1982, pp. 138-139)

If the students score on all these 17 variables can be controlled in the analysis then it means when we come to look at achievement scores we are doing so for students who have been equalised on all these variables. Any academic differences that show up may then be attributed to the schools themselves.

Coleman's criterion achievement measures were standardised tests in the areas of reading, vocabulary, mathematics, science and civics. When the variance in test scores is analysed across schools the fraction of between school variance is 11% in Catholic schools, 18% for public schools and 28% for other private schools. This means that Catholic schools are more homogeneous while the other two groups are more varied in the factors that control achievement.

> Students in the (Catholic) schools came from backgrounds that are more homogeneous in education and income level than those students in either public schools or other private schools. In addition the schools themselves are more homogeneous, all operating under the same Church, and with some common practices. (Coleman, 1982: p. 128).

Could this be acknowledgment from a secular researcher for a distinctive Church related climate or ethos in Catholic schools that impinges directly on their academic educational outcomes. Flynn (1985, pp. 275-289) will cast further light.

Table 6.3

Uncorrected raw mean scores on subtests that are identical for Seniors and Sophomores.

	Public		Catholic	
Subtest Grade	Yr. 10	Yr. 12	Yr. 10	Yr. 12
Reading (8)	3.60	4.48	4.38	5.00
Vocabulary (8)	3.69	4.48	4.59	3.35
Mathematics (18)	9.40	10.63	11.05	12.10

(adapted from Coleman, 1982: p.126)

What are the results of this massive effort first uncorrected for family background (raw mean scores) and secondly statistically corrected for the 17 family variables (standardised mean scores). Table 6.3 shows the raw scores in reading, vocabulary, mathematics for sophomore (Year 10) and senior (Year 12). It is clear that on the raw scores both Catholic sophomores and seniors do better on all but one, of reading, vocabulary and mathematics subtests than do public school students. The exception is Year 12 public schools do better in vocabulary. But is this overall result just due to better Catholic home background with a more favourable academic expectation? We must look at the scores adjusted for home background; that is, how much more or less would Catholics score if the family background was controlled. Table 6.4 shows the important results against a base line of public school sophomores.

The numbers in Table 6.4 are *increments*, how much higher was the Catholic mean score over the public mean score. If the increment is *negative* Catholic schools have done more poorly than public when home environment is controlled. If the increments are *positive* Catholic schools, even when adjusted to equal home background, still do better than public schools academically.

Table 6.4

Estimated increments to test scores in public and private schools with family background standardised.

	Reading	Vocab.	Maths
1. Raw scores/public school sophomores (Year 10)	3.60	3.69	9.40
2. Standardised increments Catholic schools sophomores (Year 10) over public schools sophomores	.32	.36	.58
3. Senior increment in public schools (Year 12)	.73	.63	.88
4. Raw increments for seniors in Catholic schools (Year 12)	.74	.90	1.65
5. Raw senior increment in public schools (Year 12)	.88	.79	1.23

(Adapted from Coleman *et al*, 1982, p. 138)

The most obvious immediate result is that *all the Catholic sophomore (Year 10) increments are positive.* When Catholic sophomores (Year 10) are compared with the public sophomores (Year 10) then the Catholic youth perform better on all three key criterion tests (Reading, Vocab, Maths) even with the wide range of home background factors controlled.

There is no specific Catholic home background effect evident here. This is the first definitive evidence from a well conducted study with a national sample that the old myth of Catholic family background accounting for the improved performance of Catholic school students *really is a myth.* When 17 family background variables are controlled Catholic sophomores (Year 10) do better on all achievement tests than their public school counterparts. There is a genuine school specific effect operating here.

Looking at Table 6.4 and seniors (Year 12) Coleman presents two lines of increments for public ('senior increment') and Catholic ('raw increment'). It is not clear what two numbers are being subtracted to obtain the increment. It is unclear if the senior increment in public schools (Year 12) is a raw or standardised one although the heading of the table suggests standardised. Only a raw increment for Catholic school seniors (Year 12) is given, making it impossible to compare the effects of public and Catholic schools with home background standardised. This was the point of this section of Coleman's work. A re-examination of this part of his raw data and standardisation is necessary.

The age old question, 'Does the distinctive selectivity of Catholic parents with higher aspiration seeking out Catholic school environments which then produce better academic climates? is to be answered at last in the *negative.* If you consider the list of seventeen (17) home background factors as reasonably representative set for the aspiration of parents, then even when these are controlled, a national sample of sophomore (Year 10) pupils in Catholic schools shows they do better on a range of reading, vocabulary, maths tests than do a similarly home-controlled set of public school students. This is certainly true at the Year 10 (sophomore) level and seems likely at the senior, Year 12 level with higher raw increments in Reading and Maths.

Coleman (1982, pp. 135-136) points to a defect of the family variable controlling procedure in that not all the right variables may be matched or controlled. If parents are prepared to pay for alternative education then this may be an additional difference over and above the 17 mentioned above. We can't equate public and private on this factor, since one system is funded by taxes while the other, parents pay twice, once in taxes and once in school fees. Yet we are equating on parental income, educational level, educational aspiration, socio-economic status and many other relevant variables. These would be strong predictors of fee paying. So, we have in effect a fee-paying factor.

However the overriding conclusion is that even when the strict statistical controls for family background are exercised that students from Catholic and other private schools have higher achievement on these tests than do public school students. Catholic and Private schools do seem to be having a unique effect. Coleman says:

> the increments for each type of private school are positive, showing that students of the same (family) background characteristics have generally higher achievement in both of these types of schools than in the public school (Coleman, 1982, p. 139).

Coleman has been strongly criticised especially on this private-school effect on achievement. The first critique is that if only the correct selection variables had been taken into account, the private schools would have shown no greater cognitive achievement. It is not clear what these selection variables are.

On the issues of race and ethnicity Coleman faced the critique that private schools are socially divisive claiming that a high proportion of parents go to them to avoid the more racially integrated public schools. Coleman (1982, p. 144) found this *not* to be the case.

> thus we have the paradoxical result that the Catholic schools come closer to the American ideal of the 'common school', educating all alike than do the public schools. Furthermore ... a similar result holds for race and ethnicity. The achievement of blacks is closer to that of whites and the achievement of Hispanics is closer to that of non-Hispanics in Catholic schools than in public schools.

There was also some sense of a specific school effect in Catholic schools with the variation in school achievement at Year 10 level becoming smaller in Year 12. The Year 12 groups were more homogeneous in achievement suggesting a specific school effect. Perhaps a secondary socialising effect which takes place more forcefully with exposure to the school and its climate such as Fahy (1980b) found for religious variables is operative. Coleman (1982, p. 146) found that in the public and other private sectors the achievement of students from different backgrounds diverges. In contrast the achievement of Catholic students converged in Year 12. Perhaps there is a cohesive academic and social benefit from a clearly defined religious climate or ethos which leads to a relatively homogeneous vision and common learning.

In conclusion Coleman (1982, p. 185):

1. Points to the greater academic demands and more ordered environment (fairness and firmness of discipline) as important factors in bringing about higher scholastic achievement in private schools than public schools;
2. Calls for support for policies that would facilitate use of private schools rather than policies that would constrain their use;
3. Regarding reductions in school authority, he comments that (p. 190):

ironically the protection of individual student rights and the attendant reduction in school authority has sometimes meant loss of the right to an orderly environment in which to learn;

4. Need for secure family environments for both academic and personal growth. We are living in a period of family disintegration when some seek to be free of their responsibility for their adolescent children. Coleman suggests that early withdrawal of family attention and interest could have serious consequences for an increasing fraction of our youth;
5. Coleman (1982, p. 194) points to the smaller size of Catholic schools with fewer resources, yet greater achievement. He suggests the reason is greater concentration on courses that continue to require effort and lead to acquisition of the skills and knowledge students will need in later life.

2. ANDREW GREELEY: '*Catholic high schools and minority students*' (1982)

Coleman's massive High School and Beyond data set attracted the attention of other researchers. Andrew Greeley (1982) examined the subset of minority students in Catholic schools and asked:

> why black and Hispanic students who attend Roman Catholic secondary schools display much higher levels of academic effort and achievement than black and Hispanic young people attending public schools.

White, black and Hispanic in Catholic schools are higher on an academic performance composite, lower on discipline problems, do more homework and have higher aspirations for a College education than public school counterparts. How to explain this? Greeley groups the predictor variables into family characteristics, student characteristics and school characteristics (although there are not many variables in each set considering the large High School and Beyond data variable set).

On academic criteria Greeley (1982: p.51) finds that:

> students who go to Catholic schools come from more affluent and educationally ambitious family backgrounds and have more powerful personal motivations.

But there are also school factors of better discipline, more academic press, higher grade point average. The old problem is how to separate these home and school effects uniquely. Greeley does not uniquely achieve this separation.

Greeley (1982, pp.53-56) raises the issue of religion in Catholic schools in a very cursory way. There are no specifically faith questions (faith in God, faith in Jesus) but birth control and attitudes to women feature. Greeley (1982, p.58) argues that the school factors of better discipline and press for academic achievement add to the home and personal aspiration factors to explain improved academic outcomes. However, his regression-causal path model has all the flaws discussed in Chapter 3 where this study was critical of Greeley, McCready and McCourt (1976). The problem of order of entry remains with the first variable entering soaking up its own plus overlap variances and no clear conclusion can be made. The real situation is too complex for even the most simple causal path diagrams in the absence of a strong body of theory. Feedback relationships are likely and cannot be handled by causal path methods.

Thus this study is likewise critical of Greeley (1982) and his analysis of the High School and Beyond data does not uniquely separate home, personal and school effects. By the lack of a faith or religious climate block of variables, it fails to match the reality of Catholic schools.

This has been a detailed analysis of Coleman *et al* (1982) and Greeley's (1982) examination of Catholic minority school but it lays a useful foundation of key concepts about the effectiveness of Catholic schools to affect academic outcomes even when differences in home background are controlled. It also lays a useful background for comparing the work of Marcellin Flynn (1985) who also tackled the academic effectiveness of Catholic schools in Australia. Some useful comparisons will be made in the following section.

3. MARCELLIN FLYNN: '*The effectiveness of Catholic Schools*' (1985)

Having examined two American studies it is appropriate to turn to an Australian study to see what factors are found to influence academic achievement. One initial marked difference is that the American studies relied upon standardised norm-referenced tests of ability. These are designed to measure and maximise differences between students rather than between courses of study in the school curriculum. If we are looking for school effects on learning it would seem more appropriate to use curriculum-sensitive measures. Public examinations, such as the Higher School Certificate in New South Wales are designed to assess students' mastery of the content of specific curriculum areas. They are state-wide and assess all senior students at the same point in time. Madaus *et al.* (1980, p. 167) agree that such public examinations are curriculum-sensitive measures of students' achievement

> ... public examinations are excellent criterion measures of specific achievement areas. Each test is geared to a separate prescribed syllabus. Tests are administered at the same time after a fixed period of study to all students in all schools ...

Thus Flynn (1985) used as his criterion measure with 2041 students the weighted average of performance in best 10 units. Subjects can be taken at one, two, three, four unit level. The Higher School Certificate was in 1982 a weighted average out of 500. In 1982, the year of his data collection, the average was 264 out of 500 with a range of 480 to 57. For the 23 schools of his sample there was no significant difference in the average Higher School Certificate mark over the ten year period (1972-1982), giving no evidence of higher achievement, merely consistent scaling procedures. Unlike Coleman (1982) with extensive public school – Catholic school comparisons, Flynn could only compare the percentage of Catholic students in the top one per cent of Higher School Certificate candidates. He found 1.6 per cent of the Catholic sample in this top one per cent of overall Higher School Certificate students. It follows that Catholic students are more highly represented in this one per cent group than the state average.

We return now to the question at the heart of the chapter. How do you estimate the effect of schooling upon achievement free of the confounding influence of different home backgrounds and expectations? Can we separate the effects of home and school on Higher School Certificate as we have on faith variables?

Again the method we use is that developed by Beaton (1973, 1974) and applied by Madaus *et al.* (1980) to the Irish schools. It is the method of systematic decomposition of variance and avoids all the unjustified assumptions about order of entry and causal paths which hampered Coleman (1982) and Greeley (1982).

Flynn sets up five blocks of variables and does preliminary screening to select the significant predictors. He names the five blocks:

1. Home background
2. Formal curriculum of school
3. Informal curriculum (Climate, Ethos)
4. Religious Education Curriculum
5. Quality of School Life.

When these blocks are entered into the analysis they are able to account for 62 per cent of the variance in Higher School Certificate score. This is an amazing result by educational standards and shows he is on the right track to find some very significant predictors for academic achievement.

The breakdown of the per cent total variance explained is also equally amazing. Table 6.5 shows the details.

Table 6.5

Per cent of the total variance in HSC achievement uniquely explained by five predictor blocks (Flynn, 1985, p. 314).

Predictor block	% Total variance explained
1. Home background	4.36
2. Formal Curriculum of school	5.98
3. Informal Curriculum (Climate, Ethos)	45.60
4. Religious Education Curriculum	1.66
5. Quality of School Life	0.92

This very large 'unique' effect (recall not causal, but concomitant variation) of informal curriculum, controlling for home and all the others, was totally unexpected by Flynn. Its magnitude shows up more clearly when the per cent of explained variance is estimated. (See Figure 6.1 and Table 6.6)

Figure 6.1

Per cent of explained variance in HSC achievement uniquely accounted for by five predictor blocks.

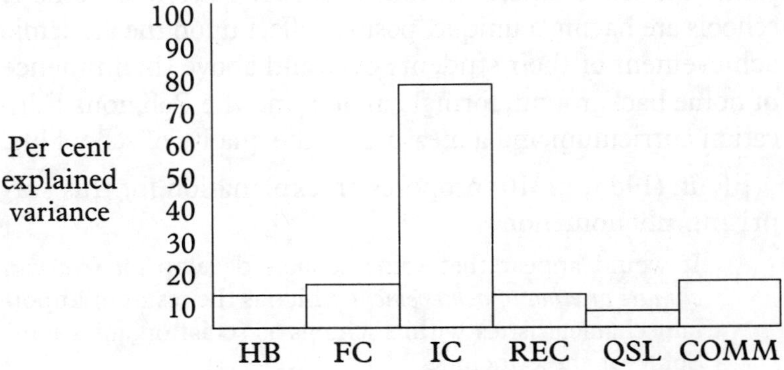

Where, predictor blocks are:

HB = Home Background
FC = Formal Curriculum
IC = Informal Curriculum
REC = Religious Education Curriculum
QSL = Quality of School Life
COMM = Commonality

This is a quite remarkable result. One would have thought that students' perceptions of the formal curriculum, what they had actually been taught, status variables of teachers would have been the key predictor of actual learning. But no, it is the informal curriculum, the climate, ethos, the students' sense of happiness in school, and personal development expectations that are the key factors covarying with actual HSC achievement keeping all other blocks constant. So when home background is controlled for, and all the other blocks for that matter, it is the informal curriculum that predicts concomitantly to a very high degree variation in academic achievement.

This result is the equivalent of Coleman's results discussed in Table 6.4. that even when a wide range of home background factors and aspirations are controlled that Catholic schools themselves are still having a very significant influence on the academic achievement of students. It is not a matter of parents with higher expectations selecting and generating a better school climate and aspiration.

Flynn also is able to point to the key focus of that academic achievement, surprisingly not the formal curriculum, but rather the school informal climate factors. Therefore Catholic schools are having a unique, positive effect upon the academic achievement of their students over and above the influence of home background, formal curriculum, the Religious Education curriculum and a measure on the quality of school life.

Flynn (1985, p. 316) proposes an explanation for this surprising phenomenon.

> It would appear that some schools develop *an informal climate or ethos of achievement* which is the result of important characteristics within schools as social organisations. Some of these include:
>
> 1. the pervasive values of the school
> 2. the morale and spirit of students
> 3. the importance of the development of each student
> 4. the pastoral care of the school

What then were the actual items in the block of informal curriculum that best predict academic achievement. They are listed in Table 6.6.

Table 6.6

The Informal Curriculum Predictor Block used in the Commonality Analysis (from Flynn, 1985, p. 317).

A. Students' Morale

1. Relations between parents and staff are very friendly
2. Students think a lot of their school
3. Students understand and accept the religious goals of the school
4. Counselling help is available to students
5. This Catholic school is making a worthwhile contribution to Australian life
6. Everyone has a lot of fun at this school
7. On the whole I have been happy at school
8. I would send my children to a Catholic school
9. If I had to do it all over again I would attend a Catholic school
10. Everyone tries to make you feel at home at the school
11. My experience of this school has been a happy one

B. Students' Personal Development Expectations

Catholic schools should:

1. Help students discover and fulfil themselves as persons
2. Develop personal qualities of independence and initiative
3. Respect each student individually
4. Give all students a chance of success in some aspect of school life
5. Help students develop their personality and character
6. Help students learn how to get on with other people
7. Provide counselling help to students on their problems

These then are the informal curriculum variables that predict so well academic achievement. When students are equalised on home background, formal curriculum perceptions, Religious Education curriculum and Quality of School Life factors, then it is those schools with a more positive morale, climate, values, ethos, mutual care and respect who produce significantly happier pupils and higher levels of academic achievement. Clearly, these are the areas schools need to strengthen (without neglecting quality of formal instruction) to promote academic outcomes. It is evident that happier students in a school with a strong tendency for academic learning as well as caring functions, will do better.

So we have come a half circle in our thinking about predictors of academic success.

Coleman *et al.* (1966) in USA invested a tremendous amount of effort into estimating physical resources only to find little significant effect.

Leavey (1972) began to point to the importance of climate variables in the informal curriculum of Catholic schools in Australia.

Flynn (1975) in Australia made these more explicit but did not have the statistical methodology needed to separate home and school factors.

Rutter *et al.* (1979) in England began to pick up some informal social factors creative of an ethos, or set of values, for sound academic performance.

Rutter had only a small sample (12 schools) but he analysed the processes and climate of these schools in great detail. Coleman's (1982) critique of Rutter that he does not have enough schools to draw valid school-effect conclusions is offset with his precise measures of the internal processes of discipline, order, settling down and ending lessons, group management in classes. There are valuable insights in Rutter which support the general notion that climate, ethos and values are key predictors of learning and this study would support Rutter's general findings.

Madaus, Airasian, Kellaghan (1980) in USA/Ireland reviewed the secular school effectiveness debate drawing on their large study of Irish schools and using curriculum sensitive measures as criteria. They too pointed to the improved validity and reliability of these measures. Their improved method of analysis (commonality analysis) also enhances the credibility of their finding. They discuss the importance of climate factors in the school such as a general press for achievement, a general tone of high morale. Policy planners need to think more clearly about the goals of schools and schooling:

> What effect they (goals) can and should have upon pupils and society ... The single most important finding of school effectiveness studies is our inadequacy of knowledge in this regard. (Madaus, 1980, pp.189-190).

Then followed Coleman, Hoffer and Kilgare (1982) in USA who began to accept the importance of climate variables, but still had inadequate criterion measures and analysis methodology limiting usefulness of their findings.

Then Flynn (1985) in Australia with a clear comparison for the first time of a curriculum sensitive achievement measure (the HSC) with a wide range of home and school (informal, formal) curriculum variables. The large amount of variance explained by informal curriculum suggests we are looking at an 'unique' effect of importance. It is the informal climate, ethos, a sense of happiness, values, morale and spirit, the importance placed on personal development of each student, the pastoral care of the school that is important. Where students experience those things they do better in final external academic performance.

It is interesting to conclude with an observation on the convergence of research findings from purely secular to religious studies, that the academic performance is not effected by resources (above a given minimum) but is determined more by the climate or morale of the student environment, the fair and reasonable discipline being a key factor, the press for academic excellence, the pastoral care of the school, a sense of values, norms, standards to be kept. These factors appear as key predictors when the home background is controlled.

This suggests a real effect of school upon the academic achievement of students and is beginning to point to the underlying ethical values and moral tone of the school climate. The academic achievement in Catholic schools bears a distinct relation to the pervading values of the school, the care for each individual pupil, the overall pastoral care. Catholic schools are having a unique, positive effect upon the academic results of students over and above the home background and hence must be termed to be effective in this regard. This very significant effect of the informal curriculum is beginning to accord with other purely secular researchers and provides mutual confirmation.

It is also compatible with the curriculum model presented in this book which gives a dual place to formal and informal curriculum circles, lying one on the other, linked by a faith vision based on the person of Christ. The informal curriculum impinges directly on the academic achievement at the heart of the formal curriculum. The formal curriculum provides the matrix through which the faith values of school and teachers can be considered by pupils.

From Flynn (Table 6.7 below) it is possible to determine those aspects of the informal curriculum that are the most significant predictors of academic outcomes. It is also possible to recast them into language compatible with common usage in Catholic schools.

Table 6.7

The Informal Curriculum cast into Catholic school terminology.

A. Students' General Happiness

1. Sense of Christian community, parents/teachers
2. School Spirit
3. Student's understand and accept the Christian goals of the school
4. Pastoral care via counselling help
5. Vision of Catholic school in community
6. Happy community spirit
7. General sense of happiness
8. Support for Catholic schools for our children
9. Overall sense of satisfaction
10. A sense of community spirit like home
11. Happy fulfilling experience

B. Students' Personal Development Expectations

1. Discover and fulfil their identity and purpose in life
2. Develop independence and initiative to live out God's purpose for them creatively
3. Mutual respect for each other
4. A chance of success to improve self-esteem
5. Develop character and moral fibre
6. Co-operative relations – help students to learn
7. Pastoral care and counselling – to care for others in trouble

Many of these are seen as a fulfilment of the Christian Gospel sense of values and the Trinity its source. Thus at the heart of the Informal Curriculum of Catholic schools lies the Gospel of Christ and indeed the person of the living Christ who gives meaning to that Gospel, love and care for others, happiness discovered in a loving community, moral principles for right living, help for poor or troubled, determination to build a better world for our children. Schools where these Trinity values are promoted are ones that tend to have higher levels of academic achievement.

This chapter has reviewed four studies on academic achievement of schools (Coleman *et al*, 1982, 1987; Greeley *et al*, 1982; Flynn, 1985).

Coleman for the first time has shown a Catholic school effect independent of the always implied selectivity of Catholic homes. Catholic schools in America are in their own right able to exert a positive impact on norm-referenced academic outcomes independent of any variation in their home background from public schools. Those who criticise Coleman for the choice of home variables, such as willingness to pay fees (which at first sight would nulliffy any comparison with non-fee paying state school parents) forget that the key ingredients (income, education, race, aspiration for educational advancement of youth) were in the analysis.

Coleman's results (especially 1987) deserve greater attention for clues towards academic achievement in the public and Catholic high schools of America.

Greeley *et al.* (1982) in selecting a subset of Coleman's data set fell into similar pitfalls as in his previous Greeley, McCready and McCourt (1976). Choice of measures, the lack of the religious climate block that Leavey (1972) found so important and an inappropriate strong inference causal path model hampered their analysis.

Flynn (1985) with a curriculum-sensitive achievement measure across a range of subjects at the senior (Year 12) level inserted this into a commonality analysis of several hundred predictors. These were grouped into five conceptual blocks and the analysis revealed a surprising predominance of the Informal Curriculum Block. Closer inspection revealed it as a matrix of ethos, values about a caring community in

Catholic schools in line with the Christian Gospel. Schools with the same stress on formal academic curriculum could be very different in academic outcomes depending on this general informal climate of happiness and care.

Many of the features of the Informal Curriculum that Flynn has pointed to as having a concomitant influence upon achievement are present in all schools, public and private. Now that this result is clear, efforts could be made to enhance them in both school systems. Catholic schools with a special commitment to these as religious goals and part of their ethos are strengthened thereby to seek for both religious and secular reasons to work together. So, the secular researchers have detected evidence of a particular climate, ethos in the Catholic community conducive to school achievement. Religious researchers have shown this to be uniquely explained by a wide range of human and faith-related values. The present research shows the key role of the formal classroom as the matrix in which these secular and religious values of the informal curriculum intermix. Truly the model of faith-theology-knowledge interplay describes the reality of Catholic classrooms in both academic and religious terms. They cannot be separated.

CHAPTER 7

WHAT HAVE WE LEARNT?

1. A FAMILY SCENARIO

A difficult and complex situation which faces many Catholic parents is that after 6 years of fee paying for a Catholic primary (elementary) schooling they are faced with the question of a more expensive Catholic secondary (high) school. Some believe with some justification that the sound basic education in faith and values of the primary will stand their child in good stead even if secondary schooling is in a public school environment. They believe that religious values come ultimately from the home. They believe that a good elementary Catholic religious education and good home values are enough. They see no need to send their child to a secondary religious school especially if they feel that school's religious curriculum is questionable in some ways. Other issues such as friendship needs for their child with friends transferring to the public system they recognise as important but secondary.

What stance would the present research take upon this family scenario?

The study would reinforce (as Elkind, 1962; Godin, 1971; Hallez and Godin, 1964 did) the primary socialisation in religious values of the home. A good Catholic elementary school is also assumed to have a positive influence on religious formation of primary children. We do not as yet have conclusive proof for this *independent* effect of the *Catholic primary school* vs the home because the measures of faith development in elementary children are far harder to construct reliably and validly than for secondary students.

Given that, what can we say about the transition to secondary Catholic (high) school. The research here has shown that the Catholic high schools studied are having a unique, independent effect upon several key Christian outcomes of Catholic boys and girls. We have clear evidence for these youth at the end of their high school education and those two years younger at a terminal exit point, of unique effects of school over and above a range of home climate factors (happiness, trust, communication, liking for siblings and parental religious behaviour and expectation for children to do likewise). The school exerts a unique influence on Christian faith, through a combination of its informal (ethos, climate, values, rituals) and formal (Religious education curriculum, quality of teachers). These are areas the home can touch by its own values and climate but in a different manner from the systematic processes of the school.

Home climate is important. When we even out the variation in students' Christian faith due to school there is still some that may be attributable to home. Students from schools with similar informal and formal climate will still have varying levels of Christian faith depending on their home religious values.

Also we have evidence of secondary socialisation by the school of the sensitive stage of religious faith/values formation independent of the home background. This and the academic program must be the data that Catholic parents look to in making the choice depicted above.

Where in the parental view or several parents' view the formal Religious Education curriculum may be deficient, this would need to be examined/discussed with teachers, Religious Education Coordinator and other parents. Yet this research shows one needs to balance the formal curriculum with the informal climate (ethos, disciplinary policies, general happiness of students) before making a decision. Both influence Christian faith.

Faith is 'personal knowledge of God' – it involves an integral mix of belief and knowledge. If parents decide through whatever circumstances that they must send their adolescent to a public school they would need to carefully prepare themselves with up to date methods and materials to assist their son/daughter to be challenged faith-wise and build a reasonable faith-vision relevant to the modern world.

In this way it can be asserted that the values of the home climate have a significant effect while *both* the climate and the formal processes of the school have a significant effect also. To assert that the love and values of the home are sufficient for faith development is true – witness the many fine Catholics who are products of public school education. This study of 3431 adolescents currently in Catholic high school education can only assert that these Catholic schools *do make a difference* in the direction of improved faith values, social justice values, knowledge and vocational interest. Home climate certainly does have the strongest effect on Catholic Practice (Prayer, Mass, Communion).

To parents faced with the difficult decision of trying to decide where to send their young son or daughter, this study can only point to the above conclusions and urge parents to consider these as well as the more immediate concerns of ability to pay fees (many schools have schemes of loans or reduced fees which may assist), friendship needs of children (need to be talked through with the underlying values in family meetings), concerns about religious education curricula (need to be talked through with Religious Education Coordinator, teachers, other parents, children).

Ultimately a time of prayer and reflection for all involved will ask for God's Spirit and power in discernment and decision-making.

2. AN ADMINISTRATOR'S SCENARIO

A second situation may involve a Catholic school administrator (lay or religious) at local or diocesan level who is confronted with the problem of estimating effectiveness of Catholic schools and making appropriate policy or remedial recommendations. A local principal/head mistress may desire to involve his/her staff in an ongoing self evaluation of school climate and function. How are these administrators to go about their tasks with confidence in the process and outcome of the effectiveness study.

This study provides a wealth of effectiveness theory, data and discussion. It has methods for handling general climate, religious educational and academic outcomes. The scales have reliability and validity constructed on a large 3431 sample of Year 10 (Sophomore) and Year 12 (Senior) boys and girls (larger for boys, fewer for girls, yet still reliable girls' scales developed). These scales show evidence of construct validity, that they are actually estimating the underlying constructs such as Christian faith, Catholic practice, Social Justice Awareness, School Community, Religious Education Curriculum, Home Climate and 14 others. In addition 8 scales for school staff, Morale, Lay Administration, Job Satisfaction, Religious Goals of Staff and others have also been validated. There are many more in Appendix A.

Thus administrators charged with the task of improving the effectiveness of their educational system have a wide range of valid and reliable measures to choose from. They will of course wish to adapt these to their own needs while maintaining the essential integrity of the scale meaning.

Having selected the key questions and purposes of their investigation, administrators will choose a sample methodology and ethical guidelines suited to their purposes. There is ample computing power available in schools and people skilled in design and analysis of surveys. Administrators can delegate these functions to capable assistants, being sure they understand the basic purposes, methodology and ethics of this effectiveness investigation.

The results compiled in tables of comparative scale scores (between schools, between staff groupings, between pupil groups or parent groups) become the basis for a simple report. Reporting back to all right-to-know audiences should always highlight strengths as well as deficiencies. Highlight those areas where some action might be easily taken. Seek support and cooperation from the group.

Such simple evaluation action-research is no longer the province of skilled researchers, research assistants, big budgets. What is being described here is as simple as taking two scales of interest, putting them through staff, students or a series of schools in a system and tabulating the results with a little computing help on a stand alone microcomputer. Useful and valid results for the sample chosen could be generated quickly and feedback and informal discussion could begin.

This study and the scales generated can well form the core for a wide range of informed evaluation-action-research in a wide range of settings in many countries. It is hoped this book and the information here and in Appendix A will be of use in this process.

3. RATIONALE

Having come towards the end of this extensive exploration into faith in Catholic schools and classrooms, one may well ask where has the journey led us. It has been a novel approach of linking educational theory and statistical concepts with the theological categories more common to Catholic thinking. One may well ask if such reasoning has benefit for the school systems we seek to serve. This chapter will seek to show the very real benefits by a summary of the key arguments and findings in each chapter and an overall concluding reflection.

4. FAITH IN CATHOLIC SCHOOLS

This initial chapter outlined the basic orientation of the study. A review was made of the theoretical and empirical studies relating to the place of faith in Catholic schools and classrooms. The dual contributions of the secular school effectiveness debate and the Catholic school effectiveness debate were highlighted. As a check on the reality of these theoretical models it was proposed that a set of data gathered from 23 Australian secondary schools, 103 Catholic classrooms and 3431 students (Sophomores, Year 10; Seniors, Year 12) could help resolve some differences.

It was hinted that the level of statistical sophistication in the study went beyond previous studies in two ways: firstly, in being able to separate uniquely home and school effects and secondly, in being able to capture in a single analysis a total population of 103 separate religious education classrooms in these schools. This enables a clear test of previous theoretical predictions about the relationship of education-in-faith and education-in-religion in Catholic classrooms.

An examination of key definitions of the book focused on the distinction between efficiency and effectiveness and showed the latter to be a more holistic term unrelated to a mechanical view of school but more with goals, objectives, morale and a curriculum model. Following the work of Philip Phenix (1964, p. 28) a meaning view of curriculum was adapted. The six concentric realms divide the curriculum into the following groups.

Symbolics – language, mathematics, non-discursive symbolic forms.

Empirics – physical sciences, life sciences, psychology, social sciences.

Esthetics – music, visual arts, arts of movement, literature.

Synnoetics – philosophy, psychology and religion in their existential aspects.

Ethics – moral reasoning, ethical concern.

Synoptics – history, religion, philosophy.

(Phenix, 1964, p. 28.)

For Phenix a social system can be seen to be effective only if it is progressing towards the essential meanings inherent in its nature and drawing it towards a Transcendent, Ultimate Truth.

Another model useful for Catholic schools is the viewpoint of Pierre Teilhard de Chardin (1959) who proposed an evolution of matter, energy and life towards a final omega point. The stages are:

Alpha point – the beginning, the Big Bang 15 000 million years ago.

Cosmogenesis – evolution of stars and galaxies into observed structures.

Geogenesis – the evolution of rock structures from star remnants, into rocks and continents.

Biogenesis – the evolution of plant and animal life forms. The power of radial energy, the spirit of love, guiding this evolution.

Noogenesis – the evolution of human persons. A realm of thought and love begins to grow around the earth.

Christogenesis – the realm of thought and love finds its highest expression in evolution most fully in the mind and Spirit of Jesus.

The omega point – when all will through Jesus and the Spirit be drawn back to God the Father, who is 'all in all'.

This progressive evolutionary model fits well with modern scientific models and links them well with a solid Christian theological framework. 'Evolution is God's method of Creation leading us back to God.' God brought the Big Bang into existence out of nothing and has guided all evolution with his love (radial energy). All schools are an essential component of the evolution and spread of knowledge and love (noosphere) and Catholic schools have the dual role of integrating that evolution of knowledge and love into the mind and Spirit of Christ (Christogenesis).

Thus the valid insight of Phenix into the meaning system of the curriculum is closely linked to the evolutionary Christian view of Teilhard and together provide a firm foundation for conceptualising the purpose of Catholic (Christian) schools.

This allows a clear link with a religious meaning system of Catholic schools to follow. The Catholic school is founded on a dual vision. It seeks to become a community of parents, teachers and students that attempts a genuine integration of both human knowledge and religious faith around the

PERSON OF JESUS CHRIST.

The effectiveness of Catholic schools in using a wide range of processes and attaining a key number of educational and religious objectives has been a key focus of this study. The long debate about the relative unique influence of home, school and peer group has been reviewed and the former studies (except for Flynn, 1985) shown to be deficient. Flynn's (1985) study is based upon the methodology developed for this present work but extends it to new religious and academic criteria. Where Flynn, (1985) and this study overlap there is good agreement on criteria and predictors.

Flynn (1985) examined whole school groups which tends to bias the results towards whole school climate variables. This present book nests religion classrooms within schools, a better way of determining relative school and classroom effects.

To help focus the reader's attention one of the several arguments developed by this book will be presented here. An *argument* of this book may be summarised as follows: *If Catholic schools* are having a unique positive effect on a range of religious variables among students *independent* of home environment (i.e. when statistical controls are applied children from poor religious homes do just as well as those from good religious homes in schools with a good religious climate); *and if further it can be shown that Catholic classrooms* likewise account for a wide range of the religious objectives of students even when controlling for home background; *then theoretical analysis* which suggests that catechesis as such should be removed from school classrooms and confined to voluntary out-of-class activities *is in error; in addition the theoretical distinction education-in-religion/education-in-faith* will have been shown by an analysis of the nature of faith to also be *suspect*, not respecting the nature of faith or religious education.

A discussion of the nature of bias in social science empirical research shows it to be compatible with a modern view of knowledge and education. In particular the fears of the Catholic thinkers that empirical social science is locked into an Enlightenment atheistic model are shown to be unfounded. The bias inherent in social science measures can be reduced by careful measures but must still be evaluated in looking at the final conclusions of any study.

5. THE SECULAR SCHOOL EFFECTIVENESS DEBATE

The secular school effectiveness debate was initiated by the post-Sputnik (1957) scare and the attempt by Coleman (1966) and his co-workers to find the factors behind school effectiveness on the grounds of achievement. The amazing result from 645 000 students in 4000 schools and a sophisticated analysis that

> 'schools bring little influence to bear on the child's background that is independent of his (home) background and general social context'. (Coleman, 1966, p. 325)

seriously undermined confidence in the institution of schooling as a social leveller. On the basis of the study the hope to raise the children of the lower classes so that they can compete more equally with those from more fortunate home backgrounds seems ill founded.

This seemingly intolerable conclusion led to many reanalyses and new studies with new criteria. Essentially similar results were found. This pessimistic malaise about schools affected both secular and religious theorists (Ivan Illich, 1970 and John Westerhoff, 1972, 1976).

Subsequent workers pointed out errors in Coleman's measures and methods of analysis. Madaus (1980, p. 40) pointed to the inappropriate use of norm-referenced achievement measures which become essentially IQ measures unrelated to school factors. He proposed as better measures curriculum-sensitive measures such as the exam-based, subject-specific to a curriculum, measures as found in the school systems of Ireland, England and Australia.

In addition Mayeske (1972) and his co-worker illustrated problems with Coleman's regression analysis approach which could be avoided by a more symmetric variance decomposition (Beaton, 1974). The use of scales using factor analysis yields measures of greater reliability as in Madaus and this present book. With these better approaches significant school effects were found for a sample of Irish schools.

In England a major study by Rutter (1979) called *15 000 Hours* looked at the effectiveness question also stressing more the process variables in the climate of schools and classrooms. Rutter analysed his data by the less than adequate multiple regression approach and attempted some causal analysis. He was thus unable to extract the unique contribution of the measures to the criteria. Only a symmetric decomposition of variance can do that. In spite of this Rutter found a number of school effects between the 12 schools linked to social variables of school environment especially a sense of ethos, a set of values, attitudes and behaviour which seem to be important for Catholic schools also.

These several studies point to the key role of *climate* in school effectiveness – a concept well developed earlier in Australian studies by Leavey (1972), Flynn (1975, 1985). Taken together these findings suggest that *climate* involves norms, expectations and feelings about the school held by parents, staff and students, a sense of high staff expectation and morale, a good degree of control by the staff over instructional decisions and a set of clear goals and a sense of order, discipline in the school. Student morale, support for the goals of the school and satisfaction with the instruction received are also key elements.

A school viewed from a climate model seeks change not by a massive influx of resources but by helping people to change themselves. Indeed as Coleman shows increasing resources above a necessary minimum does little for achievement indices.

Studies of the English and Irish educational systems by Madaus and his colleagues (1975, 1977, 1980) have questioned the Coleman study and endorsed a climate view of schools arrived at by a correlational not regression approach.

Madaus identifies six major critiques of Coleman's study which can be overcome by better curriculum-sensitive criteria measures, which detect differences between schools and between classroom climate.

The measures in this present book were obtained in just this way, being Catholic schools and formal religious education classroom groupings of students. The data was thus ideally suited to test theoretical formulations about faith in Catholic classrooms. Using classes as the unit of analysis shows there are specific effects within certain class groupings and also when individual students are examined. Resources are downplayed and climate variables examined closely in antithesis to Coleman's approach. All schools, classes and pupils are included in successive analysis for maximum heterogeneity; only then is the full range of, say Christian faith, examined.

Schools are not *impotent* (as Coleman, 1966 and Illich, 1970 once thought), yet as Madaus (1980, pp. 173-190) explains they are not the sole instrument of social and economic reform. The home background does account uniquely for some of the variation in academic (and religious) variables. School and home have independent but complementary roles in the process. The data of this book show the relative roles of home, school and classroom environments.

6. THE CATHOLIC SCHOOL EFFECTIVENESS DEBATE

A critical review of Catholic school effectiveness studies in the light of the limitations of the secular debate has been reported in Chapter Three. The relative contributions of home, school, peer group, school staff and the internal world of personality factors goes well beyond previous Catholic school and classroom studies. The claim that this book avoids the pitfalls of previous Catholic research, especially the causal approach of Andrew Greeley (1976, 1982) has been established in the review. Greeley was also limited in his choice of 'years of Catholic schooling' as his measure of school exposure. The English and Australian research has shown that the quality of the ethos or climate is what is critical not the mere years spent in the system. Above all Greeley and Rossi (1966) argued for a 'multiplier effect' where schools could build only on good homes. This present work and Flynn (1985) proves good schools can have a unique positive effect (concomitant not causal) even for students from poor religious homes.

Other significant Australian studies (Mol, 1978; Flynn, 1975) and American studies (Strommen, 1974; Potvin, Hoge and Nelson, 1976) have been reviewed and all found to be flawed in their basic attempt to separate home and school effects compared to the better statistical approach of Fahy (1980b), Flynn (1985) and this book.

In Australia the pioneering work of Carmel Leavey (1972a, 1972b) in establishing for the first time valid and reliable scales of theological items checked by professional theologians must be regarded as a breakthrough in this area of research. She developed the most important concept of *climate* in Catholic schools and began to classify schools on climate and ethos measures. This opened the way for Marcellin Flynn's massive (1975) study which took these scales further and used extensive statistical analysis. He hinted at a unique home, school effect but could not prove it. Later he adopted the symmetric decomposition of variance from Fahy (1980a). This made Flynn's (1985) book '*The Effectiveness of Catholic Schools*' much more than a follow-up on the 1975 book but a whole new discussion of the problem this time with definitive answers to what constituted the climate of Catholic schools. In addition it told how much of key religious *and* academic processes and outcomes could be attributed uniquely to home, school, peer group, staff environments. This provides a wealth of information for educational planners and teachers in the Catholic system to pinpoint observable and modifiable aspects of schools to improve climate and academic outcomes.

Flynn's (1985) other key contribution was to have simultaneously data on religious climate, processes and academic indices enabling for the first time comparison of these two essential aspects of our definition of Catholic schools as combining human learning and religious faith in the person of Christ. The model stands up well theologically and empirically. Those students who express stronger faith tend to be those better satisfied with the climate of Catholic schools and they perform better on academic criteria. Growing wholeness in Christ opens a young person to all that is best in Catholic schools and the schools themselves profit thereby.

Many other significant Flynn (1985) findings explain the relationship between the academic and religious measures and the environments of home, school, informal curriculum, and formal curriculum.

The work of Greeley, McCready and McCourt (1976) has been reviewed and found to be inadequate on grounds of
(1) sample and data collection,
(2) measures chosen for use, and
(3) statistical procedures employed.
One example, Greeley *et al* analysed 927 American Catholic adults whose age ranged from 20 to 59. Thus when subjects respond concerning their religious experience their lived life since school no doubt has an impact. For some this could be 40 years of life experience, the effects of which Greeley *et al* (1976) implicitly ascribe to the foundation of their early school experience. This may be questioned.

It has been shown by this review of the Catholic school effectiveness debate that some professional Christian educators and administrators, generally lacking empirical skills, have accepted uncritically the findings of previous research and have been led to form erroneous conclusions regarding this relative influence of home, school and peer group upon the religious outcomes of students. For many people, both in USA and Australia this became associated with a lack of confidence in the effectiveness of Catholic schools. A number of bishops in the USA, religious educational theorists in France and the Catholic press in USA have uncritically adopted the incorrect Greeley findings and a serious pessimistic view about schools in the Catholic community of the USA has developed. A move towards 'family catechesis' and home based learning is occurring among Catholic theorists in USA and Australia. The effect has been less marked in Australia because of the vigorous research defence of the place of faith in Catholic schools, initiated by Leavey (1972) and carried on by Flynn (1975, 1982, 1985), Fahy (1980) and others.

To move the burden of faith education out of the classroom and into 'out-of-school' activities is unjustified theoretically and empirically by the nature of religious education classrooms. Alternatively to place the task of catechesis back to parents in the home, the majority of whom are untrained for the specialist catechetical task, would be an unjustifiable imposition. Parents should certainly be involved in and assist with their child's religious education but many of them freely choose to seek the assistance of well-qualified and dedicated Catholic teachers. Why should we deny that right for those parents who are able to get access to Catholic schools? Certainly for those Catholic children in State-run schools there needs to be urgent provision of catechetical and sacramental formation in the context of a caring parish team of pastor, catechists and parents.

7. RELIGIOUS EDUCATION EFFECTIVENESS

We provided in Chapter Four a review of definitions of faith based on the work of Rahner (1975) and McBrien (1980) with a high level of agreement on the knowledge aspect of faith. The fundamental direct relationship with God is called 'grace' by Rahner and faith is the ongoing explication in human language and symbols (hence involving knowledge and theological categories however simple) of this core grace experience. Faith comes into operation when knowledge categories are applied to that fundamental experience.

The implications for religious education are clear. If religious education is about assisting people develop a deeper faith awareness then the definition that faith always exists in some theological form applies. If theology is the process by which we bring our knowledge and understanding of God to the level of expression then religious education must be about a *faith-theology-knowledge* interplay. It is impossible to separate out one or other component and seek to separate it conceptually or in institutional structure. This inclusive interplay stands in contrast to Rossiter's (1983) dichotomy education-in-faith/education-in-religion which does not respect traditional Catholic views of faith.

A review of the religious element in a true education led into a discussion of parental rights to establish and support schools of their particular religious orientation. There students can be challenged to consider simultaneously secular and religious knowledge, looking for a faith-filled integration in Christ. Flynn's (1985) model supports this view but Rossiter (1983) stands in danger of relegating explicit faith-filled knowledge to out-of-classroom activities. A faith-theology-knowledge interplay *within* genuine classroom religious education can avoid that danger.

When Eleanor Roosevelt as Chairperson of the United Nations Commission on December 10, 1948, obtained ratification of the *Universal Declaration of Human Rights* she enunciated again the age-old right of parents to determine the shape and form of their children's life and education.

Forced after long debate to omit a word for God or Creator the document still stands as a charter for the rights of women and men.

In the area of education these complementary universal rights of parents, Church and State were spelt out in more detail by Austin Woodbury (1962). He reasoned that if the *Universal Declaration of Human Rights* was based on a sound understanding of the human person it should be possible to develop the reciprocal rights of three key educative groups, the parents, the Church and the State.

The parents he saw as always having the prior fundamental right to determine the shape and form of the education of their children. Where they need help with this parents freely choose to ask others they rely upon to assist them in this task. If parents freely amalgamate into groups with a similar purpose then a school structure may develop.

The State does *not* have a right *in itself* to directly educate children. Such a right is claimed by totalitarian regimes. It does of course have the right to ensure that adequate standards are maintained so that well trained and motivated citizens be prepared to carry on the society. This does *not* confer the right automatically to set up public schools. Only if sufficient parents by choice or default ask the State to set up such schools is the State thereby empowered to do so.

Where all citizens pay taxes for education costs then all citizens having prior rights have a right that those tax monies be directed to the school of their choice. In this way a system of 'double taxation' whereby minority groups fund their own school while contributing to the educational costs of 'public schools' is avoided.

The Church is a Teacher in its own right and has a duty to teach the message of the Gospel using available means of social communication. Because the Word is incarnate in flesh, the Gospel message of that word needs to be incarnate in the fleshy existence of human life and thought. Accordingly the Church has the right to set up both specifically theological schools (seminaries, colleges) as well as high schools and elementary schools and encourage those parents who subscribe to the Church to send their children there.

A disciple of Woodbury, Emmanuel Azzopardi (1988) has extended this theory of human rights into the context of one global nation. He looks at the nature of rights, fundamental Human Rights and the role of the State and Government. Disputing parties need a coherent theory of rights to resolve differences without gun or missile. If a theory of consistency of human rights could be developed it could help even disagreeing parties to think out their alternative views.

Through its teacher, Christ the Lord, the Church also has a right to use the means of social communication to speak to women and men of goodwill about moral/ethical values and indeed its key belief in Christ.

Other religious educational theorists such as Moran (1966, 1974, 1981, 1984) find a viable place for faith and religious education linked with learning. An interplay model is stressed between religious education and education in the classroom.

McBrien's (1977) work on Christian education likewise poses the need for clear categories. A focus on Christ who is the Lord of all creation does not constrict the view of religious searchers but expands it. Thus 'Christian education' is the more appropriate category.

Groome (1980) provides a five step praxis model for Christian religious education which links the educational and faith aspects.

Having reflected on one's own story individually and as a group, the Christian story relevant to the issue at hand is proclaimed and then discussions applying the process to one's own life and the life of the Community follow. The overall category of the present and coming Reign of God is seen as central. Simple faith sharing between pupils would be a key feature of this model.

For Moran, Groome and McBrien then there is still an essential place for catechetics (faith dialogue between believers) in its religious education in classrooms and other learning environments.

A theoretical critique comparing the work of other religious educators casts doubt on some of the Rossiter and Crawford formulations. In particular the foundational definitions of 'education-in-religion/education-in-faith' are inconsistent with accepted definitions of faith, religion, theology, education, religious education and Catholic school formal and informal curriculum.

Flynn (1984) disagreed with Rossiter on the dichotomy of education-in-faith and education-in-religion. He called for an integration of the two each providing a challenge to the other. Flynn's fundamental distinction between the formal and informal curriculum, both at the heart of sound religious education, holds up well both theoretically and empirically. This is the focus of the integration he argues for at the basis of the religious life of the school and students. This distinction opens up a way by which empirical research may check these claims since formal and informal curriculum are amenable to investigation.

Rossiter had a distinction between classroom and out-of-classroom settings. Flynn's position is more nuanced and his key point of integration gives a more balanced view.

A view of the validity of assessment in religious education follows from this faith-theology-knowledge interplay model. Table 7.1 shows the possible elements:

Table 7.1

Validity of assessment in Religious Education

	Knowledge	Attitudes	Skills
Individual Student	*Yes*	*No*	*No*
Classes Curriculum	*Yes*	*Yes*	*Yes*
School climate	*Yes*	*Yes*	*Yes*

Because knowledge of facts, language, symbols is so integral to the Catholic tradition then students may be assessed individually on that knowledge at all levels of Bloom's (1960) taxonomy of educational objectives without delving into their personal faith construction. They cannot be individually assessed on their attitudes since these form key elements of their personal theology. They cannot be assessed on skills such as religious art expressing personal symbols, interpretation of scripture passages, helping skills towards the poor, because these too involve personal faith positions.

Within this area of knowledge all possible methods of assessment should be used (essays, exams, norm-referenced and criterion-referenced assessment, computer programmed learning modules with built-in questions, diagnostic tests of knowledge of the Our Father, Hail Mary, etc.).

At the classroom curriculum level all forms of formative and summative evaluation are valid since we are now seeking to evaluate not students but the curriculum itself. Such data is always anonymous and is reported as curriculum data with the idiosyncratic faith views of students embedded within.

Likewise measures accumulated to the school climate level (both formal and informal climate) maintain student anonymity.

This study therefore supports the cautions and distinctions made by MacDonald (1989) in her doctoral work *Assessment in religious education in Catholic Secondary Schools*. She distinguishes between students' knowledge and understanding of the content of the particular tradition, and the faith response of students to God. The first she sees as being amenable to the normal type of classroom assessment (either norm or criterion referenced, essays quiz, project) while the faith response expressed in beliefs, attitudes and values are *not individually* assessable because of the fundamental freedom in the act of faith. 'The act of faith is of its very nature a free act ... in matters religious every manner of coercion on the part of men should be excluded' (Vatican II, Abbott, 1967: 689). However to evaluate and develop a curriculum anonymous assessment of *groups* of students is essential for teachers using subsets of tools such as those developed here. Also, students need to be involved in *self* assessments of beliefs, values and practices without teacher collection. All who see 'religious education reports' need to be educated to the fact that it is knowledge of the tradition that is being tested, not belief, value or personal relationship to God.

8. RELIGIOUS EFFECTIVENESS OF CATHOLIC SCHOOLS — THE RESEARCH EVIDENCE

The research evidence was extensively reviewed in Chapter 5. The initial focus of the sample of the Fahy (1980) study designed to test the theoretical speculations of Chapter 2,3,4 led into a non-technical discussion of commonality analysis (or symmetric decomposition of variance) and an analysis of a hypothetical example. The power of this approach to compare simultaneously the effect of several environments such as home, school, peer group and personality upon religious faith, practice and social justice awareness controlling all others was highlighted. Only this approach can uniquely separate the effects of these environments so long a goal of research in this area.

Predictors of students' Christian faith

A reliable and construct valid scale called Students' Christian Faith has been generated by conceptual and empirical approaches. As discussed in the first chapter we cannot *capture* the beautiful reality of a person's complex relationship with her/his God. However if personally worded items are asked in an anonymous free-choice environment it is possible to obtain *rough approximations* or *estimates* to the underlying reality of faith. In this scale the item:

> *'Christ is a real person to me in my daily life'*

appears as the most central in the perceptions of these adolescents. Not that all agree (only a third do, a third are searching and a third now reject Jesus as central to their life). Yet whether they agree, search or disagree the underlying pattern is one of faith-unfaith. This is supported by the next two items in the scale being personal statements about Father and Spirit.

> *'I see God as a loving Father'* and
> *'The Holy Spirit influences my life'*.

It is very consoling that the empirical analysis of the 131 replies each by 3431 adolescents should yield so clear a picture for the Trinity at the core of Catholic schools. The other eleven (11) items found in Tables 5.3 (boys) and 5.4 (girls) also centre about Christian faith issues in the Catholic tradition. Boys tend to have significantly less levels of Christian faith even when in the same co-educational school climate. No conclusions can be drawn about single-sex girls schools not sampled.

The results of the commonality analysis of home, school, peer group, personality environments upon students' Christian faith are that the most powerful predictors for these sophomores (Year 10) and seniors (Year 12) are firstly unique *school environmental factors* when all other environments are controlled. Schools are having a unique, independent effect on students' faith development. Secondly the *home environment* exerts a unique effect through the parents' own religiosity and family climate, trusting relationships. These are obviously indices of a warm, loving Catholic home setting. This home climate has a unique and different effect on a student's faith development to the independent positive school environment.

But also very influential at this final stage of schooling, where students seek independence from home, are the following school factors:

(1) how well does the student accept the ideal religious goals of the school (informal curriculum);
(2) how well does the student like the religious education classes (formal curriculum);
(3) how well does the student like the teachers and feel they teach well (relationships);
(4) how well does the student like the way in which the school seeks to develop liberal education goals:
   (i) giving experience in main areas of human knowledge,
   (ii) providing for creative work by students,
   (iii) encouraging a love of learning for its own sake,
   (iv) making students aware of other religions,
   (v) developing independence and critical thinking.

These four scales are the most significant beacons we have to date to predicting how Catholic schools may promote students' Christian faith. Let us dwell on them for a moment.

1. *To the stronger degree that students accept the ideal religious goals of Catholic schools* (forming community, fine

liturgy, teaching religious education well, integrating secular and religious subjects and open to dedicated lay and religious staff), then they will tend to develop a stronger faith. So here are the fundamental strategies for a Catholic school true to its name:

* build genuine community,
* celebrate fine liturgy in Mass and assemblies,
* teach religious education creatively,
* seek to have all teachers integrate secular learning and religious subjects,
* develop staff (both lay and religious) towards a spirit of dedication to a Christian ideal of teaching and care for young people.

These are well known from the policy and practice of Catholic schools and the agencies that serve them. It is consoling that the same views may also be found by systematic investigation into the attitudes of boys and girls in those same schools. They are really aware of our formal and informal curriculum.

Also notice with this first scale predicting faith the recurring theme of the clear link to knowledge. Faith is intimately linked with religious education taught creatively, with integrating secular and religious learning. This confirms empirically the theoretical analysis above – faith is linked to knowledge *and* learning. Faith should never be moved away from formal religious education. The 'education-in-religion/education-in-faith' dichotomy breaks down here. Faith is always a personal knowledge of God and as such needs faith/knowledge/theology interplay.

2. *Level of Satisfaction with Religious Education Classes*
   Here again the clear integration of faith with the formal curriculum of Catholic schools is evident. For schools the strategies here are:
   * every attempt at each level be made to stimulate interest and creativity (the role of the Religious Education Coordinator to animate staff needs to be further fostered and encouraged by principals and Catholic Education Office),

* surveys of students' needs before and after units to see if they feel they have been helpful to their development,
* teachers need to be enthusiastic and show interest in the subject – hence need for refresher and release time schemes,
* students need to be able to speak easily with their teachers. Hence inservice in interpersonal or counselling skills,
* students need to be able to discuss problems they have. Hence structured units with a balance of significant input and adequate opportunity to discuss this or related issues. Either one should not dominate the other.

Where these factors are found in formal religious education classes students are much more likely to have significant faith development. These scales show a religious education classroom can be a genuine, academically sound learning environment only if there is explicit faith expression and development by teachers as well as students.

3. *Liking for teachers* is essentially a relationship scale although there is also the important sense of liking for teachers who are genuinely interested and teach well. If this is so then students sense a school climate which is a genuine school, respecting of learning and academic values. If so they accept this climate and it is predictive of a faith integration of learning and Gospel values. So good teaching in *any* subject by *any* teacher whether Catholic or not, is *not unrelated* to faith development in a Catholic school. *All* teachers by their dedication to their profession and support for genuine human/true values support the Christian mission of the school.
4. *Liberal educational goals.* This is a composite scale of several related aspects. Liberal education is an openness (typical of Catholicism) to truth no matter where found. Students are very sensitive to this and reject narrowness or parochial attitudes. The items of this scale have been given above. Strategies for schools seeking to promote *liberal education* and the associated faith development would involve:

* to be open to all areas of human knowledge. To not cut off too soon the benefits of any knowledge to the Gospel,
* to provide creative work for students. All need to find some self-expression in creative work whether in art/craft class or wider fields of work or sport or service experience. It is here that career advisement and work experience programs find such an important place. So too the efforts to involve students in Christian service programs need support and encouragement however difficult,
* to encourage a love of learning for its own sake. To develop an enquiring mind in all disciplines that seek out answers to real human problems in carefully thought out models. To encourage the thrill of posing a problem (however simple) and solving it will lay good attitudes and skills for subsequent life,
* to become aware of and tolerant towards other religions. To have well taught units in world religions examined from within the faith perspective of the Catholic tradition. This differs from a relativistic approach devoid of a faith-view,
* to develop independence and critical thinking. Do we sometimes shy away from these perhaps out of fear that these same skills will be used upon our statements. Yet if we are seeking to develop committed Christian adults then there is no other road. To be independent is to say as they think, to evaluate what is given them, to respond as they see fit; surely this should be our aim. The analysis shows that even at the individual level of faith development there is a high degree of idiosyncrasy. They are making highly independent choices about their faith stance and moral value position. School policy and curriculum must be geared to a progressive development of independence and critical thinking, respecting yet challenging them to put that thinking to the light of the Gospel of Christ.

Thus all the school strategies taken above point out *how schools might significantly* affect the faith development of their students. Where those factors of both formal and informal curriculum are strong then Christian faith will be promoted. From the empirical analysis of 103 classrooms, schools (classrooms and climate ethos) do have a unique, positive effect upon students' faith and ongoing integration of the Gospel message.

We now turn to the home background factors that were also a unique predictor of students' Christian faith. It is clear that the home climate is essential for faith development but it operates in a different way from the school. If less than ideal the home religious influence does not necessarily hinder a good religious school from having a positive effect upon a student's faith. If a good home climate is present and school climate work independently towards the same result, a young person will be assisted to integrate faith and learning. What then are the home variables that are so important?

A. *Parental religiosity* where parents' Mass attendance and expectation that the children attend also is evident. This seems to be a fundamental index of the Christian Catholic climate of the home and we shall see below is the key predictor of students' own Catholic practice. Here it seems to suggest that a faith-filled home does have a unique, positive effect on the development of individual Christian faith as would seem obvious. It stands as an encouragement for parents who seek to build a faith-filled home that their efforts (even continued encouragement of children to attend Mass when they resist) are not in the long run in vain.

B. *Home background.* This is a wide ranging scale of the home environment stressing the following strategies for parents:

 * 'I discuss problems with my mother and father.' It is interesting that this sense of open communication is the most central one in the home scale. Parents and children need to keep working at a trust level that lets youngsters feel free enough to keep bringing problem situations to their parents.

* 'I am generally happy at home.' This also is a key item. In spite of ups and downs the general mood is basically good. Home is usually a happy place to be. Mum and Dad work to make it a happy place and minimise disputes or seek quickly for reconciliation between family members. Where this is so a positive climate of reconciliation in the Lord Jesus develops.
* 'My parents like my friends.' This seems to do with a sense of acceptance of others I value into the family circle. A family that is too insular does not meet the social needs of the emerging adult-adolescent. Where there is a fair degree of tolerance by the family of the lifestyle and values of their friends, adolescents seem more comfortable to maintain their own faith commitment. They do not need to win acceptance by modelling themselves on the friends' values which may or may not reflect their family. Thus faith of one's children is supported by being open and accepting of their friends even if those may vary from family views, values.
* 'I enjoy helping my parents, brothers and sisters at home.' This is a sense of cooperative teamwork which organisational studies describe as *morale*. The morale of the home, cooperative teamwork builds a spirit of togetherness and love. Indeed the Holy Spirit of unity and love flourishes here. No wonder a high unity home links with a faith scale where the Spirit has a direct place.
* 'My parents are interested in my school work.' Here is a powerful home climate variable that predicts Christian faith. Why? Parents have not only chosen by personal sacrifices a Catholic school for their children but are actively interested in the progress of youth both academically and religiously. The students are clear on this. The expectations are clearly communicated. The parents by their own faith implicitly or explicitly know the value of the Catholic school in the genuine integration of secular and religious learning. This expectation is clearly communicated to youth and is a key motivation for their faith development forming integrated life values.

* 'My parents find it hard to accept my faults and failings.' This is a sense of little reconciliation in the family. A negative spirit develops, trust declines. Parents in this situation may need to seek outside professional family counselling or the intervention of clergy or school professionals. The Spirit can break through these knots.

Thus all these home background factors taken together predict uniquely faith development of adolescents. In any discussion the independent (not 'multiplier') effect of school and home upon these late adolescents needs to be mentioned. Home and school have different effects aimed at the one central purpose to promote the academic and faith development of our young people. Both can do this as the research shows and the strategies outline basic ways it is being achieved. This gives reassurance to the good work of parents, teachers and administrators and clearer direction to future efforts.

Another related aspect of the research on students' Christian faith development relates to school and classroom effects. We saw in Chapter Three this was an important theoretical question in the critique of the Rossiter position (1983) and Crawford and Rossiter (1985). Now we have an empirical check on the effectiveness of schools and classrooms as such. There were total populations of 23 schools and 103 intact religious education classrooms analysed. The method looked at the *variance* (a measure of variation in a set of scores; if the scores are tightly bunched then little variance; if the scores are widely spaced then high variance) and how well that is spread firstly between the 23 schools and secondly between the 103 classrooms nested within them. If it is spread significantly that indicates that schools and/or classrooms are having a significant effect. There is something in the school or classroom environment covarying with religious variables and having an effect on spreading students' Christian faith development.

When the analysis is done it is found that there is only *one chance in 10 000* that schools are *not* having an effect. Thus it is very strongly probable that schools as such *are* having an effect. Schools vary in climate indices (morale of students and staff, press for academic achievement, clarity and strength of religious goals, sound discipline policy, friendly relations between staff and students), some will be higher. But it is the very way these climate factors covary that links significantly with the faith measures.

Likewise the 103 classrooms show less but still statistically significant amounts of variance (only *one chance in 20* of being wrong). This is saying that for faith development, classrooms are an important grouping that *must be considered in all subsequent research*. Classrooms have a unique character or climate, some more fully supportive of religious values than others, that interacts with class religion teacher and religion class pupils seeking to examine and develop their faith vision. Not that they will all have a common view. There is enough strong evidence for a *high degree of idiosyncratic faith development* from the mix of school climate, classroom climate effects and individual freedoms.

Indeed the individual level accounts for a high proportion of the variation in faith scores. Here is very strong evidence of this idiosyncratic faith development view. Students will watch, be influenced by what the school and classroom presents to them, media, peer group build those elements that appeal to them into their own synthesis (their theology) and base their life values on this process. So it will be individualistic yet if kept in dialogue with the Spirit and sound Catholic theology, a valid reinterpretation of that Catholic tradition in modern times for them.

This idiosyncratic view of the religious education process puts paid to attempts to treat religious education as equal to any other academic subject. This has been posited by some in Catholic Education Offices in Australia. There is also a view by some teachers that religion as a State endorsed Other Approved Subject would be easier to teach with the motivation of inclusion on final academic certification. Both these views are ill-founded in the light of this research.

(Refer to discussion of Marie Macdonald's thesis (1989) above.)

Thus we have seen that the wide variation in individual faith development between students (N = 3431) in this book clearly points to an *idiosyncratic view of faith*. Such a reality allows a norm-referenced mode of individual assessment on strictly knowledge aims (not attitudes or skills) linked to the theology of curriculum designers. Submission of specifically Catholic religious education to curriculum approval by Government examiners, lacking professional awareness of the theological faith vision of the designer, is an invalid process.

Catholic practice of students

The extensive treatment of the above section has shown the reader how to translate the results of the previous chapters into useful insights and strategies. Accordingly subsequent sections will be more summary in character.

The criteria of Catholic liturgical practice and prayer is conceptually and empirically distinct from faith. Key predictors of Catholic practice are firstly, home background:

1. parents' own Mass attendance,
2. parents' expectation that children go, and
3. climate of trust and warmth in the home.

All point to a genuine Christian home built on love, trust and shared religious rituals.

However there were also lesser effects from the school informal and formal curriculum especially:

1. religious goals of the school,
2. social educational goals of the school as an ideal,
3. satisfaction with religious education classes, and
4. satisfaction with teachers.

Again we have a sense of a school climate high on trust, openness to teachers, willing to look at religious goals of the school but wanting socially relevant education. Where the students feel they are being listened to and respected they will be more open to the sacramental catechesis of religious education and more willing to participate in school liturgy.

Home and school have unique positive impacts upon the sacramental and prayer life of adolescents but each acts in a different mode. The scales above point to many strategies that parents and educators can use to foster the liturgical and prayer life of those in their charge. One example, for schools, a socially relevant education, one that looks at pressing social problems (such as world hunger, AIDS) gives adequate sex instruction to develop sound knowledge and attitudes, that is open to the religious traditions of other church schools, gives a chance to discuss controversial topics, and provide counselling help for personal problems. Where the school is making an attempt to come to grips with these issues then the religious and sacramental catechesis takes on credibility and students are more responsive. Where those and the other issues listed for home and school are being considered the research shows youth will be more open to the mystery of the Mass, Jesus and prayer in the Spirit.

Flynn (1985, pp. 356-364) speaks of the school providing a *credibility structure* for the gospel message. Here we see *both* the home and school providing that credibility structure for a life of prayer, relationship to God and the expression of that in the parish Sunday liturgy.

Social justice attitudes of Catholic students

In spite of the limitations of the scale lacking parents' own views schools were found to have a unique positive impact on students' social justice attitudes. This must be encouraging for all those working in justice and peace education. No doubt parental attitudes would also have been important had they been included in initial survey. Flynn (1985, p. 327) also finds informal curriculum as most important but still had limited parental measures (1985, p. 389).

The key predictors of students' Social Justice Awareness are:

1. importance to be attached to social education goals,
2. satisfaction with religious education classes,
3. their view of ideal religious goals for the school,
4. liking for Principal and teachers.

This suggests that formal curriculum areas (2) as well as informal (1,3,4) operate together. If a climate of respect and trust with staff has been established, if the school has a relevant program for social education, if the religious goals really inform the classes then students will tend to adopt more just attitudes in the school and be concerned about wider social problems.

Two other factors were important. If students see religious giving a credible witness of gospel peace and justice then they will be impressed more by the gospel message they proclaim. Finally if the students sense just working relationships between religious and lay then they are likewise open to justice values.

Vocational awareness and interest

Two valid scales were developed. One tapping general sense of worth of priestly or religious life, the other a more personal choice or interest. About two-thirds of boys and girls saw religious life as worthwhile while one tenth expressed a more personal interest.

The key predictors for this awareness and interest were very similar:

1. Christian faith
2. Social Justice Awareness
3. Catholic practice
4. Personality variables (self-esteem)
5. Formal currciulum
6. Informal curriculum.

The centrality of faith items shows we are dealing with youth with a clear view of the Christian ideal. Likewise more altruistic students were more interested.

A study of self-esteem showed low self-esteem associated with low faith and practice as expected but also high self-esteem students had lower levels of faith and practice. Perhaps they are so independent they see no place for God in their lives. Low self-esteem youth feel no one loves them, even God. The home has a real role by establishing a Christian climate and supporting Mass attendance. Schools formal and informal curriculum has a role also in promoting vocations. Friendly relationships with Principal and staff helps to make youth more open. However students seeking a more liberal education (open and critical thinking) are *less* interested in religious life. Perhaps their strong desire for independence and freedom puts them at odds with what they think is the nature of religious life. Some strategies are discussed for encouraging interested youth to consider religious life more closely and correct distorted notions.

Staff community

Beginning as a staff morale study for 629 staff (religious 277, lay 352) this aspect of the project generated a great deal of interesting data. Morale (a sense of teamwork; integration of lay, religious; good communications; sharing in decision making; enjoying each other's company; good school discipline) was found to be positively associated with sense of religious goals of staff but negatively associated with a push for a share in lay administration.

The fact that religious goals are so closely tied to the morale scale shows that it is in a genuine sense a measure of Christian Community. The push for lay administration shows there are justice factors as well as faith ones that are important. This is shown in Figure 7.1.

Figure 7.1

Competing effects on sense of Christian Community

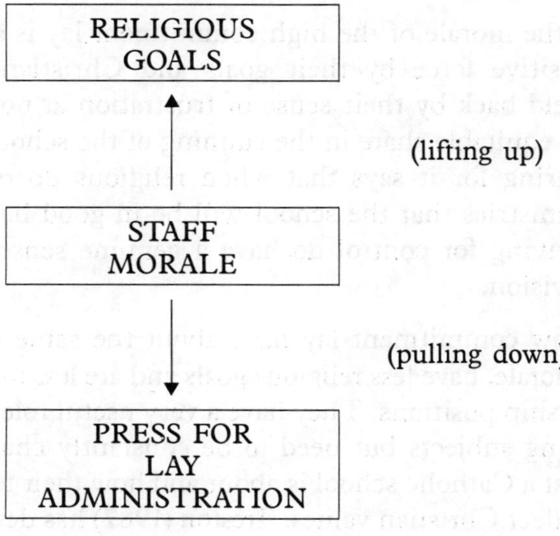

This morale dynamic is an important one for Catholic schools. The centrality of morale to the effectiveness of the school is evident. What can enhance it? Firstly the morale of lay and religious is enhanced most effectively by a sense of shared religious goals, of shared vision and purpose. Where staff share a common set of goals including religious and educational ones then they tend to have higher levels of morale together. Their happiness and communication together is better.

The other factor is the press for lay administration. This is essentially an issue of power as control of the school system is being transferred from religious to lay people. This is a phenomenon evident in the United States of America, Australia and England. The research finding here for these 23 schools is that it is the group of high religious goals (high committed lay) who are pressing for more share in administration. Those less interested in helping run the school (low committed lay) tend to have a weaker grasp of the Christian vision of the school.

Thus the morale of the high commitment lay is affected by a positive force by their goals and Christian vision but is held back by their sense of frustration at not being given an equitable share in the running of the school. This is reassuring for it says that when religious do move to other ministries that the school will be in good hands for those striving for control do have a genuine sense of the Gospel vision.

The low commitment lay have about the same level of overall morale, have less religious goals and are less interested in leadership positions. They have a very useful role to play in teaching subjects but need to be constantly challenged as to what a Catholic school is about and how their teaching might reflect Christian values. Treston (1987) has developed this distinction into two models in Catholic schools. He calls them 'the Vocation and Industrial Models'.

Administrators can best promote the staff community of their schools by attending to these significant predictors. There were three (3) general school scales and three (3) staff scales.

School scales

1. Students' press for a more liberal education (positively associated with Christian community).
2. Students' view of the actual importance being attached to religious goals of the school (positively associated with Christian community).
3. Students' view of the importance that ought to be attached to social education goals (Students with a strong desire for socially relevant education are found in schools where staff sense of community is low).

Staff scales

1. Staff degree of support for the religious goals of the school (Faith index) (positively).
2. Job satisfaction of lay staff (Justice index) (positively).
3. Press for lay administration (Staff pressing for more share in policy and administration tend to be those who are more *highly* committed to goals but their level of community is negatively affected).

A full discussion of these scales and their probable bearing on staff morale/Christian community is given in Section 5.6.

9. ACADEMIC EFFECTIVENESS — THE RESEARCH EVIDENCE

America's High School achievement study (Coleman, 1982)

The question of academic effectiveness in Catholic schools is a complex one for it may unjustly lead to comparisons between public and Catholic schools. If achievement or its predictors such as sound discipline atmosphere are found to be more positive in Catholic schools the reply can be made 'You can select out who you take, we must take all comers'. There is also the widespread belief that Catholic schools are supported by parental backgrounds richer in financial, personal interest and expectations.

In the USA too there is the common belief that Catholic schools are a haven for those parents who do not wish to send their children to the racially integrated public schools. To date, as with religious variables until Fahy (1980a) and Flynn (1985), there has been no appropriate way of sifting out the influence of the home to make an assessment of academic achievement of the school free of home bias.

The first researcher in the USA to take on this question of High School Achievement was Coleman *et al* (1982). A massive study of 1004 schools, 28 450 seniors (Year 12) and 30 280 sophomores (Year 10), yielded the following results:

1. On racial composition there are just as many Hispanics in Catholic as in public schools,
2. There are slightly fewer blacks in Catholic schools, but the difference is not significant,
3. Similar curriculum patterns but Catholic schools have more focus on languages and rigour in the curriculum,
4. Staff patterns (teachers, counsellors, librarians) are similar per student head of public and Catholic schools, other private schools had higher numbers of staff,
5. Catholic schools have fewer work experience and career preparation programs,
6. Students are happier with discipline policy in Catholic schools. At a time when State authorities are legislating for students' rights in areas such as suspension Coleman finds the more flexible Catholic system meeting students needs better and a happier overall climate than public schools,
7. Coleman discusses school spirit under strictness and nurture. He finds Catholic schools the strictest but also strong sense of nurture.

If 17 home background variables such as income, socioeconomic status and parental aspiration for their children are controlled then this national sample shows on standardised achievement tests of Reading, Vocabulary and Mathematics that Catholic Year 10 (Sophomore) students do better on all three than do public schools. This is the best evidence to date that of themselves, Catholic schools have an impact upon three key academic criteria independent of the income or aspiration of the home. The effect has been demonstrated convincingly for Year 10 (Sophomore) students and puts paid to the old myth of the unfair selectivity of Catholic schools. When public and Catholic schools are matched on 17 home background selectivity based on income, social class and aspiration the academic outcomes directly attributable to schools stand out in favour of Catholic schools at the Sophomore (Year 10) level.

What is the situation with the more developed seniors (Year 12) preparing for tertiary/college work? Here the position is not clear for Coleman gives us only the raw increment scores. In two of these the mean for the national sample of Catholic schools was superior to that of public schools (Vocabulary and Maths), but less in the case of Reading. No home standardised Year 12 (Senior) figures were reported so it is difficult to infer the effect of controlling for home.

The convincing results at the Year 10 (Sophomore) level shows that Catholic schools even when controlled for home background are more effective academically (at Year 10 level certainly) than a corresponding national sample of American public schools. This is distinguishing Catholic schools from the other private schools with many more resources and staff.

Many people have criticised Coleman for his presentation of these findings, especially on the issue of fee paying. This is interesting for there can be no comparison on fee paying of the two systems one of which depends on it and another is district or federally funded through taxation. Yet we know from Coleman's 17 home background variables that parents' total income, education, educational aspiration for their children which must all be direct predictors of fee paying ability are taken into account. Controlling the 17 variables controls fee paying ability and still gives a valid measure of Catholic school academic effectiveness independent of the home.

Thus we see key evidence that the old myth of family background accounting for the better climate and improved performance of Catholic students *really is a myth*. When family background is controlled Catholic (Year 10) sophomores and most likely seniors do better on most achievement tests than their public school counterparts. There is a genuine school specific effect on achievement operating here. The Catholic school seems to come closer to the American ideal of Horace Mann's (d. 1859) 'common school'. American Catholic schools are not just better because of better home selectivity and expectation but are better in their own right.

Catholic high schools and minority students (Greeley, 1982)

Greeley took the Coleman data set and sought to answer the question as to why do minority students, black and Hispanic, do better in Catholic schools than their public school counterparts. However his poor choice of measures, inappropriate analysis by strong inference causal path approach gives little confidence in his findings. Chapter 6 gives a fuller analysis.

The effectiveness of Catholic schools (Marcellin Flynn, 1985)

Using curriculum sensitive measures of the Higher School Certificate Examination in New South Wales, Australia, Marcellin Flynn empirically and conceptually collapsed a wide range of items into five blocks. They are as follows:

Home
Formal Curriculum of School
Informal Curriculum (Climate, Ethos)
RE Curriculum
Quality of School life

The HSC is a State wide examination set in some 50 subjects around a fixed curriculum which all have followed. It is a good example of a curriculum sensitive measure. It determines entry to university and colleges. Taking the aggregate HSC mark (the weighted average of the students' five best subjects – most subjects can be taken at one, two, three and four unit level) as the criterion, he simultaneously used the five blocks as predictors. Thus there is simultaneous control of all blocks and unique results are obtained. His major finding was a *most unexpected one*. He found that the most important unique effect could be attributed to the *Informal Curriculum* (Climate, ethos) when home, formal curriculum, religious education and School Life are controlled for. One would have thought that formal curriculum with subjects taught, skilful teachers, policy on papers, exam and assessments would have been most important but no, it was informal curriculum.

Some aspects of the informal curriculum which were found to be important for success in the HSC are shown in Table 7.2 (Not in any particular order).

Table 7.2

Informal Curriculum (Flynn, 1985, p. 317)
MORALE:

1. Friendly relations between parents and staff,
2. Students think a lot of their school,
3. Students understand and accept religious goals,
4. Counselling help is available to students,
5. This Catholic school is making a worthwhile contribution to Australian life,

6. Everyone has a lot of fun at this school,
7. On the whole I have been happy at school,
8. I would send my children to a Catholic school,
9. If I had to do it all over again I would attend a Catholic school,
10. Everyone tries to make you feel at home at this school,
11. My experience of this school has been happy.

PERSONAL DEVELOPMENT:
Catholic schools should:

1. Help students discover and fulfil themselves as persons,
2. Develop independence and initiative,
3. Respect each student individually,
4. Give all a chance of success,
5. Help students develop personality and character,
6. Help students learn to get on with other people,
7. Provide Counselling help to students.

Flynn (1985, p. 316) points to an informal climate or ethos of achievement which is even more important than resources (above a certain minimum). Even poor resource schools with Principal and staff (and parents) working together to build a good informal climate can help students produce good academic results. Coleman (1982) and certainly Rutter (1979) seem to be moving in this same direction.

Certainly Madaus (1980) agrees that schools can have an independent positive effect on the academic achievement of students mainly through their informal curriculum.

> Overall ... the processes, press, and atmosphere of schools and classrooms seem to be more highly related to variation in pupils' measured achievement than does the physical presence of particular types of resources and facilities or the status characteristics of teachers. (Madaus, 1980, pp. 107-108).

Madaus, himself very sensitive to the place of religious goals and values for Catholic schools, also points to the key role for common goals, clearly discussed.

> It is what people do in schools and classrooms – how they reinforce, interact, spend their time, and pursue common goals – which seems to influence performance on specific achievement measures. (Madaus, 1980, p. 108).

10. CONCLUSION

As Lewis Carroll (d. 1898) says in his famous *Through the Looking-Glass and What Alice Found There* (1872),

> The time has come the walrus said to speak of many things,
> of shoes and ships and sealing wax,
> of cabbages and kings,
> and why the sea is boiling hot,
> and whether pigs have wings.

So we must 'speak of many things' if we are to draw this book to some kind of conclusion.

The initial question posed, 'Faith in Catholic Classrooms', begot two kinds of responses. Did it mean a faith or a confidence in Catholic classrooms to promote religious and secular learning or did it mean the place of a personal faith response to God in Catholic classrooms?

It meant both these and the analysis shows that faith does have an essential place within Catholic classrooms on both theoretical and practical grounds. Catholic classrooms are places of faith where the individual faith vision of young people is fostered by a subtle blend of school and home effects, each independent but complementing each other. By an interaction of education and faith in a simple theology vision the young person comes to her/his own personal knowledge of God.

The key finding of the effectiveness of Catholic schools on both secular and faith criteria must give great encouragement to the two groups of people discussed in our leading scenarios.

For Catholic parents agonising over the choice of school for their children the precise data of this study can reassure them of the value of secondary Catholic education. That while the values of home are essential Catholic schools bring a whole new dimension to bear and ably assist the young person to integrate secular knowledge with her/his own evolving faith vision. Both are needed home and school independent but complementary to each other. This is analogous to the effect of pressure and temperature upon the volume of a fixed mass of gas.

Figure 7.2
Gas model of home/school relations

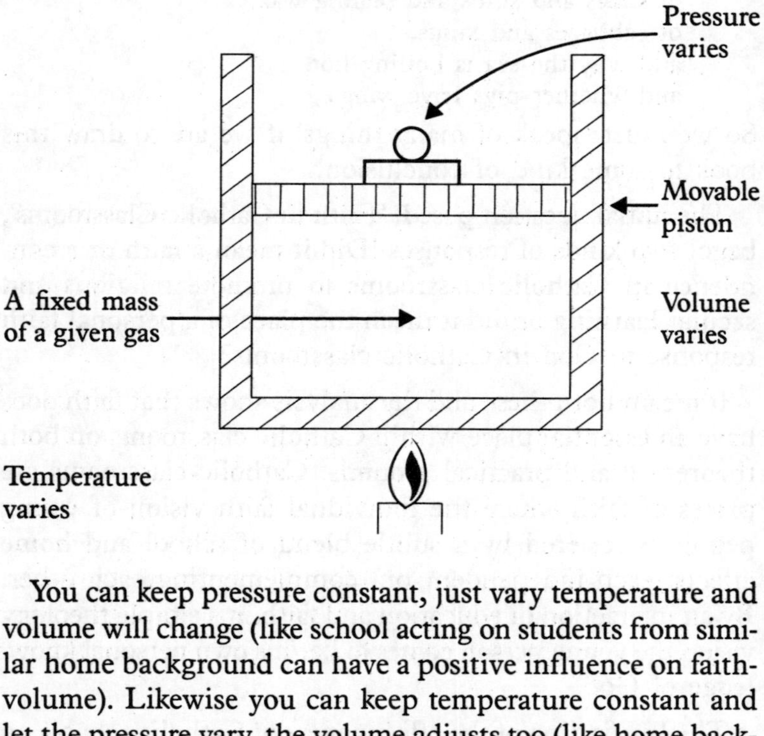

You can keep pressure constant, just vary temperature and volume will change (like school acting on students from similar home background can have a positive influence on faith-volume). Likewise you can keep temperature constant and let the pressure vary, the volume adjusts too (like home background varying with schools of equal climate, the faith development would differ). Pressure and temperature, estimated separately, complement each other in the real world where they both vary simultaneously.

So home and school, while being independent factors of the faith process, can and do complement each other in the process of faith development.

When parents are making decisions about schooling for their children they would be wise to weigh up the weight of the gospel message, encouragement of the Church, the research findings of this study and their own situation and resources. By prayer and seeking advice they bring their discernment process to a point where they can be at peace with their decision.

Simultaneously the Church school administrator has a sacred responsibility under the direction of appropriate Church authorities to work for the increased effectiveness of his/her school. This study of *Faith in Catholic Schools* has pinpointed a philosophy, a methodology and resources for carrying out sound evaluation of Catholic school effectiveness. There is little reason why Catholic school administrators could not select and adapt the scales of this study to their own needs, delegate data collection and analysis tasks and receive and write final reports for teachers, parents and governing bodies that would be a systematic encouragement of the good work being done in the school. It would focus on the essential nature of Catholic schools and avoid ancillary questions.

The further specification in the subtitle of 'theory and practice in 103 classrooms' hinted at the methodology to be used – an in-depth theoretical analysis of the nature of faith, in place the formal and informal curricula of Catholic schools and an empirical check of such theoretical formulations against the reality of 103 Catholic classrooms.

The approach has always been to balance theoretical speculation against the reality check of empirical measures. This is not blind imposition of social science method onto the faith area but a carefully nuanced application acknowledging the presence of bias in all social science data and showing that probable, suggestive knowledge replaces certainty. It is claimed here that the valid and reliable measures developed by this study give a limited but still genuine insight into the views of Catholic adolescents about their faith life. And who better should know? In addition the scales indicate many aspects of parental/home background, the school climate and procedures, and the influence of peers.

The first step in the argument of the book has been that we need first of all to understand the method of secular school effectiveness studies based upon academic achievement. A review of these in Australia, Ireland and the United States reveals a convergence of opinion. Academic achievement is best explained by the informal curriculum. This is unexpected since one may have expected that subjects taught, the students' perceptions of the quality of teachers and formal school structures would be the major determinant. But it is not so. With all those controlled, the major effect upon achievement is the informal climate and ethos, the conformity of student and school goals, the friendly, happy climate, the feeling of respect from teachers, the press or expectation for academic achievement from parents and teachers. All these explain a very significant proportion of the variation in curriculum-sensitive achievement measures. The methodology (commonality analysis) developed by the secular school effectiveness studies enables one to separate uniquely, without any other prior causal assumptions, the effects of a series of environments (home, school, peer, personality, school staff) upon key religious and secular estimates. It is the method adopted in this study to separate home and school effects uniquely and isolate the important factors in Catholic classrooms, contrary to the inappropriate causal path analysis.

So we have come full circle.

Faith in Catholic Classrooms?

In the sense of confidence in the academic and religious effectiveness of good climate Catholic schools, the *answer must be YES*. Schools and classrooms have their own unique positive role in academic and faith development. Home and school work in independent but complementary ways just as pressure and temperature are two independent factors affecting in a complementary way the volume of a given mass of gas. Where academic/religious climate is lacking from either school or home there is some evidence to suggest that the other environment can compensate. So we should have confidence in both Catholic classrooms and Catholic homes.

Faith in Catholic Classrooms?

In the sense of the place of faith in the formal curriculum processes of the Catholic classroom. For the first time we report data on 103 specific religious education classrooms and, using the basic definitions of faith as a personal knowledge of God, show that such classrooms are seen by students as developers of personal faith. The dual role of formal and informal curriculum in this faith development argues against a too-simplistic dichotomy between faith and religion in the context of Catholic schools. Rather an integrated approach that brings together the idiosyncratic personal faith vision (own theology) of the adolescent with faith and sound educational strategies is needed.

Individual classroom units showed specific faith and learning effects, on both religious and academic criteria. So the answer to the question:

Faith in Catholic Classrooms?

In the sense of a presence of belief in the fundamental mystery of God and our response in the person of Jesus, in the power of the Spirit which lies at the heart of both formal and informal curriculum, *must be YES*. We cannot seek to separate faith away from formal Catholic classrooms and the informal climate of the school, just as we cannot separate the personal theological construction going on in students' hearts and minds from the sound educational strategies in the teachers' intention.

But the central place of all must belong to

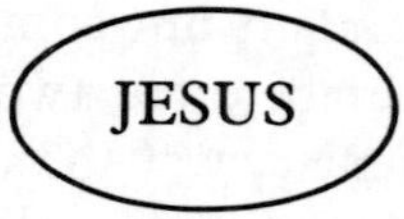

who stands at the centre of every Catholic school, in the middle of every classroom, in the heart of every student and teacher and in every loving interaction between teacher-pupils or between pupils.

Figure 7.3

Central place of Jesus

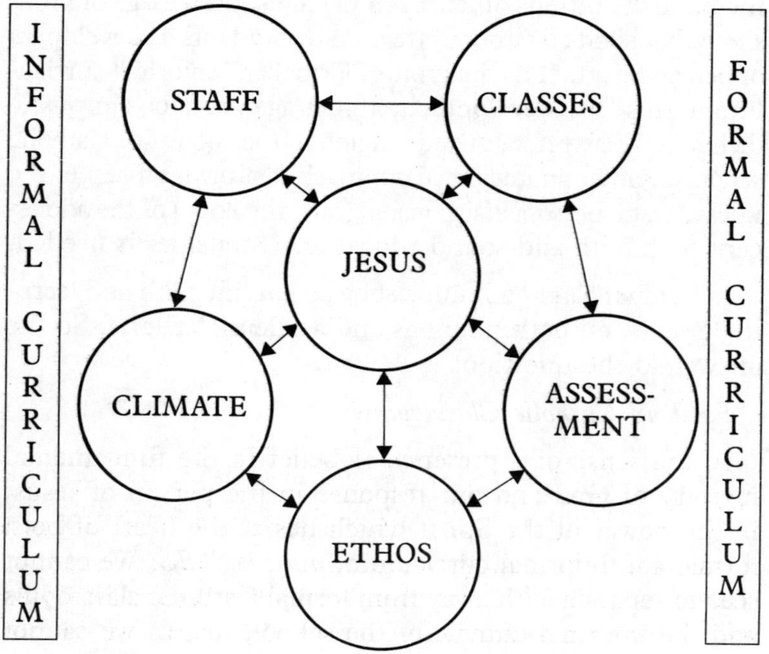

and the Mystery of the Trinity which we see here empirically to be at the centre of the deepest perceptions of these 3431 boys and girls.

Figure 7.4

Central place of Trinity

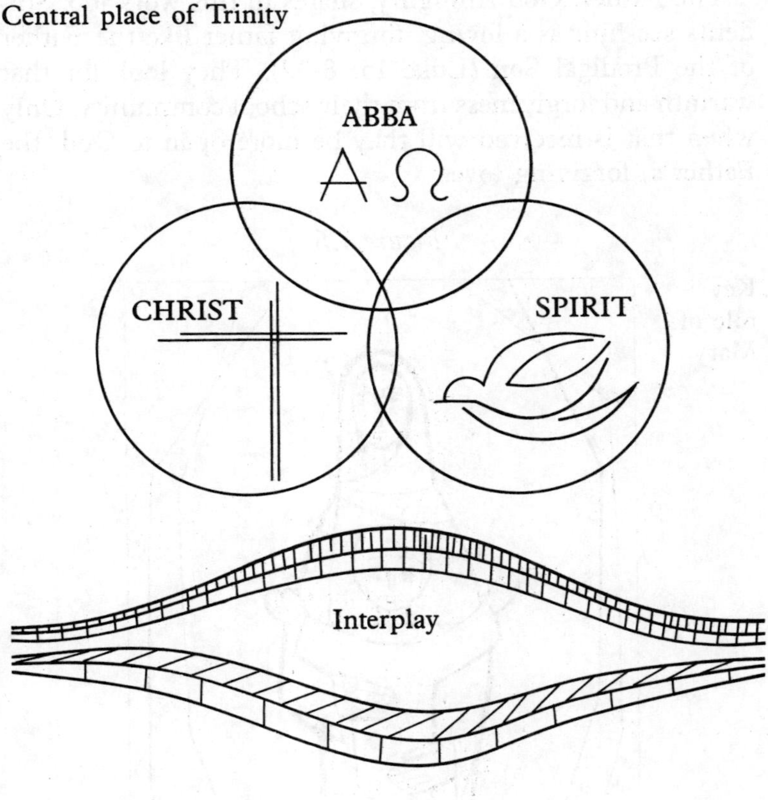

Christ, and Christ alone in his risen and glorified state gives meaning and purpose to all the goals and hopes of all the above. Catholic schools are meaning systems educating for meaning.

By the Spirit of Wisdom, manifest in his Holy Spirit, that is being sent forth over the world he seeks to create a new world of peace, harmony, justice and true freedom. By the faith-theology-educational efforts of teachers and students his Spirit and his life are becoming more evident in the human consciousness and loving foundation for a just world order.

The Father, God Almighty, shares in this work too. Students see him as a loving, forgiving father like the Father of the Prodigal Son (Luke 15: 8-32). They look for that warmth and forgiveness from their school community. Only when that is received will they be more open to God, the Father's, forgiving love.

Figure 7.5

Key role of Mary

Mary, mother of Jesus, has a key role in Catholic schools which has been apparent here in the Catholic practice scale (Table 5.7). At the Cana Wedding Feast (John 2: 1-12) she identifies the need of the young couple, 'They have no wine'. She is attentive to their need. The author is telling us of a key characteristic of hers, to be attentive to other people's needs. And so too in Catholic classrooms Mary assumed and alive and symbolised oftentimes by a statue or picture, is attentive to the deepest needs of students and teachers as they grapple with educational and faith tasks. She is a constant source of support in the complexities of modern life.

This book could end nowhere else but at the centre towards which all Catholic classrooms and the mystery of our faith is tending. Faith in a God who loves, forgives, redeems, enlivens us, Father, Son and Spirit and the mother of Jesus, Mary, who is attentive to all our needs and urges us to pray to her Son and act for him. Only a response of praise and gratitude is appropriate as we do whatever we can to promote the welfare of Catholic schools and those they seek to serve.

APPENDIX

Scales used in this study of use for school effectiveness study.

Contents

1. Per cent response to items defining CHRISTIAN FAITH SCALE N = 2821 students, male.

Item	Per cent Agree	Per cent Disagree	Factor Loading
Christ has become a real person to me in my daily life	33	37	0.71
I see God as a loving Father	55	21	0.62
The Holy Spirit influences my present life	29	32	0.61
I intend to base my life on the teaching and example of Christ	22	50	0.59
I would like to know more about Christ and his teachings	36	36	0.57
I believe God forgives me	74	9	0.57
I appreciate the chance to go to the New Rite of Reconciliation	32	44	0.41
I like to take an active part of singing, reading at the liturgy	26	63	0.38
Even if necessary precautions are taken, sexual relationships outside marriage are still wrong	23	63	0.36
I believe in God	62	8	0.32
I appreciate the opportunity to go on a religious camp or weekend	59	25	0.18
The religious experience of a Christian living weekend, camp or retreat has made a lasting impression on me	43	34	0.17
Christ lived 2000 years ago, in another culture and has no relevance for today (R)	13	62	−0.27
Christ has no relevance for me today (R)	12	62	−0.31

When I see all the war, poverty and cruelty that exists in the world, I have trouble believing in God (R)	34	47	−0.35

No. of items 15, Range 15-75, Scale mean 47.8, S.D. 10.8, Alpha Reliability 0.85. R = item is reversed in scale addition.

HIGH SCORE: Students with a strong commitment to aspects of their Christian faith.

LOW SCORE: Students with a weak or little commitment to a Christian faith in their lives.

2. Per cent response to items defining CHRISTIAN FAITH SCALE N = 323 students, female.

Item	Per cent Agree	Per cent Disagree	Factor Loading
Christ has become a real person to me in my daily life	40	31	0.71
I see God as a loving Father	62	15	0.62
The Holy Spirit influences my present life	35	30	0.61
I intend to base my life on the teaching and example of Christ	22	49	0.59
I would like to know more about Christ and his teachings	39	29	0.57
I believe God forgives me	74	7	0.57
I appreciate the chance to go to the New Rite of Reconciliation	34	45	0.41
I like to take an active part of singing, reading at the liturgy	34	53	0.38
Even if necessary precautions are taken, sexual relationships outside marriage are still wrong	34	51	0.36
I believe in God	59	7	0.32

I appreciate the opportunity to go on a religious camp or weekend	60	18	0.18
The religious experience of a Christian living weekend, camp or retreat has made a lasting impression on me	40	25	0.17
Christ lived 2000 years ago, in another culture and has no relevance for today (R)	11	58	−0.27
Christ has no relevance for me today (R)	10	62	−0.31
When I see all the war, poverty and cruelty that exists in the world, I have trouble believing in God (R)	39	42	−0.35

No. of items 15, Range 15-75, Scale mean 50.6, S.D. 9.4, Alpha Reliability 0.85. R = item is reversed in scale addition.

HIGH SCORE: Students with a strong commitment to aspects of their Christian faith.

LOW SCORE: Students with a weak or little commitment to a Christian faith in their lives.

3. Per cent response to students' reported CATHOLIC PRACTICE
N = 2821 students, male

Item	Per cent (*)	Factor loading
I normally attend Mass		
on the weekend at least	56	0.67
a few times a month	11	
once a month	6	
a few times a year	11	
rarely or never	15	

I normally receive Holy Communion		
on the weekend at least	37	0.63
a few times a month	18	
once a month	9	
a few times a year	17	
rarely or never	19	
I normally go to the Sacrament of Reconciliation		
once a week	1	0.53
a few times a month	2	
once a month	14	
a few times a year	44	
rarely or never	38	
I normally pray (apart from school prayers)		
each day	21	0.51
a few times a week	24	
a few times a month	18	
a few times a year	13	
rarely or never	23	
I pray to Our Lady		
each day	11	0.55
a few times a week	18	
a few times a month	17	
a few times a year	18	
rarely or never	36	

No. of items 5, Range 5-25, Scale mean 14.6, S.D. 4.3, Alpha Reliability 0.60.

HIGH SCORE: Those students who attend Mass and sacraments regularly and who pray frequently.

LOW SCORE: Those students who do not attend Mass or sacraments frequently and who pray little.

(*) Missing data (some 4 per cent) not included in these per cents but assigned the median response (code = 3) in the scale score.

4. Per cent response to students' reported CATHOLIC PRACTICE
N = 323 students, female

Item	Per cent (*)	Factor loading
I normally attend Mass		
on the weekend at least	57	0.67
a few times a month	14	
once a month	10	
a few times a year	11	
rarely or never	8	
I normally receive Holy Communion		
on the weekend at least	39	0.63
a few times a month	27	
once a month	10	
a few times a year	15	
rarely or never	10	
I normally go to the Sacrament of Reconciliation		
once a week	1	0.53
a few times a month	4	
once a month	42	
a few times a year	32	
rarely or never	21	
I normally pray (apart from school prayers)		
each day	23	0.51
a few times a week	15	
a few times a month	41	
a few times a year	10	
rarely or never	11	
I pray to Our Lady		
each day	9	0.55
a few times a week	18	
a few times a month	39	
a few times a year	12	
rarely or never	22	

No. of items 5, Range 5-25, Scale mean 14.9, S.D. 4.1, Alpha Reliability 0.60.

HIGH SCORE: Those students who attend Mass and sacraments regularly and who pray frequently.

LOW SCORE: Those students who do not attend Mass or sacraments frequently and who pray little.

(*) Missing data (some 4 per cent) not included in these per cents but assigned the median response (code = 3) in the scale score.

5. Per cent response to items defining SOCIAL JUSTICE AWARENESS N = 2821 students, male.

Item	Per cent Agree	Per cent Disagree	Factor Loading
White people in Australia have a Christian obligation to repair the damage done to Aboriginal people	42	24	0.45
I worry about people in countries where there is starvation	56	29	0.37
I would like to be part of a group that helps others e.g. by visiting hospitals, working with the poor	25	36	0.32
I have tried to be a friend to people who are lonely and rejected	62	21	0.24
I have taken part in some activities helping other people organised by the school	49	25	0.12
I think that other students would be prepared to help me in some charitable work	47	24	0.23
I have worked with other people on community projects helping needy people	49	43	0.04

Black people are inferior by nature to white people (R)	14	69	−0.36
Companies should be allowed to mine on Aboriginal land (R)	23	51	−0.50

No. of items 9, Range 9-45, Scale mean 30.4, S.D. 5.9, Alpha Reliability 0.60. R = item is reversed in scale addition.

HIGH SCORE: Students who are concerned about social justice issues and have taken some steps to help the poor.

LOW SCORE: Students who are not aware of social justice issues, have not helped the poor and may have some racial prejudice.

6. Per cent response to items defining SOCIAL JUSTICE AWARENESS N = 323 students, female.

Item	Per cent Agree	Per cent Disagree	Factor Loading
White people in Australia have a Christian obligation to repair the damage done to Aboriginal people	39	20	0.45
I worry about people in countries where there is starvation	78	11	0.37
I would like to be part of a group that helps others e.g. by visiting hospitals, working with the poor	48	13	0.32
I have tried to be a friend to people who are lonely and rejected	70	12	0.24
I have taken part in some activities helping other people organised by the school	46	20	0.12
I think that other students would be prepared to help me in some charitable work	56	16	0.23

I have worked with other people on community projects helping needy people	46	45	0.04
Black people are inferior by nature to white people (R)	13	60	−0.36
Companies should be allowed to mine on Aboriginal land (R)	10	58	−0.50

No. of items 9, Range 9-45, Scale mean 36.2, S.D. 4.9, Alpha Reliability 0.60. R = item is reversed in scale addition.

HIGH SCORE: Students who are concerned about social justice issues and have taken some steps to help the poor.

LOW SCORE: Students who are not aware of social justice issues, have not helped the poor and may have some racial prejudice.

7. Per cent response to items defining RELIGIOUS EDUCATION GOALS IDEAL, ACTUAL N = 2821 students.

Item	Per cent Import.	Per cent Unimport.	Factor Loading
Catholic schools ought to provide an atmosphere of Christian community. Ideal	57	14	0.62
Christian community – how important actually	56	17	0.50
Catholic schools ought to provide youth with a chance to participate in the liturgy. Ideal	40	27	0.51
Liturgy – how important actually	38	27	0.45
Catholic schools ought to teach Religious Education classes at a level comparable to other subjects. Ideal	33	37	0.40

Religious Education comparable to other subjects – how important actually	26	38	0.59
Catholic schools ought to integrate Religious Education and other subjects. Ideal	29	43	0.43
Integrate Religious Education and other subjects – how important actually	20	51	0.59
Catholic schools ought to give an example of dedicated life through lay and religious staff. Ideal	51	24	0.90
Dedicated life of lay and religious – how important actually	38	31	0.44

No. of items 5 in each scale, Range 5-25.

Ideal Scale: Mean 15.9, S.D. 4.4, Alpha Reliability 0.75.
Actual Scale: Mean 15.1, S.D. 3.8, Alpha Reliability 0.67.

HIGH SCORE: Students who attach strong importance to religious educational goals (ideal) and who see the school supporting religious educational goals (actual).

LOW SCORE: Students who do not attach importance to religious educational goals (ideal) and who do not see the school doing so (actual).

8. Per cent response to items defining SATISFACTION WITH RELIGIOUS EDUCATION CLASSES N = 2821 students.

Item	Per cent Agree	Per cent Disagree	Factor Loading
I find religious education lessons interesting	25	48	0.68
My religious education classes at school have been helpful to my religious development	40	41	0.60

My religion teacher teaches religion in such a way that you know he/she is interested in it	70	13	0.38
I could talk easily with one of my religion teachers	48	32	0.34
In religion classes we are encouraged to discuss any problems we have	37	48	0.15
There is too much emphasis on religion in this school (R)	34	45	−0.33
What we do in Religious Education classes does not mean much to my daily life (R)	33	45	−0.38

No. of items 7, Range 7-35, Scale mean 21.6, S.D. 5.3, Alpha Reliability 0.65.

HIGH SCORE: Students who like religious education classes and feel that they have helped them grow in faith.

LOW SCORE: Students who do not like the religious education classes and feel there is no connection with life.

9. Per cent response to items defining SATISFACTION WITH TEACHERS N = 2821 students.

Item	Per cent Agree	Per cent Disagree	Factor Loading
Most of my teachers take a genuine interest in me	45	20	0.63
Generally my teachers teach well	69	18	0.61
Some of my teachers do not like me (R)	38	39	−0.33

No. of items 3, Range 3-15, Scale mean 9.9, S.D. 2.6, Alpha Reliability 0.50.

HIGH SCORE: Students who are satisfied that teachers take a genuine interest in them and teach well.

LOW SCORE: Students who are dissatisfied with their relationship with their teachers and feel they do not teach well.

10. Per cent response to items defining HOME BACKGROUND N = 2821 students.

Item	Per cent Agree	Per cent Disagree	Factor Loading
I can discuss problems with my father or mother	59	26	0.56
I am generally happy at home	77	5	0.48
My parents like my friends	75	9	0.41
I enjoy helping my parents, brothers and sisters at home	59	14	0.39
My parents are interested in my school work	89	5	0.29
I find it hard to get on with other members of my family (R)	24	68	−0.53
My parents find it hard to accept my faults and failures (R)	26	59	−0.56
My parents do not trust me (R)	17	73	−0.70

No. of items 8, Range 8-40, Scale mean 31.1, S.D. 5.4, Alpha Reliability 0.72.

HIGH SCORE: Students who feel trusted and happy at home and able to communicate with their parents.

LOW SCORE: Students who do not feel happy or trusted at home and who have difficult relationships with parents and siblings.

11. Per cent response to items defining PARENTAL RELIGIOSITY – STUDENTS' VIEW N = 2821.

Item	Per cent Agree	Per cent Disagree	Factor Loading
My parents expect me to go to Mass on Sunday (or Sunday vigil)	73	20	0.85

At least one of my parents goes to Mass on Sunday (or Sunday vigil)	75	21	0.76

No. of items 2, Range 2-10, Scale mean 8.0, S.D. 2.7, Alpha Reliability 0.77.

HIGH SCORE: Students from homes where at least one parent attends Mass weekly and expects the student to do so also.

LOW SCORE: Students from homes where parents do not attend Mass weekly and do not expect the student to do so.

12. Per cent response to items defining SOCIAL EDUCATION GOALS N = 2821 students.

Item	Per cent Agree	Per cent Disagree	Factor Loading
Catholic schools ought to make students aware of pressing social problems. Ideal	58	7	0.63
Awareness of social problems – how important actually	34	22	0.54
Catholic schools ought to give adequate sex instruction. Ideal	64	4	0.56
Adequate sex education – how important actually	26	33	0.55
Catholic schools ought to create friendly relations with other church schools. Ideal	63	12	0.36
Friendly relations with other church schools – how important actually	30	38	0.45
Catholic schools ought to provide the chance to discuss controversial topics. Ideal	69	9	0.40

Discuss controversial topics – how important actually	30	35	0.59
Catholic schools ought to give counselling help in personal problems. Ideal	68	11	0.32
Counselling for personal problems – how important actually	31	40	0.47

No. of items 5 in each scale, Range 5-25.

Ideal Scale: Mean 19.6, S.D. 3.4, Alpha Reliability 0.64.
Actual Scale: Mean 14.7, S.D. 3.7, Alpha Reliability 0.55.

HIGH SCORE: Students who want more stress on social education (ideal) and/or feel the school is giving it.

LOW SCORE: Students who do not stress social education and do not want the school to stress it (actual).

13. Per cent response to items defining SATISFACTION WITH PRINCIPAL N = 2821.

Item	Per cent Agree	Per cent Disagree	Factor Loading
The Principal is a good leader of the school	51	26	0.81
The Principal is ready to listen to students	43	23	0.77
The Principal takes a real interest in the school	66	16	0.76

No. of items 3, Range 3-15, Scale mean 10.4, S.D. 3.4, Alpha Reliability 0.77.

HIGH SCORE: Students who think the Principal is a good leader, takes an interest in the school and is ready to listen to them.

LOW SCORE: Students who are dissatisfied with the Principal feel that he is not a good leader and does not listen to them.

14. Per cent response to items defining RELIGIOUS GOALS OF STAFF N = 448 staff.

Item	Per cent Agree	Per cent Disagree	Factor Loading
I think that some Christian commitment should be expected of all teachers in Catholic schools	81	9	0.59*
The Catholic School should offer experience in Christian living through the liturgy, sacraments and prayer	92	3	0.58
Classroom prayers should be said daily in Catholic schools	85	5	0.57
The Catholic school should integrate religious and secular studies as far as possible	88	6	0.57
I think that teachers in Catholic schools should be practising Catholics	39	48	0.50
Lay teachers are able to give a witness of Christian living in the daily life of the school	90	3	0.46
Catholic schools should provide a witness of dedicated Christian life through its religious teachers	96	1	0.45

No. of items 7 in each scale, Range 7-35.

Religious: Mean 25.3, S.D. 2.2, Alpha Reliability 0.28.
Lay staff: Mean 21.9, S.D. 4.6, Alpha Reliability 0.74.

HIGH SCORE: Staff who strongly support the religious goals.

LOW SCORE: Staff who have little or no support for religious goals of the school.

* Religious agreed strongly with all items and hence had little variance in their scores. The factor loadings are for the lay staff and reflect a useful scale.

15. Per cent response to items defining OPENNESS TO RELIGIOUS LIFESTYLE N = 2821.

Item	Per cent Agree	Per cent Disagree	Factor Loading
I feel that brothers and sisters have a worthwhile part to play in today's world	67	16	0.81
I feel that a priest has a worthwhile part to play in today's world	67	17	0.71
I would be happy if one of my friends became a priest, brother or sister	30	29	0.49

No. of items 3, Range 3-15, Scale mean 10.5, S.D. 2.9, Alpha Reliability 0.71.

HIGH SCORE: Students who feel that a religious or priestly lifestyle is a valuable one in the present world.

LOW SCORE: Students who do not feel that the priestly or religious life is useful in the modern world.

16. Per cent response to items defining INTEREST IN A RELIGIOUS VOCATION N = 2821.

Item	Per cent Agree	Per cent Disagree	Factor Loading
I would like to talk to someone about a religious or priestly way of life	11a	77	0.70
I have thought seriously about being a priest or a brother (or sister) over the last year or so	14b	75	0.64
I have spoken to an adult about being a priest or brother (or sister) over the last year or so	8c	80	0.58

No. of items 3, Range 3-15, Scale mean 5.3, S.D. 2.8, Alpha Reliability 0.71.

HIGH SCORE: Students who have a serious interest in a religious lifestyle for themselves.

LOW SCORE: Students who have no interest in a religious lifestyle.

a 310 students who would like to talk to someone about religious or priestly life;

b 395 students who have thought seriously of a religious lifestyle;

c 226 who have spoken to an adult about a priestly or religious life in the last year or so.

17. Per cent response to items defining ALTRUISM SCALE N = 2821 (After Strommen, 1974).

Item	Per cent Agree*	Per cent Disagree	Factor Loading
FORGIVENESS (being willing to pardon)	51	37	0.34
SERVICE (helping others)	51	40	0.33
HONESTY (being frank and genuine with everyone)	70	22	0.32
RELIGION (religious beliefs, relationship with God)	44	47	0.30
FAMILY HAPPINESS (caring among family members)	72	18	0.29
LOVE (warmth, caring, giving and receiving love)	80	12	0.22
ETHICAL LIFE (responsible living toward others)	36	51	0.15
PERSONAL FREEDOM (independence, making own choices) (R)	64	27	−0.14
RECOGNITION (being important, well-liked) (R)	43	47	−0.40
PHYSICAL APPEARANCE (attractiveness) (R)	35	55	−0.55

PLEASURE (excitement, fun, satisfaction) (R)	57	35	−0.56
PERSONAL POWER (influence over others) (R)	20	70	−0.60
MONEY (plenty of money for things I want) (R)	32	59	−0.66

No. of items 13, Range 13-65, Scale mean 42.8, S.D. 8.6, Alpha Reliability 0.71. R = item is reversed in scale addition.

HIGH SCORE: Those who tend to have altruistic life priorities.

LOW SCORE: Those who tend to have more self serving life priorities.

* Per cent agree includes those who responded 'most important' or 'quite important'. Per cent Disagree includes those who responded 'somewhat important' and 'least important'.

18. Per cent response to items defining student's SELF ESTEEM N = 2821.

Item	Per cent Agree	Per cent Disagree	Factor Loading
My friends listen to my suggestions	82	8	0.55
I think most people like me	71	8	0.46
I am good at organising things	58	21	0.31
When I try, I usually succeed	76	11	0.22
I am concerned that I do not get along well with or know how to talk to members of the opposite sex (R)	29	62	−0.28
My friends seem more sure of themselves than I am (R)	24	40	−0.30
I am concerned that members of the opposite sex are not interested in me (R)	26	57	−0.31

I am afraid my friends may think I am boring (R)	27	54	−0.47
My friends often forget me (R)	23	59	−0.52
My friends do not listen to what I say (R)	13	75	−0.69

No. of items 10, Range 10-50, Scale mean 36.4, S.D. 6.2, Alpha Reliability 0.73.

HIGH SCORE: Students with a high self-esteem and sense of self worth.

LOW SCORE: Students with a low sense of self-esteem and self worth.

19. Per cent response to items defining LIBERAL EDUCATION GOALS IDEAL, ACTUAL N = 2821 students.

Item	Per cent Import.	Per cent Unimport.	Factor Loading
Catholic schools ought to give students experience in the main areas of human knowledge. Ideal	56	4	0.66
Experience in the main areas of human knowledge. How important actually	35	20	0.47
Catholic schools ought to provide for creative work by students. Ideal	55	7	0.56
Chance for creative work. How important actually	26	32	0.51
Catholic schools ought to encourage love of learning for its own sake. Ideal	65	10	0.38
Love of learning. How important actually	32	32	0.51

Catholic schools ought to make students aware of other religions. Ideal	54	19	0.27
Awareness of other religions. How important actually	20	53	0.41
Catholic schools ought to develop independence and critical thinking. Ideal	72	8	0.40
Independence and critical thinking. How important actually	33	30	0.53

No. of items 5 in each scale, Range 5-25.

Ideal Scale: Mean 19.0, S.D. 3.4, Alpha Reliability 0.58.
Actual Scale: Mean 14.6, S.D. 3.5, Alpha Reliability 0.52.

HIGH SCORE: Students who attach strong importance to liberal educational goals (ideal) and who see the school supporting liberal educational goals (actual).

LOW SCORE: Students who do not attach importance to liberal educational goals (ideal) and who do not see the school doing so (actual).

20. Per cent response to items defining CHRISTIAN COMMUNITY OF STAFF N = 448 staff.

Item	Per cent Agree	Per cent Disagree	Factor Loading
I think that staff morale in this school is high	78	9	0.79
Religious and lay work together harmoniously as a staff community or 'team' in this school	82	9	0.75
There is a high degree of integration of lay and religious to form one staff	62	12	0.68

Adequate channels of communication between the headmaster and staff exist	74	15	0.65
Lay teachers have a genuine share in the decision-making and policy-making of this school	49	31	0.60
Teachers, both lay and religious, enjoy being together at morning tea and other informal occasions	87	4	0.58
Religious staff in this school carry out their work with energy and enthusiasm	89	3	0.56
Lay staff in this school carry out their work with energy and enthusiasm	86	4	0.53
General discipline in this school is humane and reasonable	89	4	0.51

No. of items 9, Range 9-45, Scale mean 37.1, S.D. 2.8, Alpha Reliability 0.84 (religious), 0.86 (lay staff).

HIGH SCORE: Those staff with a strong sense of Christian community and cohesion.

LOW SCORE: Those staff with a weak sense of Christian community or cohesion.

21. Per cent response to items defining JOB SATISFACTION LAY STAFF N = 299 lay staff.

Item	Per cent Agree	Per cent Disagree	Factor Loading
Satisfied with teaching subjects	80	6	0.42
Satisfied with number of periods taught	70	16	0.52
Satisfied with size of classes	46	39	0.44
Satisfied with salary provisions	57	30	0.53
Satisfied with promotional opportunities	34	41	0.68

Item	Per cent Response	Factor Loading
Concern about superannuation:		
1. greatly concerned	57	−0.13
2.	14	
3.	12	
4.	1	
5. no concern at all	12	
Degree of involvement of lay teachers in administration:		
1. very involved	15	0.33
2.	26	
3.	24	
4.	18	
5. no involvement	11	

No. of items 7, Range 7-35, Scale mean 24.6, S.D. 1.4 Alpha Reliability 0.63.

HIGH SCORE: Lay staff well satisfied with their teaching conditions, high job satisfaction.

LOW SCORE: Lay staff dissatisfied with teaching conditions, low job satisfaction.

22. Per cent response to items defining PRESS FOR LAY ADMINISTRATION N = 149 religious and N = 299 lay staff. Religious N = 149

Item	Per cent Agree	Per cent Disagree	Factor Loading
Positions of responsibility such as Deputy Headmaster should be open to lay teachers	62	21	0.69
Suitably qualified lay teachers ought to be offered the position of Headmaster in Catholic schools	44	31	0.67

Lay Staff N = 299

Item	Per cent Agree	Per cent Disagree	Factor Loading
Positions of responsibility such as Deputy Headmaster should be open to lay teachers	74	14	0.71
Suitably qualified lay teachers ought to be offered the position of Headmaster in Catholic schools	63	20	0.73

No. of items 2 in each scale, Range 2-10.

Religious: Mean 7.8, S.D. 0.8, Alpha Reliability 0.74.
Lay staff: Mean 8.6, S.D. 0.6, Alpha Reliability 0.79.

HIGH SCORE: For religious indicates those open to lay staff as taking positions of responsibility. For lay staff it indicates a press for such positions.

LOW SCORE: For religious indicates resistance to lay staff in positions of responsibility. For lay staff indicates little desire to see lay staff in positions of responsibility.

23. Per cent response to items defining OPENNESS TO DRUGS AND ALCOHOL N = 2821.

Item	Per cent Agree	Per cent Disagree	Factor Loading
I use drugs occasionally	20a	76	0.84
I think trying out drugs is all right if I do not go too far	26b	51	0.62
I worry that I am becoming addicted to drugs	8c	88	0.58
I think I sometimes drink too much alcohol	30d	64	0.54

No. of items 4, Range 4-20, Scale mean 8.1, S.D. 4.0, Alpha Reliability 0.68.

HIGH SCORE: Students who use drugs or too much alcohol and are open to further usage.

LOW SCORE: Students who do not use drugs or excess alcohol and are less open to such usage.

a) 564 students who report using drugs occasionally;

b) 733 students who think trying out drugs is all right;

c) 224 students who worry they are becoming addicted;

d) 846 students who think they sometimes drink too much alcohol.

BIBLIOGRAPHY

Anderson, D.S. & Weston, J.S. (1972), Denominational Schooling and Religious Behaviour. *Australian and NZ Journal of Sociology*, 8, 19-31.

Anderson, D.S. (1971), Do Catholic Schools Cause People to Go to Church? *Australian and NZ Journal of Sociology*, 7, 65-67.

Armor, D.J. (1976), School and Family Effects on Black and White Achievement. In F. Mosteller & D.P. Moynihan (Eds). *On Equality of Educational Opportunity*. New York: Vintage Books.

Azzopardi, E. (1988), *Human Rights and Peoples*, Drummoyne: Marist Brothers.

Barakat, H. (1969), Alienation: A Process of Encounter Between Utopia and Reality. *British Journal of Sociology*, 20 (1), 1-10.

Beaton, A.E. (1973), *Commonality* Unpublished Paper, Educational Testing Service, Princeton: N.J.

Beaton, A.E. (1974), Multivariate Commonality Analysis. In G.W. Mayeske, A.E. Beaton, C.E. Wisler, T. Okado, W.M. Cohen Technical Supplement to *'A Study of Achievement of Our Nation's Students'*. US Dept. of Health, Education and Welfare.

Berger, P.L. (1973), *A Rumour of Angels*, Harmondsworth: Penguin.

Berger, P.L. & Luckmann, T. (1966), *The Social Construction of Reality* New York: Doubleday.

Bloom, B.S. (1976), *Human Characteristics and School Learning*. New York: McGraw-Hill.

Bookover, W.B. *et al.*, 'Elementary School Social Climate and School Achievement', *American Educational Journal*, 15, 301-318.

Brimer, M.A., Madaus, G.F., Chapman, B., Kellaghan, T, & Wood, R. (1978), *Sources of Difference in School Achievement*, Slough: NFER Publishing Co.

Campbell, D.T. & Stanley, J.C. (1963), *Experimental and Quasi-experimental Designs for Research*. Chicago: Rand McNally.

Carroll, L., Through the Looking Glass and What Alice Found There, in *Alice in Wonderland*, London: Bell Publications, 1872.

Chardin, de Teilhard (1959), *The Phenomenon of Man*, New York: Harper & Brothers.

Chardin, de Teilhard (1965), *The Appearance of Man*, London: Collins.

Chardin, de Teilhard (1966), *The Vision of the Past*, London: Collins.

Cronbach, L.J. (1951), Coefficient Alpha and the Internal Structure of Tests. *Psychometricia*, 16 (3), 297-334.

Coleman, J.S., Hoffer, T., Kilgore, S. (1982), *High School Achievement: Public, Catholic and Private Schools Compared.* Washington DC: National Centre for Educational Statistics.

Coleman, J.S., Campbell, E.O., Hobson, C.J., McPartland, J., Mood, A.M., Weinfield, F.D. & York, R.L. (1966), *Equality of Educational Opportunity*. Washington DC: Office of Education, US Dept. of Health, Education and Welfare.

Coleman, J.S., Hoffer, T., Kilgore, S. (1982), *High School Achievement, Public, Catholic and Private Schools Compared*. New York: Basic Books.

Coleman, J.S. & Hoffer, T. (1987), *Public and Private High Schools: The Impact of Communities*. New York: Basic Books.

Crawford, M. & Rossiter, G.M. (1985), *Teaching Religion in the Secondary School: Theory and Practice*. Strathfield, NSW: Christian Brothers Province Resource Group.

Crawford, M. & Rossiter, G. (1987), What is the Place for 'Academically' Challenging RE in Catholic Schools? in *Catholic School Studies*, 60 (1), 20-24.

Crawford, M. & Rossiter, G.M. (1988), *Missionaries to a Teenage Culture*. Sydney: Christian Brothers Province Resource Group.

Dewey, J. (1916), *Democracy and Education*. New York: Macmillan.

Dunkin, M.J., & Biddle, B.J. (1974), *The Study of Teaching*, New York: Holt, Rinehardt and Winston.

Elford, G. (1978), Religious Education Outcomes Inventory (REOI) Defended. *The Living Light*, 15 (4), 549-553.

Fahey, J. (1987), Self-Concept and Schooling. *Catholic School Studies*, 62 (1), 27-31.

Fahy, P.S. (1976), School and Home Perceptions of Australian Males Attending Catholic Schools. *Our Apostolate*, 24 (3), 167-188.

Fahy, P.S. (1977a), *Staff Environment of 41 Catholic Schools*. Sydney: Macquarie University, M.A. Thesis.

Fahy, P.S. (1978), Religious Beliefs of 15 900 Youth Attending Australian Catholic Schools. *Word in Life*, 26 (2), 66-72.

Fahy, P.S. (1980a), *The Effectiveness on Christian Criteria of 17 Australian Catholic High Schools*. PhD Thesis: Boston College, Institute of Religious Education and Pastoral Ministry. Uni Microfilms 80-17609.

Fahy, P.S. (1980b), The Religious Effectiveness of Some Australian Catholic Schools. *Word in Life*, Aug. 86-98.

Fahy, P.S. (1980c), Scientific Cosmology and Biblical Traditions of Creation. *Lumen Vitae*, 35, 333-353.

Fee, J.L., Greeley, A.M., McCready, W.C., Sullivan, T.A. (1980), *Young Catholics*. Los Angeles: Sadlier.

Fitchter, J.H. (1966), *Send Us a Boy. Get Back a Man*. Cambridge, Mass: Cambridge Centre for Social Sciences.

Flynn, M. (1975), *Some Catholic Schools in Action*. Sydney: Catholic Education Office.

Flynn, M. (1977), *Faith, Socialization and Education in Faith with Reference to Australian Catholic Schools*, Doctor of Education Dissertation, Columbia University Teachers College: New York.

Flynn, M. (1979), *Catholic Schools and the Communication of Faith*. Homebush: St. Paul Publications.

Flynn, M. (1985), *The Effectiveness of Catholic Schools*. Homebush: St. Paul Publications.

Flynn, M. (1989), The Culture of Catholic Schools. *Catholic School Studies*, 62 (2), 22-28.

Fowler, J. (1978), Life/Faith Patterns: Structures of Trust and Loyalty. In Fowler, J. & Keen, S. *Life Maps*, Waco, Texas: Word Books.

Frankl, V. (1963), *Man's Search for Meaning: An Introduction to Logotherapy*. Boston: Beacon Press.

Friere, P. (1970), *Pedagogy of the Oppressed*, New York: Seabury Press.

Ganss, K.P. (1979), *American Catholic Education in the 60s*. PhD Dissertation: Loyola University of Chicago.

Goodman, L.A. & Kruskal, W.H. (1954), Measures of Association for Cross-classification. *Journal of the American Statistical Society*, 49, 732-64.

Greeley, A. (1982), *Catholic Schools and Minority Students*, New Brunswick, USA: Transaction Books.

Greeley, A.M. & Rossi, P.H. (1966), *The Education of Catholic Americans*. Chicago: Aldine.

Greeley, A.M., McCready, W.C., and McCourt, K. (1976), *Catholic Schools in a Declining Church*. Kansas City, Kansas: Sheed and Ward.

Greeley, A.M. (1989), Catholic Schools: A Golden Twilight. *Catholic School Studies*, 62 (2), 8-12.

Greer, J.E. (1971), Religious Belief and Church Attendance of Sixth Form Pupils and Their Parents. *Irish Journal of Education* 2, 98-106.

Groome, T.H. (1977), The Critical Principle in Christian Education and the Task of Prophecy. *Religious Education*, 72, 262-272.

Groome, T.H. (1980), *Christian Religious Education: Sharing our Story and Vision*. New York: Harper & Row.

Hamilton, A. (1981), *What Has Been Happening in RE in Australia?*, Blackburn, Vic, Australia: Dove Communications.

Hancock, P. (1989), Prophetic Union: Catholic Schools As Agents of Social Change. *Catholic School Studies*, 62 (1), 7-9.

Hoge, D.R. & Petrillo, G.H. (1978), Determinants of Church Participation and Attitudes Among High School Youth. *Journal of Scientific Study of Religion*, 17 (4), 359-379.

Hoge, D.R. & Petrillo, G.H. (1979), Youth and the Church. *Religious Education*, 74 (3), 305-313.

Hornsby-Smith, M. & Petit, M. (1975), Social, Moral and Religious Attitudes of Secondary School Students. *Journal of Moral Education*, 4 (3), 261-272.

Hornsby-Smith, M. (1972), A Sociological Case for Catholic Schools. *The Month*, 5 (10), 298-304.

Hornsby-Smith, M. (1978), *Catholic Education: The Unobtrusive Partner*, London: Sheed and Ward.

House, G. (1977), The Logic of the Evaluative Argument. CSE Monograph. Series in Evaluation. Los Angeles: University of California, Centre for the Study of Evaluation.

Illich, I. (1971), *Deschooling Society*. New York: Harper & Row.

Jencks, C.S., Smith, M., Acland, H., Bone, M.J., Cohen, D., Gintis, H., Hyns, B. & Michelson, S. (1972), *Inequality: A Reassessment of the Effect of Family and Schooling in America*. New York: Basic Books.

Kerlinger, F.N. & Pedhazur, E.J. (1973), *Multiple Regression in Behavioral Research*, New York: Holt, Rinehardt and Winston.

Kerlinger, F.N. (1973), *Foundations of Behavioral Research*. (2nd Edition) New York: Holt, Rinehardt & Winston.

Leahy, M. (1991), The Catholic School – Servant of Education or of Religion?, *Word in Life*, 39 (2), 5-8.

Leavey, M.C. (1972a), *Religious Education, School Climate and Achievement: A Study of Nine Catholic Sixth Form Girls' Schools*. Unpublished PhD thesis: Australian National University, Canberra.

Leavey, M.C. (1972b), The Transmission of Religious and Moral Values in Nine Catholic Girls' Schools. *Twentieth Century*, Dec. 167-184.

Lee, J.M. (1973), *The Flow of Religious Instruction*. Dayton, Ohio: Pflaum Press.

Little, A. (1981), *Contemporary Issues in Education. Block 4, 20, Educational Standards*, Milton Keyner: Open University Press.

Maafe, K. (1980), Does a Catholic School Make or Break a Parish? In *US Catholic*, 45 (2), 34-39.

Macdonald, M. (1989), An Assessment Dilemma: What to Assess in Religious Education? *Catholic School Studies*, 62 (2), 39-41.

Madaus, G.F., Airasian, P.W. and Kellaghen, T. (1980), *School Effectiveness: A Reassessment of the Evidence*. New York: McGraw-Hill.

Madaus, G.F. (1983), *Evaluation Models*, Boston: Kluwer-Nijhoff.

Madaus, G.F., Kellaghan, T., Rakow, E.A. & King, D. (1975), *A Study of the Sensitivity of Measures of School Effectiveness*. Report submitted to the Carnegie Corporation of New York: Educational Research Centre, St Patrick's College and Chestnut Hill, Mass: Boston College.

Madaus, G.F., Kellaghan, T., Rakow, E.A. & King, D.J. (1979), *The Sensitivity of Measures of School Effectiveness*. Harvard Educational Review, 49 (2), 207-230.

Madaus, G.F. & Linnan, R. (1973), The Outcomes of Catholic Education? *School Review*, 81, 207-232.

Marthaler, B.L. (1973), *Catechetics in Context*, Huntington, Indiana: Our Sunday Visitor.

Mayeske, G.W., Okada, T., Cohen, W.M., Beaton, A.E., & Wisler, C.E. (1973), A Study of the Achievement of Our Nation's Students. *DHEW. Publication* No. (OE) 72-131. Washington, DC: US Department of Health, Education and Welfare.

Mayeske, G.W., Wisler, C.E., Beaton, A.E., Weinfeld, F.D., Cohen, W.M., Okada, T., Proshek, J.M. and Tabler, K.A. (1972), *A Study of Our Nation's Schools: A Working Paper* Washington, DC: US Dept. of Health, Education and Welfare. Publication No. 10E/72-142.

Mayeske, G.W., Wisler, C.E., Beaton, A.E. (1973), *A Study of Our Nation's Schools. A Working Paper*. Washington, DC: US Dept. of Health, Education and Welfare.

McBrien, R. (1977), *Basic Questions for Christian Educators*, Winona, Minn., St. Mary's College Press.

McBrien, R.P. (1980), *Catholicism*. Melbourne, Australia: Dove.

Mol, J.J. (1968), The Effects of Denominational Schools in Australia. *The Australia and NZ Journal of Sociology*, 4, 18-35.

Mol, J.J. (1971), A Rejoinder. *The Australia and NZ Journal of Sociology*, 7 (1), 68-69.

Moran, G. (1966a), *Theology of Revelation*, New York: Herder and Herder.

Moran, G. (1966b), *Catechesis of Revelation*. New York: Seabury Press.

Moran, G. (1974), *Religious Body*. New York: Seabury Press.

Moran, G. (1981), *Interplay: A Theory of Religion and Education*, Winona, Minn.: St Mary's Press, Christian Brothers Publications.

Moran, G. (1989), Religious Education in Australia, *Catholic School Studies*, 62 (1), 27-28.

National Conference of Catholic Bishops (1979), *National Catechetical Directory Sharing the Light of Faith*. Washington, DC: United States Catholic Conference.

Nelson, C.E. (1972), Is Christian Education Something Particular? *Religious Education*, 67, 2-10.

Nelson, H.M., Potvin, R.H. & Shields, J. (1976), *The Religion of Children*, Washington, DC: United States Catholic Conference.

Neuwien, R.A. (1966), *Catholic Schools in Action*, Indiana: Notre Dame Press.

Oakeshott, M. (1972), Education: The Engagement and Its Frustration. In *Education and the Development of Reason*. Dearden, R.F. (Editor), London: Routledge and Kegan Paul.

Pastrick, D. (1978), A Critical Review of the Religious Knowledge Component of the Religious Education Outcomes Inventory (REOI). *The Living Light*, 15 (3), 406-416.

Phenix, P.H. (1964), *Realms of Meaning*, New York: McGraw Hill.

Piveteau, D.J. & Dillon, J.T. (1977b), *Resurgence of Religious Instruction*, Notre Dame, Indiana: Religious Education Press.

Potvin, R.H., Hoge, D.R. & Nelson, H.M. (1976), *Religion and American Youth*. Washington, DC: United States Catholic Conference.

Rahner, K. (Editor) (1975), *Encyclopedia of Theology: The Concise Sacramentum Mundi*. New York: Seabury Press.

Rossiter, G.M. (1983), *An Interpretation of Normative Theory for Religious Education in Australian Catholic Schools*, Ph D Thesis: Macquarie University, Sydney.

Rossiter, G.M. (1984), *A Review of Australian Research Related to Religious Education in Schools*, Sydney: National Catholic Research Council.

Rossiter, G. (1986), The Place of Faith in Classroom Religious Education, in *Catholic School Studies*, 59 (2), 49-55.

Rulla, L. (1976), *Entering and Leaving Vocation*, Rome: Gregorian University Press, Chicago: Loyola University.

Rutter, M., Maughan, B., Mortimore, P., Ouston, J. (1979), *Fifteen Thousand Hours: Secondary Schools and Their Effects on Children*. Cambridge, Mass: Harvard University Press.

Stake, R.E., The Countenance of Education Evolution, in Worthen, B.R. & Sanders, J.R. (1973), *Educational Evaluation: Theory and Practice*, pp. 106-126, Belmont, California: Charles A. Jones.

Starratt, R. (1988), Teaching Justice in Catholic Schools, in *Catholic School Studies*, 61 (2), 29-30.

Strommen, M.P. (1974), *Five Cries of Youth*. New York: Harper and Row.

Stufflebeam, D.L. (chairman) (1978), *Standards for Evaluation of Educational Programs, Projects and Materials*, Joint Committee on Standards for Educational Evaluation, New York: McGraw Hill.

Stufflebeam, D.L. (1974), *Meta-evaluation*, Occasional Paper 3, Kalamazoo, Michigan: The Evaluation Centre, Western Michigan University.

Stufflebeam, D.L., *Decision Management Strategies*, in Worthen, B.R., & Sanders, J.R. (eds.) (1973), *Educational Evaluation: Theory and Practice*. Belmont, California: Wadsworth Publishing.

The Sacred Congregation for Catholic Education, (1988), *Religious Dimensions of Education in a Catholic School*, Homebush, NSW, Australia: St Paul Publications.

The Sacred Congregation for Catholic Education, (1977), *The Catholic School*, Homebush, NSW, Australia: St Paul Publications.

Tillich, P. (1957), *Dynamics of Faith*. New York: Harper and Row.

Tracy, D. (1975), *Blessed Rage for Order*. New York: Seabury Press.

Treston, K. (1987), The Relationship Between the Vocation and Industrial Models of Teaching in a Catholic School, *Catholic School Studies*, 60 (1), 47-50.

Tyler, R. (1954), *Basic Principles of Curriculum and Instruction*, Chicago: University of Chicago.

Warren, M. (1986), Ministry, Catechesis and Religious Education: Implications for Youth Ministry and Catholic Schools, in *Catholic School Studies*, 59 (2).

Westerhoff, J. (1972), *A Colloquy on Christian Education*. Philadelphia: Pilgrim Press.

Westerhoff, J. (1976), *Will Our Children Have Faith?* New York: Seabury Press.

Whitehead, A.N. (1967), *The Aims of Education*. New York: Free Press.

Woodbury, A.M. (1962), *Educational Rights of Family, Church and State*. Sydney: Aquinas Academy Press.

Wright, S. (1960a), Path Coefficients and Path Regressions, in *Biometrics*, 16, 189-202.

Wright, S. (1960b), The Treatment of Reciprocal Interaction, With or Without Lag, in Path Analysis, in *Biometrics*, 16(3), 423-445.

INDEX